Ambivalent Encounters

The Rutgers Series in Childhood Studies

The Rutgers Series in Childhood Studies is dedicated to increasing our understanding of children and childhoods, past and present, throughout the world. Children's voices and experiences are central. Authors come from a variety of fields, including anthropology, criminal justice, history, literature, psychology, religion, and sociology. The books in this series are intended for students, scholars, practitioners, and those who formulate policies that affect children's everyday lives and futures.

Edited by Myra Bluebond-Langner, Board of Governors Professor of Anthropology, Rutgers University and True Colours Chair in Palliative Care for Children and Young People, University College London, Institute of Child Health.

Advisory Board

Perri Klass, *New York University*

Jill Korbin, *Case Western Reserve University*

Bambi Schieffelin, *New York University*

Enid Schildkraut, *American Museum of Natural History and Museum for African Art*

Ambivalent Encounters

Childhood, Tourism, and Social Change in Banaras, India

JENNY HUBERMAN

RUTGERS UNIVERSITY PRESS

NEW BRUNSWICK, NEW JERSEY, AND LONDON

Library of Congress Cataloging-in-Publication Data

Huberman, Jennifer.
    Ambivalent encounters : childhood, tourism, and social change in Banaras, India / Jenny Huberman.
       p. cm. — (Rutgers series in childhood studies)
    Includes bibliographical references and index.
    ISBN 978-0-8135-5407-5 (hardcover : alk. paper) — ISBN 978-0-8135-5406-8 (pbk. : alk. paper) — ISBN 978-0-8135-5408-2 (e-book)
     1. Child labor—India—Varanasi. 2. Tourism—India—Varanasi. 3. Tourists—India—Varanasi. 4. Social interaction—India—Varanasi. I. Title.
    HD8039.T642I44 2012
    331.3'18—dc23
    2012005167

A British Cataloging-in-Publication record for this book is available from the British Library.

Copyright © 2012 by Jenny Huberman

All rights reserved

No part of this book may be reproduced or utilized in any form or by any means, electronic or mechanical, or by any information storage and retrieval system, without written permission from the publisher. Please contact Rutgers University Press, 106 Somerset Avenue, 3rd floor, New Brunswick, NJ 08901. The only exception to this prohibition is "fair use" as defined by U.S. copyright law.

Visit our website: http://rutgerspress.rutgers.edu

Manufactured in the United States of America

For my parents

CONTENTS

Preface ix
Acknowledgments xiii
Note on Translation and Transliteration xv

PART 1
Introductions

1. Children, Tourists, and Locals — 3
2. A Tourist Town — 18

PART 2
Conceptions of Children

3. Girls and Boys on the Ghats — 35
4. Innocent Children or Little Adults? — 67
5. The Minds and Hearts of Children — 93

PART 3
Conceptions of Value

6. Earning, Spending, Saving — 119
7. Something Extra — 141
8. Money, Gender, and the (Im)morality of Exchange — 165
9. Conclusion — 182

Notes 189
References 205
Index 221

PREFACE

The idea for this book initially developed when I was a graduate student and I went to the city of Banaras for nine months to study Hindi at the American Institute of Indian Studies. The language instruction that I received and the camaraderie of my fellow classmates rendered it an invaluable experience. It certainly was integral in preparing me for my subsequent research. However, as someone prone to cabin fever, the long hours spent sitting inside were a source of frustration for me. By the time the late afternoon rolled around and our classes were finally adjourned, I would head to the city's famous riverfront, hoping to burn off my restlessness with some exercise.

My initial forays into power walking on the riverfront were not very successful. For the first few weeks, it seemed impossible to make it more than several yards without having an eager child stop me and offer to sell me postcards or trinkets, or guide me to city's "best" sights and stores, where promises of handsome commissions awaited them. The children greeted me with flashy smiles and optimistic persistence. "You want postcard?" "Would you like to see the temple?" "You come to my silk shop?" "Would you like to buy a candle to put in Ganga?" In my head the answer was always "No! No! No!" But occasionally their charm, and in some cases badgering, proved too much for me to resist, and I would end up sending twenty flickering candles down the river, or return home with a stack of postcards, most of which I never sent.

As the weeks passed, it became clear to the children that I was not a great customer. It became even clearer to me that I was going to have to develop a more flexible conception of "the power walk" in order to successfully navigate the *ghats* of Banaras, the broad stone landings that stretch along the river's edge. On both sides, we adjusted our expectations. I surrendered to a slower-paced meandering, and most of the kids gave up trying to sell me their goods, since there were more promising tourists on the riverfront to pursue. When we met, they still smiled, and if things were slow they would come over to chat with me. I would ask questions about how business was going and often they would introduce me to their customers as though I were a fixed attraction on the tour or a character witness who could vouch for their honesty. Some of the children started coming to me with letters they had received from their other "foreign friends." I would read the letters and, when asked, help them write replies.

Most of the letters came from Western tourists who had spent just a few days with the children. Yet the emotional intensity behind these texts was striking:

> Dear Pramod,
> I was thinking what could I do for you and me to become special to each other, something like being part of the same family. I would love to know if you need anything I could do for you. I was also thinking it could be nice for you to go to school maybe, and as I always wanted to have a younger brother I could take care of it. There's the greatest Hindu School and University in Banaras, as you know. I don't really want to push you to do anything but only try and help both of us. There is a good friend of mine who lives in Calcutta who could help me talk to the authorities for the registration. This decision can only be taken from you and your family, of course; in any case I want you to know that you can count on me because my heart is always with you. I'm your loving sister and I'm here for you.
>
> Mother gives you a big kiss and hopes you are well and in health. Please don't forget you've got a loving sister who thinks and cares about you.
>
> Don't forget me and write soon.
> Hugs xxxxx
>
> Your sister
Arienne
(Italy)

After reading many more letters of this kind, I began to wonder what exactly was being produced and consumed in this informal economy. It seemed clear that, for Western tourists at least, much more was at stake than just postcards and souvenirs. So, with my interest piqued, I started paying closer attention to the interactions between these foreign visitors and children. Many of the tourists whom I observed and spoke with voiced similar feelings of adoration for these youngsters, but there were also many who expressed remorse and even disdain for these "relentless" young salespeople. "These aren't children," I was repeatedly told in outraged tones, "they're just little adults in kids' bodies. All they are interested in is business and making money; they are ruined!" Here too, the emotional intensity of tourists' reactions seemed out of proportion.

I wondered how people in Banaras felt about the children who worked along the riverfront. I assumed they would have more measured responses than foreign tourists. When I began to talk with locals in the neighborhood, however, I found that their reactions were also emotionally charged and frequently conflicting. Some spoke admiringly of the children and their willingness to subordinate their own interests in order to help their families, while others bitterly lamented how the children had relinquished their sense of familial responsibility and, instead, were being corrupted by their access to foreign wealth.

As I drifted in and out of conversations with tourists and locals and registered the praise and criticisms that were mounting on both sides, I continued to spend time with the children. Many of the adults I talked with either idealized the children for their charm and virtue or denigrated them for their apparent "corruption." I wanted a fuller account. I wanted to know more about how the children themselves experienced and understood their work. How did they negotiate the expectations placed upon them by these visitors and by their own families? How did they mediate tourists' encounters of the city? And, in turn, how did they enable local people to express their ambivalence about the impact of foreign tourism, as well as more pervasive changes that were reshaping traditional ways of life? With the hopes of answering these questions and more, I returned to Banaras in the year 2000 to begin twenty months of fieldwork.

ACKNOWLEDGMENTS

Over the years, many people and institutions have contributed to this book. My greatest debt is to the friends and families in Banaras who shared their lives with me, took care of me, and made doing my fieldwork a real labor of love. Though I cannot name everyone here, and though I have used pseudonyms throughout the text to ensure anonymity, I would particularly like to thank: GR, Deepu, Baloo-ah-raye, Raju, Dhanu, Madan, Sambhu, Guddhu, Ajay, Pawan, Rajan, Vicky, Nirmila Didi, Maneesha, Jyoti, Sandya, Pritthi, Anita, Sitara, Sudhama, Pintu, Jagdish, Yashoda Didi, Jagdish Bhai, Pappu Bhai, Tiwariji, Sheliaji, Guddhu Bhai, Sangeeta, Soni, and Meenu.

As an undergraduate student at Boston University I had the good fortune of encountering an incredibly talented group of teachers who got me hooked on anthropology: Charles Lindholm, Robert Hefner, Jane Guyer, Shahla Haeri, Terrence Deacon, and Allan Hoben are, in large part, responsible for my becoming an anthropologist. At the University of Chicago I benefitted greatly from an intellectual environment that was both rugged and robust. During this time, John Kelly and Tanya Luhrmann offered me invaluable guidance and steadfast encouragement. My friend and fellow scholar, Jocelyn Marrow, was also a source of continuous support.

I received generous grants from the American Institute of Indian Studies, the Fulbright-Hays Program, and the Committee on South Asian Studies at the University of Chicago. I am also grateful to all of the people who have helped me navigate the publishing process and who have allowed me to benefit from their expertise and resourcefulness. I would particularly like to thank: Marlie Wasserman, Allyson Fields, and Todd Scudiere; Assa Doron, who was kind enough to let me borrow his map; and Michael Southern, who was skilled enough to redraw it for me.

Portions of this manuscript are revised versions of publications that have appeared elsewhere. Parts of chapter 6 were published in *Global Tourism*, edited by Sarah Lyon and Christian Wells (AltaMira Press, 2012) and in *A Companion to the Anthropology of India*, edited by Isabelle Clark-Decès (Wiley-Blackwell, 2011). Chapter 7 draws on my essay "Shopping *for* People or Shopping for *People?*

Deciphering the Object of Consumption among Tourists in Banaras," published in *The Lived Experiences of Public Consumption*, edited by Daniel Cook (Palgrave Macmillan, 2009). An earlier version of chapter 8 was published in *South Asia: The Journal of South Asian Studies* 33(3) (2010): 399–420, under the title "The Dangers of *Dalālī*, the Dangers of *Dān*." I am grateful to the editors of these journals and volumes for making it possible for me to reprint this work here.

Jean Pierre and Judith Huberman have loved and supported me in all of my endeavors, and it is to them that I owe and dedicate this book. Finally, I want to thank my husband, Jeff Bennett. He enriches my life everyday with his love, companionship, ideas, and delicious cooking, and he never lets me lose sight of the true meaning of human requirements.

NOTE ON TRANSLATION AND TRANSLITERATION

The statements and conversations reported in this book come from tape-recorded interviews, and from informal conversations that I either took part in, or listened to throughout the course of my fieldwork. Sometimes I was able to take notes on conversations immediately after they occurred, but often, circumstances were such that I had to wait several hours. When this was the case, I usually tried to jot down key phrases or points to help me remember what had been said. All of the interviews I conducted with tourists were done in English. All of the interviews I conducted with people from Banaras were done in Hindi. I spent several years studying Hindi prior to beginning my fieldwork in Banaras, and I was able to converse in Hindi with relative ease. However, not being a native speaker and not being trained in Bhojpuri, which was also spoken by many of the people I interviewed, I decided to hire a language teacher from Banaras to go over my interview transcriptions and translations with me. In the process I learned a great deal more about the colloquial expressions and cultural allusions that people in Banaras draw upon in their everyday speech.

This book was written with the general reader in mind. As such, in terms of translation and transliteration I have avoided the use of diacritics and I have tried to transliterate all Hindi, Bhojpuri, and Sanskrit terms in a way that most closely approximates their local pronunciation. Hindi, Bhojpuri, and Sanskrit words are italicized at first usage. Places, language names, and personal names are not italicized, nor are words that have become very familiar to English speakers (e.g., sitar, yoga, tabla). In some cases, I pluralize Hindi nouns with an s rather than pluralize them in Hindi in order to make it less confusing for the reader (e.g., *diyas*). In terms of spellings, I use the spellings found in most tourist guide books and brochures, (e.g., Dasashwamedh, rather than Dashashwamedh or Dasashvamedh). Finally, although the city is variously called Varanasi, Banaras, and Kashi, Banaras is the name I use throughout the text.

PART 1

Introductions

1

Children, Tourists, and Locals

Our lives are a stream of encounters with other human beings. Many of these encounters fade into the background of everyday life, demanding little of our attention or concern and bearing little consequence. Others, however, press themselves upon us like an itch that requires constant scratching. We return to them again and again, seeking to decipher their structures, outcomes, and significance. In so doing, we often come to suspect that the immediacy of human encounters, even when face-to-face, is in fact an illusion, and that between ourselves and others, myriad forces and relations are at work. Yet, what are they? What kind of imagination does it require to grasp their articulations?

These were the kinds of questions that initially led me to study anthropology, and at the most general level, they are the ones that animate this book. This book provides an ethnographic study of encounters between Western tourists and some of the children who worked as unlicensed peddlers and guides along the riverfront of Banaras between the years 2000 and 2001. Specifically, it focuses on the lower-class and lower-caste children who worked near the city's "Main Ghat," Dasashwamedh. From expressions of adoration and amusement, to pity, anger, or disgust, tourists' responses to the children were rarely neutral. Similarly, people in Banaras also had strong reactions to the children, variously casting them as admirable, self-sacrificing youths or as disruptive deviants. The aim of this book is to examine why these children elicited such powerful reactions from travelers and locals in their community, while also exploring how the children themselves experienced their work and rendered it meaningful. In the pages that follow, I demonstrate how the children emerged as polyvalent symbols that enabled tourists and locals to express and experience a range of desires and concerns. Yet I also show how the children played upon adult fantasies and fears, thereby actively shaping the outcome of these encounters.

Traveling between anthropological studies of childhood, tourism, consumption, and exchange, I use this particular case study to address the following questions: How do children come to be valued and devalued within the global sphere? Why do children so frequently emerge as sources of anxiety and debate? What role do children play in configuring people's experience of socioeconomic change? How do children actively navigate their lives? What might it take to more effectively inscribe their efforts within the anthropological record? How and why have children increasingly become objects of the tourist gaze? And finally, what can these encounters teach us more generally about the highly mediated and often ambivalent nature of human interaction? How are we to trace and theorize the complicated interplay of intimate and social realities?

The Anthropology of Childhood

Not surprisingly, many of these questions have been pursued within the growing literature on the anthropology of childhood. One of my goals, therefore, is to further these efforts. As an international tourist destination, the riverfront of Banaras provides a very compelling site for exploring the multiple and often conflicting ways that children come to be defined and valued within the global sphere. Indeed, the reactions that Western tourists exhibited toward the children are interesting, in part, precisely because they put these differences on display. Oscillating between "premodern" and "postmodern" conceptions of the child as a "miniature adult" (Scheper-Hughes and Sargent 1998, 13), and Romantic conceptions of the child as a "noble savage" (James, Jenks, and Prout 1998, 13–15), tourists variously praised the children for their savvy business sense; scorned them for their apparent corruption; indulged them for their playfulness and innocence; or alternatively, pitied them as neglected "street kids." What are we to make of these varied yet patterned reactions?

As will be seen, tourists' reactions to the children on the riverfront were shaped by multiple determinations. They were influenced by varying discourses on children and childhood, by the tropes and themes through which tourists came to know India, by the ways that tourist actively read and interpreted the space of the ghats and, of course, by children themselves. However, I also propose that their reactions were reflective of unconscious defense mechanisms (Klein [1955] 1987, 1975) that enabled tourists to better cope with the anxieties and guilt that the children and the surrounding environment so often evoked in them. Drawing upon concepts from psychoanalytic theory, I show how processes of splitting, idealization, and denial variously led tourists to embrace these youngsters as "innocent children" or, alternatively, castigate them as "little adults masquerading in kids' bodies." This leads me to conclude that the classification of children should not be reduced to an exclusively social or cultural phenomenon.¹ Psychodynamics also animate these processes and by attending to them in this analysis, I hope to deepen our understanding of the complex ways that children are affirmed and denied in different contexts.

The different ways that tourists and locals classified the children also affected the way they transacted with them. In many instances, the sale or refusal of postcards and souvenirs, or alternatively, the granting or withholding of a mother's praise and affection, was predicated upon a child's ability to satisfy adult demands for "innocent" or "obedient" subjects. And yet, while access to resources frequently involved conforming to adults' expectations, the children were also capable of carving out spaces where they could exercise some degree of power and control (James, Jenks, and Prout 1998, 87).²

This book traces how the children creatively engaged the institutions, structures, and people that shaped their everyday lives, as well as how they were constrained by them. Over the last few decades, there has been a sustained attempt within anthropology to reclaim children's perspectives and agency, and this study certainly contributes to such efforts. It does so in part, however, by questioning the analytic utility of concepts such as "children's culture."³ Instead of suggesting that children occupy an autonomous realm of meanings and practices, insulated from adult society (Opie and Opie 1969, 1977), my goal is to show how the children on the riverfront came to sequester spaces and produce meanings within the larger ambit of social, cultural, and economic relations that structured this transnational contact zone.

Tourism and the Turn Inward

As tourism has emerged as a global industry, children in many parts of the world have been drawn into socioeconomic relations and spaces that are increasingly transnational in nature. Even if we have not had the experience ourselves, many of us know friends or family who have come back from their vacations abroad with animated tales and endless photographs of the children whom they encountered on their travels. Often, these tales highlight a particular child who "made the trip so memorable!" In other cases, we hear "horror stories" about the "dreadful" or "pestering kids who just wouldn't leave us alone!" And yet, despite their prominence in tourist narratives and economies, very little attention has been paid to the role children play in the global tourism industry. No one has asked why children so frequently become objects of "the tourist gaze" (Urry 1990).⁴

Although I pursue this question, I also argue that many of the tourists in this study wanted much more than just to gaze at these children. Many tourists sought to develop personal connections with the children, which in turn, would provide them with a more "authentic" or "extraordinary" experience of India.

The desire for authenticity has been widely noted and debated with the literature on tourism and tourist motivations.[5] Some scholars have theorized tourists' preoccupation with authenticity as a response to the alienating conditions of modern social life. As Dean MacCannell has argued, modern-day tourists are "contemporary pilgrims," "seeking authenticity in other 'times' and other 'places' away from that person's everyday life" (MacCannell 1976, 147). Others have suggested that the search for the authentic has more to do with a desire for distinction, as it provides the discerning traveler with a highly valued form of cultural capital that reflects his or her good taste (Edensor 1998; Tucker 1997).[6]

Both of these motivations influenced tourists' attempts to establish personal connections with the children on the riverfront. However, these connections also took on significance because they made tourists feel as though they were having more *intimate* experiences. The desire to be seen and recognized as unique people or, as tourists frequently put it, as "more than walking dollar signs" was, in many cases, a central part of tourists' quests. Therefore, paradoxical as it may seem, in this book I propose that some tourists travel halfway around the world not necessarily to discover an authentic Other, but rather to have the Other discover and acknowledge them. That is, within such encounters, it is often the tourist's self that is pursued and cathected as the ultimate object of desire.[7]

What does this reorientation in both the mode and object of touristic consumption suggest about the changing nature of travel experiences, as well as the desires and subjectivities of twenty-first-century leisure-class subjects?[8] Coining the concept of *the touristic turn inward*, I theorize tourists' desires for personal relationships and recognition as a psychosocial response to the ongoing commodification of places and peoples that has accompanied the expansion of the global tourism industry and the spread of global capitalism more generally. The touristic turn inward not only represents another manifestation of the increasingly flexible nature of commodity production and consumption within the context of late capitalism (Frank 2002; Harvey 1990; Urry 1990, 1995). It also suggests that contemporary leisure-class subjects may be driven more by narcissistic needs than by modernist longings to overcome a sense of alienation (Lasch 1978; Sennett 1976, 1998).

Consumption, Exchange, and the Pursuit of Value

If it was not just postcards and souvenirs but rather personal relationships and recognition that constituted one of the central objects of consumption for many Western tourists, then how exactly were these "objects" produced, consumed, and valued? What happens when the object of consumption is not a "sign object" that already exists within a code of differences, ready to be "appropriated" by the consumer—as the theorist Jean Baudrillard has famously argued (1981, 64–65)—but is, rather, an intangible relationship or experience that is produced through the ongoing interactions and (mis)interpretations of human beings? How do we theorize the forms of production, consumption, exchange, and value that emerged in this less rationalized, informal economy? Finally, how and why did some tourists in Banaras experience this informal economy as a space of intimacy where they felt they could transcend their status as mere tourists or "walking dollar signs," while others regarded it as a threatening space in which the apparent lack of rules and regulations filled them with anxiety and recurring suspicions that they were being taken advantage of?

Although we tend to feel rather awkward about putting children and sex in conversation with each other, one of the areas that I turn to for insights into these matters includes the research that has been done on female adult entertainers and sex workers (Allison 1994; Bernstein 2007; Brennan 2004; Frank 2002). Anthropologists and sociologists have raised provocative questions about the object of consumption in these service industries. Moreover, they have provided us with very rich ethnographic accounts of the performative dimensions that enable female workers to fulfill their male clients' desires for erotic experiences, companionship, authenticity, self-aggrandizement, and even recognition. In drawing upon their work, therefore, I consider how these encounters on the riverfront also involved the articulation of material and libidinal economies, and I suggest that in many cases, the children did engage in particular forms of "emotional labor" (Hochschild 1983).

This is also to say that in their attempts to earn money from foreign tourists, many of the children learned to intuit tourists' desires, and modify their sales strategies and presentations of self accordingly. By paying close attention to these efforts, and by exploring the various ways that tourists responded, I seek to emphasize the way that markets and market transactions unfold as "lived experiences." Arguing for the need to "reaffirm the significance of place" (and I would emphasize performance) in economic life, Daniel Cook reminds us that "something irreducible occurs in the public, face-to-face encounters of buyers and sellers, of observers and participants, in the terrestrial market" (Cook 2008, 2).[9] As he suggests, "It is the tensions pertaining to the comingling of economic exchange value with other values like sentiment, love, care and belonging" that make these transactions so experientially fraught, and so analytically interesting (3). This book contributes to these efforts to take place and performance seriously while also exploring the articulations between different registers of value.

For instance, the children's pursuit of profit was far from an unbridled affair. Their participation in this economy was primarily shaped by dominant gender norms and expectations. Whereas girls were more or less limited to selling low-priced items on the riverfront, where their behaviors and activities could be monitored by kinsmen and neighbors, boys were free to wander about the city and engage in the more lucrative enterprise of guiding and commission work. This informal economy was also structured by long-standing cultural expectations regarding everyone's "right to earn." I explore how the children relied on a set of informal rules, as well as an informal division of labor, to mitigate excessive competition. Although the rules were not always adhered to in practice, in principle at least, this informal economy was supposed to operate as a "moral economy" predicated upon everyone's right to subsistence (Scott 1976; Thompson 1971). Finally, by participating in this informal economy, and by regulating their behavior in accordance with different social norms and expectations, the children ultimately sought to produce *themselves* as valued and respected subjects. It is precisely by attending to these efforts that this book contributes to larger attempts to foreground the experiences and perspectives of children within the anthropological record.

The Ambivalence of Modernity

Despite their varying efforts to perpetuate a moral economy, people in Dasashwamedh often suggested that the children, particularly the boys, were engaged in *immoral* activities. In fact, when I first began telling people in Dasashwamedh that I was doing research for a book about encounters between Western tourists and the children on the riverfront, I received puzzled, and often disappointed, reactions. There were several permutations, but the usual response ran along the lines of: "You should be writing about our priests, our religious practices, our sacred traditions! Why do you want to spend your time with those hippies and uneducated children who just cheat people?" Instead of contributing to the greater glory of the city, as other notable anthropologists had done (Alter 1992; Kumar 1988; Parry 1994), it seemed that I would be broaching a topic that might actually increase its infamy. "No one will want to come here if you tell everyone about the way these children cheat tourists!"

Although these warnings and criticisms were a bit discouraging, as I listened to people in Dasashwamedh talk about the children who worked on the riverfront, I became increasingly convinced that I was indeed on to something. Some spoke bitterly about how the children were being corrupted by their involvement in the foreign tourist economy, whereas others seemed quite hopeful that their access to foreign wealth would make new opportunities possible. Over time, I also came to realize that the ambivalent reactions that locals had to the children were also symptomatic of a more pervasive feeling tone and climate of opinion that permeated the city of Banaras during the time of my fieldwork. In newspapers, films, political debates, and in everyday conversations, people were struggling to come to terms with some of the larger, not yet fully metabolized, changes brought on by Indian modernity and the joint forces of globalization and economic liberalization that emerged with renewed strength in the 1980s. Whereas some saw these developments as cause for celebration, many others pointed to a list of widespread social ills which, rightly or wrongly, were attributed to India's growing involvement with things foreign and things new: rapacious consumerism, Westernization, the unceasing pursuit of money and luxury, a seemingly pathological individualism, and an overall loss of traditional values.

Such concerns were often voiced in rather abstract or rhetorical terms, but for people in the neighborhood of Dasashwamedh, they also found more concrete expression in narratives about the boys who worked with Western tourists. The boys were frequently criticized for their corrupt and wayward behavior. In contrast, the girls who worked in this informal economy often elicited admiration and praise. By subordinating their behavior and desires to traditional gender norms and expectations, they proved themselves to be virtuous daughters and provided people with the hope that although life might be changing, it was not changing too much. Thus, as will be seen, gender not only played a decisive role in shaping the children's experiences but it also influenced how they emerged as particular kinds of evocative symbols for locals in the city.

The City and Riverfront

As is the case with most iconic places, it is virtually impossible to describe the city of Banaras, and India more generally, without perpetuating a cliché, particularly an Orientalist one.[10] The adjectives and imagery usually associated with this "ancient," "sacred," "bustling," "chaotic," "crowded," "exhilarating," "overwhelming," "temple-topped," "spirit-seeking-tourist," and "pilgrimage" town are both exhausted and inadequate. And yet, admittedly, in some cases, they still seem appropriate for trying to provide the unfamiliar reader with at least a preliminary idea of the scenes and sensations that have both repelled and attracted Western visitors to Banaras over the years. Undoubtedly, this is one reason why, despite being tired, and criticized, clichés persist.

Stretched along the gently curving banks of the Ganga or Ganges River, the city of Banaras, also known as Kashi and Varanasi, is located in the north Indian state of Uttar Pradesh. It has a population of approximately 1.27 million people (Singh, Dar, and Pravin 2001). Dating back to the sixth century BC, it is one of the oldest living cities in the world and one of the most important pilgrimage sites for Hindus (Eck 1983, 5). Every year, millions of pilgrims arrive in the city to visit its sacred temples and crossing points (*tirthas*); to bathe and cleanse themselves in the purifying waters of the holy Ganga; to die and be cremated, or to dispose of their dead. Many Hindus still believe that death in Banaras, known also as the sacred city of Kashi, brings liberation (*moksha*) from the cycle of rebirth. As Jonathan Parry has shown in his brilliant ethnography *Death in Banaras*, this has made both pilgrimage and death booming industries there. A cadre of ritual specialists make their living from servicing the mortuary needs of the city's residents and pilgrims alike (Parry 1994).

The religious and ritual significance of the riverfront is therefore its most celebrated and often studied feature.[11] In this book, however, I explore the riverfront of Banaras as an iconic site within the international tourist imaginary. The riverfront of Banaras graces innumerable travel brochures, postcards, and guidebooks of India. Before most visitors ever arrive, they are familiar with the colorful façades of buildings and the contiguous chain of large stone landings or steps known as *ghats* that stretch almost four kilometers along the river's edge. There are over seventy bathing ghats along the riverfront, each with its own history and ambiance. At the northern end of the city, where the Malviya Bridge arches across the horizon, one finds few of the tourist accommodations and trappings that service the steady stream of itinerant backpackers near Dasashwamedh. Alternatively, at the southern end of the riverfront, Assi Ghat and the neighborhood surrounding it have emerged as popular stomping grounds for long-term "scholarly tourists."

Dasashwamedh Ghat

One could write a fascinating book about the tourist scene in Assi, but from my perspective, the most interesting tourist encounters occurred at Dasashwamedh Ghat. As Assa Doron has noted in his study of the boatmen of Banaras, "it is somewhat misleading to speak of Dasashwamedh ghat as one ghat, as its territory actually consists of several distinct ghats . . . Shitla; Dasashwamedh; Prayag; and Prachin Dasashwamedh" (Doron 2008, 100). For tourists as well as many locals, however, this general territory is usually referred to as Dasashwamedh or, alternatively, as the Main Ghat.

Located beneath the Godolia shopping bazaar, Dasashwamedh has long been a center of ritual and commercial activity, as well as a focal point on the Western tourist itinerary. Aside from being one of the key tirthas, or crossing points, that Hindu pilgrims are supposed to visit, more recently the ghat has become host to an evening ritual ceremony (*puja*), which has emerged as another major attraction for Western tourists and residents alike. It is also one the favored places for tourists to arrange boat rides down the river, and it is one of the only ghats in the city that is accessible by car—a feature that has rendered the ghat a popular place for staging cultural programs. Most of the time, the main road leading to the ghat is closed to automobile traffic, and visitors must either make their way through the congested bazaar on foot or, as I most often did, approach the ghat by walking along the riverfront.

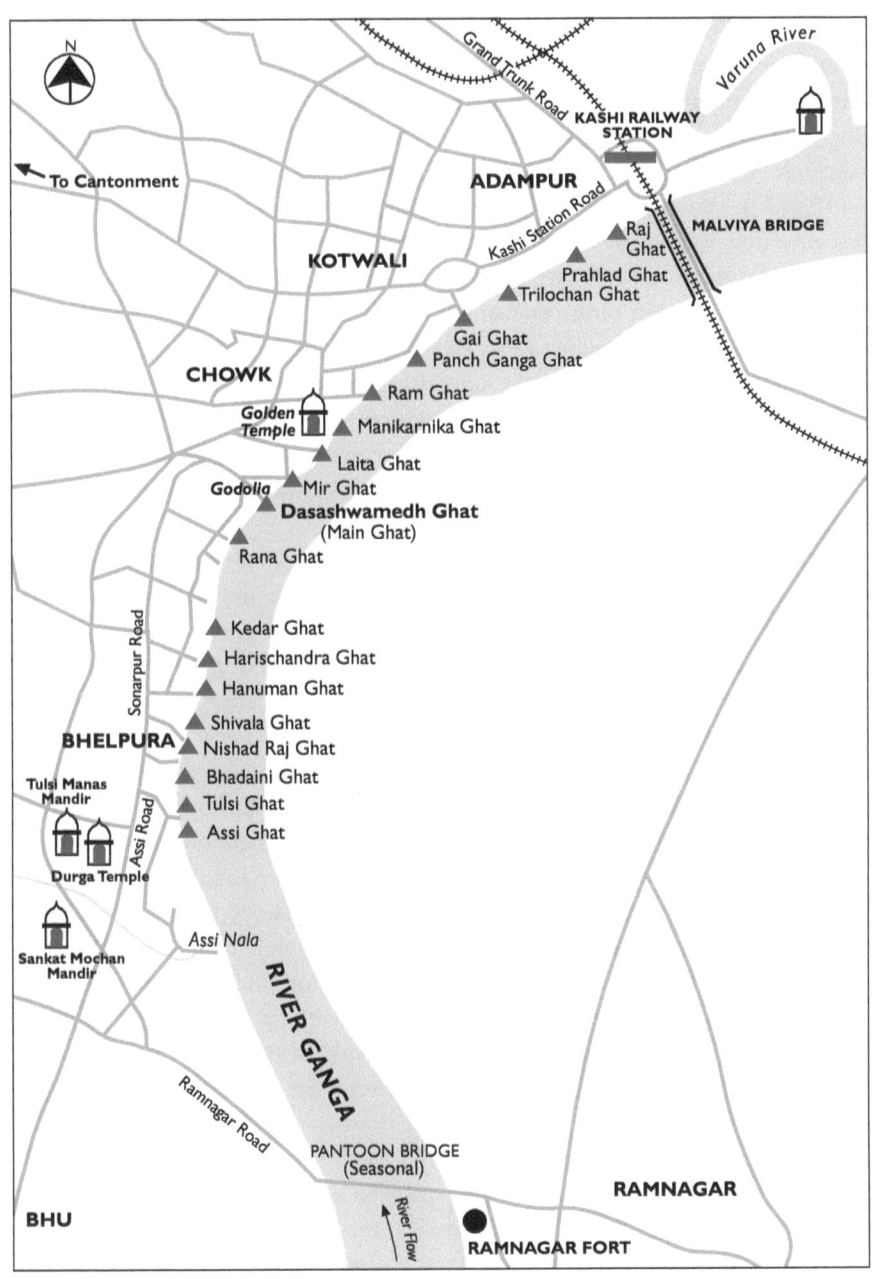

The riverfront of Banaras.
Map by Michael T. Southern.

Children and Locals

Over several months of almost daily visits to the ghat during my initial stay as a language student, I came to know many of the children and adults who worked and played at Dasashwamedh, and who, subsequently, became integral to my research. Most of the people I knew belonged to the Mallah or boatman caste and lived in the nearby neighborhood *mohalla* of Manmandir. Located just a few minutes' walk away from the ghat, Manmandir is characteristic of most neighborhoods in the "old city." The narrow multistoried buildings seem close enough to touch each other, and are arranged around a winding maze of cobbled, labyrinthine lanes called *galis*. The neighborhoods in the old city stand in stark contrast to the more recent, upscale residential "colonies," where broad boulevards and sprawling bungalows have become the fashion of the day. In Manmadir, it was quite common for families with two, three, and even four children to share a single-room dwelling that was either rented or allocated to them as part of an extended family home.

The people whom I came to know at Dasashwamedh were mostly from low-caste, uneducated, poor families. Although these were not the only terms in which they defined themselves, they were central ones, and they were usually offered to me as explanations for why their lives were difficult: "We are low people" (*ham nich log hain*). "We are poor people." "We are uneducated" (*ham pardhey likhey nahin hain*). "What shall we do?" (*ham kya karey*)? Most of the men on the ghat made their living by taking pilgrims and tourists out for boat rides on the river. Those who owned their own boats were able to earn more than those who worked for others. Yet, aside from a few successful boatmen who had established long-term relations with upscale hotels from the Cantonment area or with pilgrimage companies, most of the men complained that their earnings were meager, totaling little more than thirty or forty dollars a month. Some of the women I came to know tried to compensate for their husbands' limited incomes by selling garlands to pilgrims or by working as domestic servants in middle-class homes. However, working outside of the home also carried a stigma that for some was unbearable, no matter what the financial advantages might be.

The boys and girls who worked on the ghat, who became the focus of my research, were mostly between the ages of seven and fourteen. During the tourist season, from early October through late April, there were usually between twenty and thirty children working in the area, selling small floating lamps (*diyas*), postcards, boxes of colored powders, and souvenirs. Boys also offered their guiding services to tourists. Although boys usually referred to themselves as "guides" rather than commission agents (*dalals*), most of their earnings came from commissions they received by delivering tourists to various shops, restaurants, or hotels in the area.

The Tourists

Although the children did earn money from the organized tour groups that visited Dasashwamedh, I do not attend to these interactions or these tourists in this book. When tourists came with a group, they were usually ushered onto the ghat under the careful supervision of a tour leader and then quickly loaded onto a boat to view the riverfront from a more scenic and safe distance. As such, their interactions with the children were very limited, and from my perspective, they were of far less interest. The tourists whom I focused on actually spent time at Dasashwamedh and, whether they wanted to or not, found themselves interacting with the children who worked there. Most of these tourists were self-proclaimed "backpackers" or "independent travelers" who were between twenty and thirty-five years old. They came from America, Australia, Europe, and Israel, and their stays in the city usually ranged from a couple of days to one or two weeks.[12]

Within the last few decades, there have been numerous studies of backpackers.[13] Surveying this literature, Darya Maoz writes:

> The studies generally define backpackers as self-organized pleasure tourists on a prolonged multiple-destination journey with a flexible itinerary. They are often keen to experience the local lifestyles, attempt to 'look local,' and cite 'meeting other people' as a key motivation. Their recreational activities are likely to focus around nature, culture, or adventure. This pattern is consonant with the tendency of backpackers to travel more widely than other tourists, seeking unusual routes. Many travel under a strictly controlled budget, often due to the relatively long duration of their journey. They are described as people who search for authentic experiences, a search based on exclusion of other tourists. (Maoz 2007, 123)

Maoz acknowledges that these studies have played a useful role in delineating backpackers from other kinds of tourists. However, like other scholars, she suggests that more attention needs to be paid to the "heterogeneity in the backpacking phenomenon" and how it "is manifested in terms of nationality, purpose, motivation, organization of the trip, age, gender and lifecycle status" (2007, 124).[14] Clearly, this is an important point and one that may seem to be sidestepped in this text, for although I am very aware that these different factors influenced tourists' experiences and behaviors, in this book, I do often speak as though I were referencing a homogenous group. By invoking the terms "Western tourist," "Western traveler," and "Western backpacker" I inevitably open myself up to charges of essentialism. And yet, it is a critique I am willing to accept, for what ultimately interested me and what provides the departure point for this analysis was precisely the fact that, in spite of their different backgrounds, cultural upbringings, motivations, and stages in the life cycle, tourists' reactions to the children who worked along the riverfront frequently followed a set of patterns. There was, as I have already noted, a shared repertoire of responses, ranging from feelings of adoration to expressions of outrage, and the terms in which tourists described the children were often very similar. Understanding why this was so is one of the main goals of this book.

Methods, Data, and Positioning

When I returned to Banaras in January of 2000 to officially begin my fieldwork, I rented three rooms on the second floor of a low-budget guest house in Dasashwamedh. One served as my bedroom, another was used as an office, and the third room was designated for cooking and entertaining. Although named after the goddess of wealth, my accommodations at the Laxmi were far from luxurious. Still, there were important benefits to living there. First, the Laxmi was conveniently located just a minute's walk away from the ghat and next to one of the city's central markets. Second, considering the fact that most of the families I knew in Dasashwamedh shared a very small, single-room dwelling, it would not have been feasible for me to move in with a family. The Laxmi, therefore, seemed like a good alternative because it provided me with the space to do my work while simultaneously granting me access to the daily round of activities and goings-on in the neighborhood. It was also one of the few guest houses in the neighborhood that catered to both Western and Indian visitors, which was important to me for both practical and principled reasons. Premji, the owner of the guest house, was a friend and mentor to many of the children and young men who became my closest friends and informants during the time of my fieldwork. Like other guest house owners, he relied upon these young guides to bring him customers. However, unlike most others, Premji did permit these boys to visit their customers in the guest house and dine with them on the rooftop restaurant. Moreover, from the outset, he also agreed that the children would be allowed to visit me whenever they desired, and, as the months passed, my rooms at the Laxmi became a familiar hangout for some of the children and older guides who worked at Dasashwamedh. Finally, the Laxmi also provided me with a place to interview tourists without too much disruption. There were many occasions when I felt that my office had morphed into a therapeutic space, where tourists seized the opportunity to share their fears and fantasies about traveling in India.

By staying at the Laxmi, therefore, I was able to move between the lives and experiences of the children, tourists, and locals with relative ease. However, methodological challenges did come with trying to position myself between a diverse group of itinerant Western tourists, on the one hand, and a diverse group of Dasashwamedh residents, on the other. First, I was confronted with the fact that the tourists were not people I could come to know intimately through the traditional anthropological methods of prolonged participation observation and complete immersion in their everyday lives and environments. However, if by intimacy we mean a relationship where people disclose or share usually private parts of the self with others, then prolonged periods of time and everyday familiarity are not necessarily the criteria for its production. Indeed, in many cases I felt that the tourists whom I met and interviewed were more forthcoming with their feelings precisely because of their itinerant and "liminal" status.

Situating myself vis-à-vis people in Dasashwamedh involved a different set of challenges. These were people whom I came to know over a prolonged period of time and through daily interactions. I spent a good deal of time visiting people in their homes; chatting, sharing meals, drinking tea, watching Hindi films and sitcoms on small black-and-white television sets, and chewing betel nut (*paan*). I also spent a considerable amount of time participating in certain favored leisure activities, which variously involved attending weddings, picnics on the opposite side of the river, raucous whiskey and chicken feasts, which were usually held on a houseboat at night, and mini-pilgrimages that involved journeying, by boat, two and three days downriver.

One of my biggest challenges was balancing my relationships and interactions between the children and the adults I befriended at Dasashwamedh. There were many times when as a researcher I wanted nothing more than to play and talk with the children on the ghat, many of whom referred to me as "Jenny *Didi*" and treated me as an honorary big sister. However, often my older friends would appear and more or less demand that I give them my attention. Because they were older, and because age differences establish one set of terms for hierarchical relations in India, they often felt entitled to steal the spotlight and to shoo the children away. This frequently happened with outsiders, as well. My conversations with children on the riverfront were often interrupted by outside visitors (almost always male), who felt entitled to do so.

The other challenge, however, had to do with the way my presence influenced interactions and relationships between the children and tourists. The children and I developed a working understanding of sorts. They knew I was interested in their customers, and I knew they were interested in how I might be able to make them appear more credible. When they would deliver tourists to my office for interviews, some of the children hoped, and perhaps expected, that I would convince these tourists to assist them financially. This put me in an awkward position at times. For instance, tourists would ask me if a particular child really needed 10,000 rupees to pay for school tuition that year or needed

5,000 rupees for a family member's operation. Even when I knew the tales were fictional, the policy I ultimately adopted and tried to maintain throughout the course of my fieldwork was to plead ignorance. I tried not to disturb the children's chances of earning money from tourists, nor to be an active accomplice in their money-making schemes. Sometimes, I would accompany the children and their customers on sightseeing tours and, of course, in those situations as well my presence influenced what tourists took away from these encounters. However, it seemed like another good opportunity for observing their interactions with the children, so on the occasions when I was invited, I went along.

Much of the data I collected, therefore, came from informal conversations and from endless hours spent on and around Dasashwamedh Ghat observing interactions between children, tourists, and locals. A lot of what I report in this book also comes from taped interviews, however. Over the course of twenty months of fieldwork, I conducted sixty-three taped interviews with tourists and another thirty-five with people in Dasashwamedh. The practical and theoretically thorny issues surrounding taped interviews have been duly noted by anthropologists and sociologists.[15] I found them to be an invaluable source of data, however. These interviews enabled me to recognize responses and patterns of thinking that were not always discernable through other forms of observation. They enabled me to listen more carefully to the terms people used to express themselves and to hear the metaphors, the slips of the tongue, the expressions of frustrations that so frequently animated our conversations. Had I not been able to revisit these conversations on tape, many of the subtle yet illuminating nuances they contained would have slipped by unnoticed. Moreover, although every anthropologist develops her own strategies for trying to stay connected during the long and often frustrating process of writing up, for me, there was something particularly comforting in being able to hear the voices of my acquaintances and the conversations that we had shared.

Finally, in terms of positioning, it seems worth noting that the projects we choose to study, the "baggage" we bring to the task, and the ways we orient ourselves in relation to a set of questions and concerns are never arbitrary. In the process of writing this book, I have often been struck by a recurring childhood memory of being on vacation with my family. I was almost six years old, and my brother and I were seated in the back of a rental car while my father and mother navigated us through a slow-moving traffic jam in a run-down neighborhood in the Bahamas. I recall staring out the window and seeing a local girl, who looked to be about my age, perched on a balcony wearing a tattered dress. She was glaring down at me with a hateful expression. When our eyes met, to me, the moment felt impregnated with feelings and meanings that I could sense were important, but could not fully comprehend. I wanted to escape her gaze. I wanted the traffic to move faster. And yet, as we began to pull away, I also found myself turning my head so that I could keep her in my sight. That little girl and her piercing stare have stayed with me for all of these years. Though I never intended it to be so, I suspect that in part, writing this book has been an attempt to understand that fleeting encounter and to grasp the myriad forces and relations that positioned us within that moment.

2

A Tourist Town

My first visit to Banaras was as a tourist. It was spring of 1995, I was twenty-two years old, and I had recently graduated from college. During my junior year, I had spent a semester abroad in India, and that experience, coupled with the excellent anthropology courses I was exposed to as an undergraduate, had inspired me to apply for Ph.D. programs. Disregarding all advice to wait and figure out what I "really wanted to do," I promptly, and perhaps, even impulsively, took the GREs, submitted my applications for graduate school, and then returned to India to wait out the decision.

During my semester abroad I had been regaled with numerous accounts of the "charms" and "challenges" of Banaras. "You haven't seen India until you've been to Banaras," I was repeatedly told. Thus, when the opportunity for a week-long visit presented itself on my second trip, I went. Traveling solo by train, I arrived in the city in the early morning. I was dazed, confused, and, like many tourists, intimidated by the environment I was stepping into. Strapped under a heavy, awkwardly fitting backpack, I struggled to keep my balance as I made my way off the train, through the station, and into the crowd of shouting rickshaw drivers who immediately began barraging me with offers. "Come with me! Come with me! I take you to cheap, good guest house, Ganga view!"

Ultimately, I did not end up with a Ganga view. However, I was taken to a hotel that was cheap, relatively clean, and close enough to the riverfront to satisfy me. It was located in the Godolia Bazaar, just a minute's walk away from Dasashwamedh Ghat. After checking into my hotel, I quickly headed to the riverfront. Upon descending the steps of the ghat, I was again bombarded with offers from boatmen and young guides who wanted to show me around the city. I declined the offers and with the rudimentary Hindi I had learned during my semester abroad program, I launched into a desperate effort to break the commodifying frame of "host" and "guest" and convince them of our shared humanity. It backfired. My efforts at communing with these solicitors quickly turned into complaints and before I realized what I was saying, I was going on and on about how tourists in India were always being taken advantage of by people who seemed solely interested in making money.

The guides and boatmen who had gathered around began chiding me. From their perspective my rant reflected a gross insensitivity to the asymmetries in wealth and power that positioned us as very different kinds of subjects within the world system. They quickly schooled me in the error of my ways. "Why are you complaining? You come from a big rich country. You do not even have to work! Here you are in India wandering around. We can't do that; if we don't make money how will we eat?"

Still unable to appreciate their lesson in structural inequalities, I took their resentment personally, burst into tears, and headed back to my hotel to mend my wounded feelings with a three-course lunch of *dal makhani*, *palak paneer*, and onion *pakoras*. By early the next morning, my body began purging everything I had inside of me and I awoke sicker than I had ever felt in my life. I spent the rest of my week-long visit in the city bedridden in my hotel, and it was not until two years later, when I returned to Banaras to study Hindi, that I encountered these boatmen and guides again. They recalled the incident on the ghats, "You ran off crying like a little girl!" they laughed. I blushed with embarrassment but I was also quietly delighted that that they had remembered me. The incident from the past had emerged as an opportunity for a new beginning and this time, instead of complaining, I became much more interested in listening and watching. What kind of tourist space was the riverfront? What kinds of relations mediated interactions between hosts and guests? What had led me, like numerous other tourists I eventually came to observe, to run off the ghats in tears? And why, two years later, did I feel so pleased to be recognized?

A Tourist Destination

Westerners have been traveling through Banaras for over four hundred years, and they have penned a lengthy trail of impressions of the city. In the mid-sixteenth and seventeenth centuries, the town attracted merchants and explorers who were variously awestruck, inspired, and revolted by the religious spectacles and "idolatry" that they witnessed (Eck 1983). By the end of the eighteenth century and throughout the nineteenth, when the city was officially under British rule, Banaras, and its riverfront in particular, came to be regarded as one of the must-see destinations on the standard traveler/tourist route, and writings on the city proliferated. From a historical standpoint, this corpus of travel writings is interesting because it provides a sense of where and how Westerners spent their visits and the way this changed over time. More generally, these records display the "observational/ travel modalities" (Cohn 1996, 6) through which

Western visitors engaged, perceived, and then represented the city of Banaras to others. As the anthropologist Bernard Cohn astutely observed, what Western travelers took notice of and reported varied not only with the different sociopolitical contexts of their travels but also in accordance with certain aesthetic principles that came to dominate particular periods, such as "the sublime," the "picturesque," the "romantic," and the "realistic" (7). To talk about the history of Banaras and its riverfront as a tourist destination, therefore, is both to take account of the structural developments of the industry (the increasing number of hotels, guest houses, shops, restaurants, tourists, jobs, etc.), and also to look at the changing representational and travel practices of the tourists themselves and the conditions that have influenced them.

What follows is by no means an exhaustive treatment of this subject. Rather, in this chapter I draw upon colonial travel writings coupled with more recent guidebooks and data that I gathered on tourists and tourism workers while I was in Banaras, to sketch a general picture of how Dasashwamedh has changed as a Western tourist destination. I also consider some of the factors that may help explain when and why children in Banaras began to take to the riverfront to sell goods to foreign travelers. Finally, I explore the shift among the "observational / travel modalities" of Western visitors during the eighteenth, nineteenth, and early twentieth centuries and the emergence of a more person-centered and interactive way of travelling that characterized many of the tourists whom I observed and interviewed during my fieldwork. In so doing, I suggest that the encounters explored in this book are best understood as the historical product of both social and subjective transformations.

Observing Otherness

Colonial travel writings most often framed the city of Banaras as a site of radical Otherness. Portrayed as the ultimate icon of the mystical East, it provided a foil against which Western order, progress, and rationality could be both celebrated and critiqued.[1] For Reginald Heber, the Anglican bishop of Calcutta who visited Banaras in 1824, Banaras was "a remarkable city, more entirely and characteristically Eastern" than any which he had ever seen (Eck 1983, 13). In the travel memoirs of André Chevrillon, published in English translation in 1896, the timeless splendor of the city evoked a nostalgic remorse for a lost European past. "Today not a trace remains of our European world as it then was; it is altogether dead, finished, buried in the abyss of time. But this city of Benares remains always Kasi, 'the resplendent city,' of India" (Chevrillon 1896, 74). Like so many travelers, Chevrillon was also struck by the overwhelming displays of religious life. As he noted, "elsewhere religion is only part of the public life; at Benares there is nothing else to be seen" (75).

Although the city inspired appreciation and perhaps even sparked some longings to recover a more enchanted world at home, for Chevrillon, Banaras also clearly stood beyond the pale of Western reason. In describing his first impressions, he wrote: "Imagine yourself to have landed in a country where the inhabitants walk on their heads. This race thinks, and feels, and lives in a fashion contrary to our own; and one's first idea on arriving in Benares is that insanity is normal here" (Chevrillon 1896, 76).

Like scores of other travelers, for Chevrillon it was the riverfront more than any other site in the city that put this incomprehensible spectacle of humanity on display. In recounting his boat ride along the river, he wrote:

> We have gone over two miles, and the spectacle is the same. The crowd, the architecture, the sunlight, seem to be visions of some opium-dream, where time, space, and all that they contain, appear enormously magnified and multiplied . . . from all this moving, praying singing multitude rises a great noise, a confused rustle of human life. Everywhere on the edge of the great careless river there is the same swarming life, the same vast wave of humanity heaping itself up. (Chevrillon 1896, 79)

As continues to be the case for many tourists, the boat ride along the Ganga provided colonial travelers with a favored way of consuming "the spectacle" of Banaras. From the comparatively protected space of the boat, these travelers were able to gaze out on the city without having to immerse themselves in the "swarming" and "confused rustle" of human life that they found both intriguing and intimidating. Moreover, for the European traveler, the chaos of India was cordoned off as soon as he or she returned to the sanctuary of the hotel. As Chevrillon described: "At the hotel it is a strange sensation to come back to European tranquillity and reasonableness, fine, calm order, correct costume, commonplace and courteous conversation. You fall back into your accustomed place, and the impression of what you have just seen disappears like a dream" (Chevrillon 1896, 81). Indeed, although most European travelers were quite content if not eager to maintain the distance between themselves and India and retreat to what was familiar and comfortable at the end of the day, it is also apparent that for some, Chevrillon included, this limited access and inability to get behind the scenes was rather frustrating. As he wrote, "It is difficult to see anything in Benares beyond the streets and public buildings. Letters of introduction give you access only to European homes; and of the Hindu world you can see scarcely beyond its exterior" (108–109).

Such difficulties were also mentioned by W. S. Caine in his book, *Picturesque India: A Handbook for European Travelers*, which was published in 1890. Caine described Banaras as "the most picturesque city in India" and, as his travel handbook makes clear, by the late nineteenth century it had become a popular destination for "scoffing globetrotters from Europe and America" who would spend their days streaming "up and down the ghats" (Caine 1890, 302). In describing some of the standard touring practices of Western visitors, he noted that although they flocked to the riverfront during the day, at night almost all of these travelers resided in the British enclave of the Cantonment Area, where the city's first European hotels, and to this day most lavish ones, were constructed. Like Chevrillon, Caine too reported that it was both a common practice and "a great advantage" for Western travelers to arrive in Banaras with letters of introduction to either fellow Europeans, or to "educated Hindu gentlemen" who could properly educate them on the culture, sites, and history of the city. Advising travelers to steer clear of the "professional guides," he wrote: "The professional guides all over India are very inferior, and cannot do more than show the way through the bazaars, point out notable buildings, and keep a sharp eye on tips and commissions. Every turn of the street, every step of the ghat, every group on the platforms present some incident exciting the greatest curiosity, which can only be satisfied by someone versed in the customs of the Hindu religion" (304).

Dasashwamedh Ghat and the Magnificence of Banaras

Contemporary travel writings continue to depict Banaras as a "timeless" and "unchanging" wonder. In the early part of the twentieth century, however, local and foreign accounts of the city also emphasized the way Banaras was changing. Banaras was depicted as a city struggling to ward off the "vulgar" realities of modern life and hold onto to its "ancient glory." For many observers, the place most likely to preserve the ancient and magnificent splendor of the city was Dasashwamedh Ghat. For instance, in *Benares, the Sacred City*, published in 1905, E. B. Havell, principal of the Government School of Art in Calcutta, remarked: "The traveler who wishes to realize the magnificence of Benares on the riverside, and to catch some reflection of that Vedic brightness which still shines through all that is sordid and vulgar in the modern city, must be at Dasashwamedh Ghat before the first streak of dawn" (Havell 1905, 90).

In his book, *Benares*, published in 1930, P. Seshadri described the riverfront of Banaras as "more Indian probably than scenes witnessed anywhere else in the country" (Seshadri 1930, 12). Although he lamented many of the changes that had beset the city, like Havell, he, too, suggested that Dasashwamedh Ghat continued to be one of the few places where vestiges of Banaras's triumphant past could still be found:

> Some of the ancient glory has departed. The routes of Indian commerce have shifted their courses because of the introduction of the railway. The center of political gravity has changed in other directions. Other noble cities have sprung up elsewhere in India and have thrown elder ones

into the shade, at least with regard to the achievements of modern civilization. . . . But the locality in Benares which still retains some of all this early grandeur is the Dasashwamedh Ghat reached by a broad road from the city and pouring with a continuous crowd of pilgrims and seekers after pleasure towards the river crowded with bustling life. (Seshadri 1930, 25)

Seshadri's account of Dasashwamedh also provides some insight into the way the ghat figured into local community life as well as the importance it took on in Western representations of India:

Here are crowds of devotees listening to a sacred recitation from the scriptures; young men and women who have come in the evening by way of recreation to the river bank which is really also a fashionable promenade for the city; grave-looking elders spending the evening of their lives in peaceful retirement; men of business, artists, hawkers, listless spectators—everybody seems to be there in the evening, inviting interested observation. Many a well-known painter of the West has represented the panorama of life on this ghat, with all its wonderful grouping of colour, as seen under the brilliant effects of a tropical sun. (Seshadri 1930, 26–27)

The descriptions above make it clear that Dasashwamedh Ghat has long been a powerful signifier in representations of Banaras and more generally, of the East. These texts also evidence the fact that the ghat has served as one of the most prominent attractions for local and foreign spectators, and that its centrality to the tourism industry in the city can be traced back over two hundred years. Although it is obvious that Western travelers frequented the ghat and riverfront during the eighteenth, nineteenth, and early twentieth centuries, it is also apparent that the area was far from the bustling tourist hub that it is today. For lodging, dining, and entertainment European and American travelers were still largely confined to the Cantonment Area in the center of the city, and until the late 1970s there were no formal accommodations for Western travelers near the riverfront.[2] These impressions of the city also draw attention to the fact that even though the desire may have been there, Western travelers were quite limited in terms of their possibilities for interacting with locals. It seems that their wanderings through the city were highly mediated, either by professional guides, European residents, or "educated Hindu gentlemen" who in some cases were requested, and in others took it upon themselves, to tend to the needs and curiosity of these visitors. Moreover, it seems that these visits were largely construed as educational experiences, akin to the European and American "grand tour," and that having the proper guide, and the proper information about the city's sites, history, and culture, was of great concern.[3]

From Colonial to Counter Culture

By the mid-1960s and throughout the 1970s the Western "hippie invasion" found its way into Banaras. Although it meant more business for people involved in the tourism industry, and a higher GDP for the nation as a whole, the influx of these young, "untidy," low-budget travelers stirred up a good deal of anxiety and ambivalence throughout India. By 1968 their steady arrivals were characterized in the *Times of India* as a potentially "sinister pattern" by magistrates in New Delhi.[4] Like their colonial predecessors, these travelers were also awestruck by the otherness of the East, but instead of condemning it for its seemingly irrational religiosity, they saw it as offering promises of spiritual wisdom and potential escape routes out of the disenchanted world of Western materialism.

In Banaras, this wave of low-budget travelers had a significant impact on the infrastructure of the tourism industry, and ultimately led to the development of a low-budget tourist hub in "the old city" near Dasashwamedh. Small guest houses and hotels began to spring up in the narrow-lane neighborhoods along the riverfront, and by the mid-1980s, the Cantonment Area, which had previously lodged almost all Western visitors, increasingly became the privileged domicile for upscale tourists and organized tour groups who could afford to pay five-star hotel prices, and who preferred air conditioning and Western toilets to breathtaking views of the Ganga.

In an effort to roughly sketch out when this transformation occurred and understand its impact on the area of Dasashwamedh, I draw upon the following materials: historical accounts of the city; guide books from the sixties, seventies, eighties, and nineties that describe the city and the range of accommodations available to Western travelers; an interview with one of the first low-budget guest house owners in the Dasashwamedh area; and an interview with an English tourist who visited Banaras in 1974.

Disintegration

Kubernath Sukul was gravely dissatisfied with the books that Europeans had written about Banaras, so in 1974 he published his own historical "study" of the city, entitled *Varanasi down the Ages*. It attracted my attention not just because he spoke at length about Dasashwamedh Ghat but also because it explicitly mentioned the presence of "Hippies" in the city. It also referenced the impending development of tourist "rest houses" along the riverfront, thereby suggesting that in 1974, there were few if any, formal accommodations for Western tourists in the area. Remarking on the ghat, he wrote:

> This is the only ghat in the heart of the town where conveyances can go right up to the river bank and has consequently been ever the place where the nobility and gentry, both Indian and foreign have approached the

river for a boat-ride. It was here that queen Victoria's sons, grandsons, and great grandsons alighted from their carriages to see the glorious ghats of Varanasi by boat. . . . Again it is here that the Hippies of the present day have built their headquarters and are ruining the atmosphere of the most important Tirtha. The Municipal Corporation intends to add to this ruination by building a rest house for tourists there. (Sukul 1974, 274–275)

Sukul tried to warn his readers that the new Western "Hippie" presence would further defile the city's sacred geography and culture. However, although Sukul identified Western hippies as corrosive forces in Banaras, he also suggested that there were other invaders who were just as complicit in bringing about this state of cultural crisis. As he remarked:

Vicissitudes of life consequent on rising prices in the beginning and later on the civic invasion of Varanasi by the citizens of other provinces in numbers which exceeded the total population of Varanasi, swamped the atmosphere, and the Varanasi man found himself surrounded on all sides by this avalanche of the cultures of the Punjab and Sindh on the one hand and of Eastern Bengal on the other. He started getting suffocated, and in sheer despair had to adapt himself to these changed and changing conditions of life. The Varanasi culture is at present in the throes of an agonizing disintegration. The older representatives of that way of life still survive but their number is fast dwindling and the younger generation are keen at imbibing the culture of Varanasi's guests including the Hippies. (Sukul 1974, 320–326)

The Rise of the Low-Budget Guest House

The anxiety that surrounded the "hippie invasion" of the early 1970s was also relayed to me by Mr. Joshi, who opened one of the first and, at the time of my research, one of the most successful low-budget guest houses in the Dasashwamedh area. Mr. Joshi was a well-traveled man who had been educated in England and who spoke with a thick British accent. In March of 1978, after traveling with some British friends in Nepal, he decided to open a guest house in Banaras. "At the time," he said, "there were no clean, orderly and inexpensive places for foreigners to stay, there were no guest houses in the Dasashwamedh area. So I had this idea that I could open a place that was clean, and safe, and honest, where there wouldn't be any cheating and there would be security for tourists."

While Mr. Joshi saw the influx of low-budget travelers as an opportunity to establish a respectable and prosperous business, others, as Sukul's remarks already make clear, were extremely unhappy about the presence of these Western visitors. In recounting the beginnings of his business venture, Mr. Joshi told me that he and his wife had faced numerous difficulties and criticisms when they decided to open their lodge. Many of the residents in the area, he said, strongly objected to having "these kinds of Westerners," who were reputed to be dirty, drug users, and sexually promiscuous, so close to some of the city's holiest sites. In talking about the impressions that travelers of the sixties and seventies evoked, and those that remain today, Mr. Joshi commented:

> The impression that . . . a particular brand of foreigner I would like to say. Like in the early sixties and the seventies the Westerners who came to Varanasi, apart from the large tourists groups who stayed in five-star hotels, the average backpacker was maybe of the hippie cult, you know, lost, spiritual search, smoking pot, trying to . . . you know the anti-establishment if you would. So the impression that they created when they initially came was not a very good impression to the average Indian mind. So, that image has stuck.

In our interview, Mr. Joshi also pointed out that strong objections still persisted, and that many people in Banaras continued to frown upon Western travelers residing near the riverfront, as they were viewed as "polluting the Indian culture." He even informed me that one year prior to our interview, in an effort "to placate Hindu fundamentalists," local politicians had attempted to "remedy" the situation with an unsuccessful motion to revoke guest house licenses in the area. "Compared with a couple of thousand tourists coming to Varanasi," Mr. Joshi complained, "the effects of cable television are far worse, or the Internet. If these people want to be the protectors of Indian culture, blah, blah, blah they should focus on that."

Mr. Joshi's response opens up a much larger issue that runs throughout this book. For it raises the question: to what extent did foreign tourism function as an alibi, or provide people in Banaras with an idiom through which to express anxieties about more pervasive forms of change? While Mr. Joshi clearly denied the idea that foreign tourism was one of the main causes of cultural corruption and decline, many others whom I interviewed and spoke with in the area did feel that it was playing a leading role in this process.

A Traveler's Look Back

I also gleaned some information about what Dasashwamedh was like as a tourist destination during the 1970s from an interview I conducted with Peter, a fifty-one-year-old English traveler who first visited Banaras in 1974, the year Sukul's book came off the press. Spurred on by an account of an Italian woman who had cycled from Dublin to Kathmandu and vivid photographs in *National Geographic*, Peter and a friend decided to arrange their own bicycle tour in northern India, which eventually brought them to Banaras. Peter noted that most Western travelers were lodging in the Cantonment Area during this time, but he also pointed out that it was common for these travelers to rent house boats along the riverfront, which may help explain Sukul's claim that the hippies had established a virtual headquarters at Dasashwamedh. Recalling his first visit to Banaras in winter of 1974, Peter remarked:

> When we got to Varanasi we slept at the Tourist Bungalow in the Cantonment Area. At that time there were no guest houses near the ghats. Most of the accommodations were in the house boats, which we really thought was a little bit dangerous and it wasn't really good for keeping two bicycles. I remember still doing the tours in the morning, sort of sight-seeing down to the ghats, but there were no children selling postcards. I can remember seeing small children with their mothers but there were certainly no children selling postcards; in fact I don't remember there being postcards in Varanasi because there were very few tourists, and most of the tourists were staying in the Clark's Hotel in the Cantonment. There was no sort of tourist places or special restaurants to get Western food, or places to get bus tickets or train tickets.

In recalling his first visit, Peter not only drew attention to how different the accommodations were. He also focused on how "the people" had changed. As he went on to note:

> And the people, the people then were just curious about where you had come from and why you had an Indian bicycle and where you were going and I can't actually remember people actually trying to sell me things years ago, whereas now you get the feeling when it is "Hello, how are you? What is your name? Which country did you come from?" the next thing is going to be the silk factory. Or something like this, it gets on your nerves really, and you fall into the trap of thinking that everyone is selling you something and then you realize they're not and then sometimes you feel a bit guilty that you were a bit snappy because you think, "Oh, I've heard all this before it's going to be hello how are you?" And then just when you think it's going to be "Oh have a look at my silk shop," they say, "Oh it's been nice meeting you and sorry I have to go now." So you feel a bit guilty. You know, you're a bit snappy rather than a bit friendly. Now you're aware that everyone wants to sell you something, or most people do, and that's usually the reason to make contact with foreigners. The reason why they want to make contact with you . . . now people go out of their way because they think they might see some rupees at the end of the day. But the small children here, I don't really feel it about them, you can accept it more from children. Especially when you see where they live.

Despite the obvious nostalgia in Peter's account, his narrative is interesting for a number of reasons. First, his comments suggest that during the hippie era

Western travelers developed ways of traveling that differed considerably from those of their colonial predecessors. Instead of trying to secure letters of introduction to learned Hindu gentleman or experience the city through a safe yet distant gaze, travelers like Peter actually welcomed the opportunity to immerse themselves in the everyday hustle and bustle of urban life and establish more intimate contact with India and Indians.

Peter's recollections also go back to a time when there were considerably fewer Western travelers in the city. Although it was a popular destination, at that point Banaras was not a highly developed Western tourist hub. On his first visit, Peter did not encounter the plentiful shops, restaurants, guest houses, yoga centers, and astrologers that cater exclusively to Western visitors today.[5] A Western traveler with a bicycle may have been a curiosity but, as Peter pointed out, he was not immediately marked as a potential source of profit because the commercial infrastructure was not in place.[6]

Peter, therefore, contrasted this moment in the past with a much different picture of the present. On this trip, Peter was traveling alone, and staying in an inexpensive guest house near Dasashwamedh. Every day, he spent hours sitting on the ghat where, he told me, he met "all sorts of people." However, as he indicated in the passage above, this time, all of his interactions were laced with suspicion and second guessing. When people approached him, he assumed they wanted to try and sell him something, and if they left without making any such attempts he felt guilty for questioning their motives in the first place.

Peter's narrative thus indicates a change in the traveler himself. Over his many years of visiting India, Peter had come to occupy a very different subjective space that influenced his possibilities for interacting with the locals whom he met—a difference that, as Peter pointed out, manifested itself in a shift from "friendly" to "snappy" responses. Although he had more interactions with locals now than ever before, Peter saw them as less genuine, motivated by the desire for "some rupees at the end of the day" instead of by earnest curiosity and good will.

However, Peter also noted that he could accept and understand this kind of treatment from children. Indeed, as I discuss in chapter 4, one of the reasons I wanted to interview Peter was because he had developed a relationship with a group of young children who sold postcards and candles on the ghat, and every afternoon he would go to the ghat to spend time with them: chatting, buying them snacks and drinks, and sometimes even visiting their homes.

From Hippies, to Freaks, to Shoestring Travelers: Banaras in the 1980s

In 1981, "Varanasi and the holy Ganges" were listed in *The Lonely Planet* guidebook as one of the major "Freak Centers" in India; a place where "on-the-road-hippy-dreams" and 1960s lifestyles were still being lived out amid "India's kind climate." Compared with the three low-budget hotels that were listed in the 1975 *Fodor's India* guidebook, by 1981, there were over thirteen "bottom end" accommodations listed. Dasashwamedh Ghat was also mentioned in this edition of *The Lonely Planet* as an optimal starting point for beginning a tour of the riverfront, and the book explicitly cautioned travelers as they wandered the ghats to be "on the lookout" for "the ever present beggars giving others an opportunity to do their karma some good" (236). Although much could be said about this advice, it does suggest that by this point in time, Western travelers in Banaras were increasingly heading out on their own as they toured the city, and more open to the interventions and appeals of its riverfront dwellers.

By 1987, Banaras had been crossed off from *The Lonely Planet*'s list of "Freak Center" destinations, but the Godolia bazaar and "the old city" near the riverfront had achieved formal status in the guidebook as one of the "three important areas of accommodation" for "shoestring travelers." Now, within this area alone, there were twelve hotels and guest houses listed in the guidebook. By the time the 1980s came to a close, therefore, the low-budget travel industry in Banaras was well established and the area surrounding Godolia and Dasashwamedh was most visibly influenced by this development. The guidebook even included a map highlighting the area, and it listed the numerous restaurants that had opened up to cater to this stream of Western travelers. In the "Things to Buy" section of the Banaras review, the authors advertised the fabulous silks of Banaras, but again, imparted a warning: "Varanasi is famous all over India for silk brocades and beautiful Benares saris. However, there are lots of rip-off merchants and commission men at work. Invitations to 'come to my home for tea' will inevitably mean to somebody's silk showroom, where you will be pressured into buying things" (281).

This warning again suggests that by this point in time, the tactics and strategies of "commission men" working in the informal sector of the tourism industry in Banaras had achieved a certain level of notoriety among travelers. Guidebooks thus cautioned tourists not to confuse expressions of genuine hospitality with the workings of a savvy hospitality industry. It also suggests that travelers' desires to get behind the scenes and have more personal encounters with locals had indeed become integral to the workings of this informal economy. By holding out the possibility for a friendly exchange, or a more intimate peek into Indian life, salesmen frequently seduced tourists into buying their goods.

The Growth of Tourism and the Uncertainty of the Future

Official statistics on the influx of Western tourists in Banaras, particularly prior to the 1990s, were difficult to obtain, and those that I did procure varied dramatically in terms of the numbers they reported. For instance, according to one data set from the U.P. Tourism Department, between 1993 and 1997 the number of foreign tourists in Banaras more than doubled from 107,000 tourists to 273,956.[7] The statistics I obtained from the local Foreigners Registration Office in Varanasi, however, reported the number of foreign tourist arrivals to be 135,781 for the year 1997. Although these discrepancies are significant, both sources report that for most of the decade, foreign tourist arrivals in Banaras were steadily increasing, but then began to decline in 1998, two years before I officially started my fieldwork.

This information is significant for two reasons. The first is that most people in Banaras maintained that children did not begin to work in the informal sector of the tourism industry until the early 1990s, which would mean that their entry into this economy coincided with this increase in tourist arrivals. The other reason these numbers are significant is that when I arrived to begin my fieldwork in 2000, people in Dasashwamedh often remarked that the foreign tourism industry was itself in crisis and they even predicted that in the years ahead tourists would stop coming to the city altogether—a fear that was exacerbated in the aftermath of September 11, when tourist arrivals decreased by another 20 percent.[8] This palpable skepticism and insecurity often influenced people's reactions to tourists as well as to the children who relied upon them to make a living.

Conclusion: Not Just Commission Men Anymore

A colorful picture of Dasashwamedh Ghat bathed in morning sunshine graces the cover of the 2001 edition of the *Frommer's Adventure Guides: India, Pakistan, and the Himalaya*. The book is unconventional in its presentation; instead of providing succinct historical narratives and "useful facts for the visitor," each destination is covered by a different author who presents a diary-like entry on his or her experiences there. The effect is a guide book that reads more like a travel log. Although the Banaras entry reinscribes many of the familiar Orientalist tropes and themes that animated colonial representations of the city and does little to distinguish itself as a particularly useful aid to the traveler, there is one aspect that I find noteworthy: the explicit mention of children on the ghats. In describing his visit to the riverfront, the author writes: "As I wandered along the upper steps, boatmen persistently offered me trips on the river, some at just $2 per hour. In between the boatmen's sales pitches, pretty young girls with smiles to die for used their charm and their mantra 'No buy, just look, costs nothing to look,' to sell me dreary postcards of the city and river" (78). As the rest of this book will demonstrate, these "pretty young girls," as well as young boys, with their "smiles to die for," special "charm," and "mantras," have increasingly become objects of "the tourist gaze" (Urry 1990). Indeed, by the time of my research, they were actively influencing the ways that many of these visitors explored and experienced the riverfront.

To summarize, some of the social and subjective changes that have facilitated encounters between Western tourists and the children on the riverfront include: a significant increase in the number of foreign tourists during the 1990s; the development of a low-budget tourist hub near the riverfront and Dasashwamedh Ghat; less structured touring practices on the part of Western travelers; an increase in the number of shops and guest houses that began paying these children commissions for bringing them customers; and finally, a subjective change in the tourists themselves. For many tourists in Banaras, the yearning to establish more interactive, affectively charged encounters on their vacations has become a central part of the travel quest. And, as will be seen, when the children on the ghats were able to help tourists fulfill this desire, they were often compensated with even more "rupees at the end of the day."

PART 2

Conceptions of Children

3

Girls and Boys on the Ghats

In January of 2000, when I returned to Banaras to officially begin my fieldwork, I discovered a curious absence. Almost all of the girls whom I had met two years before and who worked on the ghat selling *diyas* (small floating lamps) and postcards were gone. There was a new batch of young girls selling these items, but it was as though the others had been sent into hiding and, as I later found out, in a sense they had been. With a few notable exceptions, by the time the girls reached the age of twelve or thirteen, they were prohibited from working on the riverfront. In an interview with Diraj Sahani, one of the older guides in the neighborhood, I asked him why this was the case, and he provided an explanation that I was to hear countless times throughout the course my research:

> After that, slowly, slowly they become [in English] "young," and there are a lot of boys on the ghats and they will look at the girls in a bad way and the girl will get the wrong kinds of feelings, so the parents have to stop the girl and say, "You stay at home and do your work, make food, help your mother." We worry about girls who have become mature (*sayana*) being on the ghats, people will say bad things about her, boys will look at her in the wrong way, they will say she is a girl who wanders around a lot, they will say she is doing some bad business. You see girls are the honor of the house, if something happens to them it is a disgrace for the whole family.

Gender, therefore, played a fundamental role in determining the way the children participated in this informal tourist economy. Girls and boys were not only exposed to different work trajectories but they were also subject to very different spatial constraints and social expectations. While boys were free to guide tourists around the city and participate in the more lucrative enterprise of commission work (*dalali*), girls were almost always confined to selling lower-priced items on the riverfront, where their behavior and activities could be monitored by kinsmen and neighbors.¹

The gendered nature of this economy and the different access that girls and boys had to various spaces in the city resonate with many of the observations made by the anthropologist Nita Kumar. Kumar argues that gender plays the most decisive role in influencing the way that space is structured, imagined, and experienced by children in Banaras. As she observes: "the most crucial lines of division within a class called children are between girls and boys: girls privilege the home, boys the neighborhood; girls know they have more than one home, boys that they will forever wander. Their personas, and their lives, as male and female, are shaped by the spaces they find themselves in, the spaces as they read and live them, and the spaces they anticipate" (Kumar 2007, 239). Following Henrietta Moore, Kumar is interested in how spatial relations both "represent and reproduce social relations." She examines how adults use space in their attempts to discipline and socialize children along gendered lines. However, she also notes that the question remains as to "how children reappropriate space" and use tactics both overt and clandestine "to escape the nets of disciplining" (246).

In this chapter, I take up this question and I introduce some of the children who worked on and near Dasashwamedh Ghat during the time of my fieldwork. I discuss the different ways that girls and boys negotiated the riverfront and participated in this informal economy. Although their accounts resonate with many of Kumar's ethnographic findings, they also diverge from them in interesting ways. Most notably, they highlight the prominent role that class, caste, and neighborhood affiliation played in configuring the children's experiences.

So Long as They Are Children

Like Diraj, numerous anthropologists have noted the relative freedoms afforded to prepubescent girls in India and the increasing restrictions that are placed upon them as they approach sexual maturity. As Leela Dube has observed, "Pre-pubertal girls can generally play with boys and other girls on streets and in parks, courtyards, and other open spaces." Moreover, in "poorer sections of the population," they often work outside of the home. However, with the onset of puberty girls are usually withdrawn from the labor market and prohibited from playing with boys in public spaces (Dube 2001, 108). Sylvia Vatuk suggests that this is because in Hindu India, "concern about how daughters turn out (*nikalna*) centers upon neither their earning potential nor their filial devotion but rather upon their sexual purity."² "In most cases," Vatuk concludes, the purity of girls is preserved by imposing "strict restraints on their freedom of movement and by close supervision of their associations and activities" (Vatuk 1990, 77).³ Such was the case with the girls who worked in this informal tourist economy. So long as the girls were still considered children (which, is also to say, so long as they were viewed as asexual subjects), their work and presence on the riverfront were socially tolerated.[4]

And yet, while the girls on the ghats were not confined by the stringent norms and proscriptions of female adolescent life, they still lived in anticipation of them. Their understandings of self, of proper female decorum, and even their imaginings of what constituted a desirable life for the future were heavily shaped by pervasive gender norms and expectations that repeatedly cast the good woman as a modest, self-sacrificing, domestic caretaker.[5] Thus, although the girls were "free" to work on the riverfront, and certainly enjoyed having the opportunity to play there, I also sensed that they felt stigmatized by their work in this highly public, male-dominated sphere. As I will discuss below, their attempts to manage and ameliorate this stigma surfaced in both subtle and overt ways.

Troubles at Home and the Virtue of Necessity

One of the more obvious ways the girls attempted to ameliorate this stigma was by "making a virtue" out of their necessity to work (Bourdieu 1980, 54). Another, related, strategy involved continually demonstrating that necessity was precisely what rendered their work on the riverfront virtuous. All of the girls who I came to know throughout the course of my research told me that they worked on the riverfront because there were "troubles at home." "Troubles at home" emerged as an organizing narrative that provided these girls with a way to explain, legitimate, and valorize their participation in this informal economy. The following account of Malika Sahani provides one such example.

Malika

In 1997 I met Malika Sahani. She was almost eleven years old at the time and the only girl I had seen selling postcards on the ghats. The first time I saw her I did a double-take, for unlike all of the other young girls whom I had encountered in the city, Malika was dressed in boys' clothes. Instead of the usual frilly dress and sandals, or the neatly pressed *salwar kamiz*, Malika stood before me wearing polyester trousers, a striped collared t-shirt, and a pair of oversized sneakers. Had there not been such an incredibly beautiful and delicate face underneath her tightly drawn pigtails, I probably would have mistaken her for a boy.

Malika's striking looks, her intelligence, and her polite demeanor made her one of the most successful children selling postcards on the ghats. After a few years of working on the riverfront, she had accumulated a considerable following of Western tourists who regularly kept in touch with her. Many of them sent her money and gifts, and one tourist had even purchased a boat for her father. Based on the letters I read, all of these "foreign friends" seemed extremely eager to help alleviate the financial stress that plagued Malika and her family.

About three years before I met Malika, her father, who was working as a house painter, fell from a ladder during an intoxicated episode and severely broke his leg. The injury left him bedridden and unemployed for almost a year, and it left his wife Sharmila frantic about how she was going to provide for Malika and their three younger daughters, Ritthi, Jaila, and Seenu. Up until that point, Sharmila had never worked outside the home, but in the wake of the accident she decided to set up a small stand on the riverfront and began to sell garlands and incense to pilgrims. Inspired by her mother's courage and resourcefulness, Malika decided that she would also take to the ghats and begin selling postcards to foreign tourists.

By her own account, and that of many others in the neighborhood, Malika was the first girl at Dasashwamedh to sell postcards to foreign tourists, and one of the only girls to eventually do some guiding. When I returned to Banaras to begin my fieldwork, Malika was fourteen. She had already retired from working on the ghats and was going to school full time, but her two younger sisters, Ritthi and Jaila, had picked up where she left off. Occasionally, Malika would come to the riverfront to bring food for her sisters and mother, but when she wasn't at school she spent most of her day in the tiny, dark room that served as home for her and her family.

I first visited Malika's home on a wintery Saturday morning in 1998. I was happy to be off from language school for the day and was taking one of my usual strolls along the river's edge when I slipped and fell into the Ganga. By the time I awkwardly made my out of the muddy water and back onto the ghat, I was soaked and humiliated. Malika and her mother had been sitting above at their garland stand and had witnessed my fall. When they saw the pathetic state I was in, Sharmila quickly instructed Malika to take me to their house and give me a change of clothes. I was grateful for their kindness, and the incident emerged as a turning point in my relationship with Malika and her family. Thereafter, I became a frequent visitor.[6]

Malika and I would spend hours chatting over tea and *papadam*, or while she prepared meals for her parents and sisters. We would also go to the movies together, and have lengthy discussions about Bollywood heroes and lifestyles, and how they differed from the world that Malika knew. It was through such informal gatherings and conversations that I really came to know Malika. However, before I left Banaras at the end of my fieldwork, I asked Malika if she would be willing to give me the "official" narrative of why and how she had begun working on the riverfront. "It's for the book," I kept urging her. She agreed. On an October afternoon, Malika and I sat on the floor of their dark blue rectangular room and she recounted her story:

MS: Well, earlier everything was okay at home, earlier my mother used to stay at home and Papa used to work, he used to work as a painter. At that time we didn't have a boat. My father drinks a bit. One day he broke his leg because of his drinking habit and no one in my neighborhood or among my relatives helped us. If anyone had stood by us at that time and helped us out financially then we would not have stepped outside the home but at that time neither those whom we called our kinsman helped us, nor anyone else. Even my grandfather and my uncles and my brothers did not help us. That is why we decided that we ought to do something to save our family and at the same time something that would not give us a bad name.

JH: So how old were you then?

MS: At that time I was about eight years old.

When Malika described the troubles that had brought her to the ghats, she referenced more than just her weak father, his crippling accident, and his drinking habit. According to Malika, she and her mother were forced into this situation because the people who traditionally should have come to their aid, that is, their neighbors and extended family, did not. In this regard, Malika understood her entry into this informal tourist economy as being directly linked to the erosion of key social relations and obligations. Her presence on the ghats bespoke a fractured "familial self" (Cohen 1998, 105).[7] Moreover, adding insult to injury, Malika had to endure criticisms and ridicule from her relatives when she first began working on the ghats, and she described the anguish that her decision had initially caused her mother:

> The first day, after I got the postcards I went straight to my mother's shop and told her that I was going to sell them so my mother began to cry, she said, "If your father didn't have a broken leg then maybe you wouldn't have to do this." So I said, "There is nothing wrong with doing this if I have no choice, if I am doing this it is good because at least you will get some help in running the family, simply because I am a girl doesn't mean that I should stay at home and feel embarrassed." Well, one should have a sense of shame but not to the extent that most girls have. You see, some people work because it is their hobby (*shauk*) and others work because they have no choice (*mazburi mein kam karte hain*). I didn't do this as a hobby, I did this because there were troubles at home.

For Malika, therefore, the emphasis on necessity provided her with a way to render her work on the riverfront legitimate and virtuous rather than shameful and transgressive. Furthermore, it enabled her to indict those kinsmen who had failed to live up to their responsibilities.

In the course of listening to these entry narratives, one of the things I found interesting about Malika, and many of the other girls I came to know, was the way they walked and talked a very fine line between critiquing gender norms and notions of femininity, and reinscribing them.[8] For instance, as Malika pointed out, while an overbearing sense of shame and modesty could be detrimental to girls' earning ability, it was also a quality they needed to possess if they were going to maintain a good reputation while working on the ghats. By working on the riverfront, these girls actively appropriated a space that was dominated by men and, as Malika pointed out, they challenged the idea that girls should be limited to the home. However, by continually emphasizing that they "had no choice," the girls also reinstated the home as the truly legitimate sphere for them to operate in. In fact, the girls on the ghats often spoke very critically of "girls from rich families" who worked in "offices," "mingled with boys," and "neglected their families" so that they could pursue their own personal interests and "hobbies." For the girls on the ghats, work was not regarded as a means for the cultivation of individual skills, talents, or interests but, rather, it was an act of necessity that one took on in their efforts to serve and support the family.

Again, this is not to suggest that the girls derived no personal pleasures or benefits from working on the riverfront. They clearly enjoyed being able to socialize with their friends, and some of them hoped that they would be able to divert part of their earnings toward their own personal consumption and pleasures. But such perks could not be represented as ends in themselves. Establishing and proving their compulsion to work, therefore, became a kind of ongoing labor for the girls, and if someone was perceived as trying to challenge their legitimacy the girls responded swiftly.[9]

For example, in the late afternoon, before it became dark and the crowd assembled for the evening puja, the girls would gather together on the lower steps of the ghat near the river. They would drink tea, share snacks, play marbles or other games, and sometimes they even took a boat out for a spirited sing-along row. Often, I joined them. I would watch and listen as they played together and gossiped about various happenings and people on the ghats. Over time, I began paying closer attention to the run-ins that occurred between these girls and some of the boys who worked and played on the ghats. While the girls were usually fairly successful at sequestering play spaces for themselves, they were also alert to the presence of young male intruders, who would occasionally interrupt their fun with a slew of obnoxious comments. The boys would tease the girls by saying that they were doing this work to "get money for their marriages," pointing out that "the girls in the boatman caste are married very quickly." Or, they would accuse the girls of working so they could buy jewelry and makeup. "Look," the boys would say to me, "they have no shame, they are wearing rings (*dekhiye unko koi sharam nahin hai, anguthiyan paheni hain*)!" Some of the boys even reprimanded the girls for "begging" tourists for cream, hairpins, and mirrors. This charge was particularly offensive to the girls, even though they wielded it among themselves in their efforts to ensure that an appropriate physical presentation was being maintained. The girls often reprimanded each other by saying: "Don't tie that *gamcha* (cloth) around your waist, it makes you look like a beggar." "Don't hold your hand out that way when you take the money from your customers, it makes you look like a beggar."[10]

Interestingly, while the girls clearly resented the boys' taunting, they usually did not fire back with insults of their own. "If you start insulting these boys on the ghats, they will just respond with even dirtier things to say," Basanti Sahani (age eleven) informed me. Instead, when such incidents did occur, the girls would quickly remind their assailants that they were doing this work because of troubles at home; a sick mother, an unemployed father, a family member who needed an operation. As was the case with Malika, they also frequently turned the tables on their critics: "Will you give me money for my family's expenses if I don't sell diyas? Will you give me food? Will you fix the problems in my home?" Though these run-ins were a source of aggravation, they also provided the girls with a valuable public opportunity to reassert their necessity to work and thereby reestablish their legitimacy on the riverfront.

Domesticating the Ghats

Another strategy the girls relied upon to ameliorate the stigma associated with their work involved domesticating the ghats. By this, I am referring to the girls' repeated efforts to cast the ghats as a virtual extension of the home; a friendly and familial space, where nurturing and protective kinsmen were on hand to ensure their safety and see to it that they were treated appropriately by others.[11] By relying on this strategy, the girls sought not to "escape" the adult "nets of disciplining" and supervision, as Kumar puts it, but rather, to productively deploy them. Malika's account, again, provides an example.

Although Malika explained that she was forced to work on the riverfront because of negligent relatives, when it came to discussing her actual presence on the ghats, she too was quick to emphasize that she was always surrounded by a watchful web of friends and family. For instance, in describing what it was like to be the only girl selling postcards at Dasashwamedh, she remarked: "I never had any fear inside of me, I never felt afraid because there were some people there who I knew. For example, my uncle, people who I knew very well, so since they were there I didn't feel afraid. Of course I felt a little bit scared but not too much. I told myself, 'If I won't have anything to do with anyone, then why would anyone bother me?'"

The presence of known family and friends did not automatically, or always, protect these girls from being harassed or teased by boys. And certainly, many of the girls were quite eager if not fond of assailing the boys' reputations and emphasizing how "rude" and "dirty" they were.[12] However, this did not prevent the girls from continually pointing out that in comparison to other alternatives, such as working in an office, or even in someone's home as a domestic servant, the ghats were a good place for them to work; perhaps, even safer and more respectable. Anjali Srivastav provides another vivid example of this.

Anjali

At the time of my research, Anjali was fourteen and her two younger sisters, Mona and Gulab, were ages nine and seven. They would arrive at the ghat every morning to sell tea. After several hours of selling they would go home to bathe, eat, and tend to their household chores. In the late afternoon, they would return to the ghats and continue selling until the evening puja had finished. Their parents' tea stall was located about ten minutes beyond the Godolia crossing near the edge of the Chowk market. Despite its central location, business there was slow, so Anjali's parents equipped the girls with a large metal kettle and a supply of plastic cups and instructed the girls to look for customers on the ghats. On an average day, the girls earned between fifty and seventy-five rupees. Their brother, Maneesh, who was twelve, also used to accompany them, but a few months into my research he got a job cleaning the floors in a nearby photo lab, and his appearances on the ghat became less frequent. Their youngest brother Dinku who was five, also occasionally accompanied the girls, but most of the time, he remained in the marketplace with his parents.

I first met the Srivastav children in the winter of 2000. Anjali reminded me of Malika, because she too was dressed in boy's clothes, had a strikingly beautiful face, and was sharp as a tack. The first time I met her I was sitting on the ghat with a friend of mine. When she overheard me speaking in Hindi she came over, and with one hand grasping her kettle and the other hand placed on her hip she asked, "Are you one of those foreigners who have come here to help poor children, the ones who take the children over to the other side of the river to swim and wash their hair in the afternoon?"

I had no idea what she was talking about, but the friend whom I was speaking with told me that Anjali was referring to the Back to Life Program, which, as he explained, was started by a group of Westerners who had come to Banaras to help poor children on the ghat with their schooling and medical needs. Sometimes in the afternoons the volunteers would load the children into a boat, take them to the other side of the river, watch the kids swim around, delouse them with a stringent shampoo, and then give them a snack as they rowed them back over to the city. Anjali and her sisters had heard about these excursions and wanted to go. They were disappointed when they found out that I was not involved in organizing such outings.

After this encounter, however, the girls and I became friendly and we started meeting on a regular basis. I also got to know Anjali's parents and paid many visits to their home. After a few months, they agreed to let Anjali serve as my "tutor." She was going to help me learn about "Indian culture," and more specifically, what it was like to be a girl working on the ghats. In the afternoon, when she had free time, Anjali would come visit me at my guest house and we would turn on the tape recorder and basically chat. The topics varied: family, friends, religion, work, and love. The latter was one of Anjali's favorite topics since she and a young boy on the ghat had recently developed a romantic interest in each other and had begun passing love letters back and forth.

Anjali told me that she had started selling tea six years before in order to help her parents pay for an operation for her paternal grandfather. At first she only sold tea near her parent's stand in the marketplace, but when business became slow she and her sisters began coming to the ghats. "In the beginning I used to feel shy," she recounted. "I just felt in my heart, 'what will it be like to sell tea on the ghats?' Then gradually after being there for some time I began to like it. People started to recognize me and speak to me, before that no one used to speak to me."

From what I could tell through our conversations and from what I observed when Anjali was on the riverfront, Anjali did, for the most part, enjoy her work.[13] She was an extremely gregarious and curious person, and she seemed to delight in the buzz and bustle of life on the ghats. She also said that she enjoyed having the chance to meet and speak with foreigners. Like Malika, she too had a large collection of letters and photos that tourists had sent to her over the years, and many stories about "the nice customers" whom she had befriended. Moreover, like Malika, Anjali also felt that it was important for her to try and help her parents financially, and she often pointed out that if she had been born a boy, she would have been able to do much more to support them. "My regret," she told me one afternoon, "is that I am a girl and all I can do is sell tea, I can't do any other work because I won't get a job in a shop." When I asked her why she wouldn't be able to work in a shop, she responded:

AS: Because it is not a good thing to work alongside boys, people are different from each other, some are good, some are bad and you can only find out about them after working with them for some time. All the girls, I mean girls from big [rich] families, who work in offices, they find that the men there are not good. Because they make taunting comments, they are dirty type of people.
JH: What does dirty mean?
AS: A dirty (*ganda*) type. [Starts making chi chi chi noises and is reluctant to answer].
JH: You mean bad manners? Do you mean that they misbehave with girls?
AS: They misbehave with girls, they tease and molest girls, meaning they touch their bodies, all this stuff.

JH: So these kinds of things never happen with you on the ghats? The boys don't bother you?

AS: They treat me like their kid sister and they joke and kid with me. Nothing more than that.

Interestingly, Anjali's explanation circumvented the primary obstacles that stood in her way of getting a well-paying shop or office job, such as the fact that she came from a poor family and had little education. Like many of the other girls who worked on the ghats, however, Anjali redeemed her class position and her limited work options by reading it as an indication of moral superiority. The children on the ghats had a very well developed set of ideas for explaining and characterizing the differences between the rich and poor, and stereotypes of these two classes of people were constantly being invoked by the children as they attempted to understand their positions in relation to their larger society. For most of these children, rich people (*amir log*), were regard as "unmannered," "selfish," "spoiled," and more corrupted by influences from the West. However, poor people, such as themselves, were seen as the upholders of traditional values and virtues and, as Anjali and Malika constantly reminded me, they were inherently more "kind" and "polite." Moreover, like Malika, Anjali also attempted to portray the riverfront as a safer and more respectable place to work. In contrast to the daughters from "big families," who had to defend against lascivious predators in the officeplace, on the ghats Anjali was the recipient of brotherly love and protection.

And yet, although Anjali clung to the idea of being treated as a little sister, according to most people in the neighborhood, she was far past the age to be working on the riverfront and joking around with boys and men, who, in actuality, had no kinship ties to her.[14] As I will discuss in later chapters, some saw her situation as heartbreaking, and pitied her for having "greedy" parents who seemed to care more about money than their daughter's well-being or reputation. Others, however, had less sympathy, and interpreted Anjali's attempts to create playful relations with boys and men on the riverfront as a sign that she herself had not been properly "domesticated."

Spaces of Reflection

The girls' attempts to represent their experiences and identities in more socially acceptable ways, did not, therefore, go unchallenged. However, there were also instances when encounters with tourists and locals could prompt the girls to reconsider, rather than defend, the usual narratives they relied upon. In the terms of George Herbert Mead, they provided these girls with an opportunity to reflect upon their situations through the eyes of the Other, and in so doing, reach a potentially revised understanding of their experiences and selves (Mead 1934). The following accounts of Jaila and Priya put this on display.

Jaila

Jaila Sahani was one of Malika's three younger sisters. At the time of my fieldwork she was eight years old, and she was working every day selling postcards and diyas on the ghats. While Jaila was adept at attracting customers and earned a fair amount of money for her family, she was not as successful or popular as Malika had been. Jaila was hot-tempered and lacked the diplomatic skill that had made Malika so well regarded by both tourists and her peers. Like Malika, Jaila also continually emphasized that she was doing this work because of troubles at home. However, unlike her older sister, Jaila was less inclined to cast these troubles as the product of an unsupportive extended family and more apt to point the finger at their alcoholic father.

For instance, one morning I found Jaila on the ghats crying because her father had taken the money she had saved to go on an overnight boating excursion with several other families in the neighborhood. Jaila had been looking forward to the trip for weeks, and had persuaded me to go along with them. When I met her on the ghats the morning of our departure, however, all of her excitement had disappeared. She was sitting with her head in her hands, while tears rolled down her face and gathered around her ankles. Through muffled cries she told me how her father had confiscated her money, pointing out that it was something he had done many times before. Then she turned and looked at me and said, "Jenny *Didi*, don't you think it is wrong for a father to take his daughter's money for liquor?" "Yes," I emphatically replied. Sensing my sympathy, Jaila asked if I would loan her fifty rupees for the trip. I agreed, and as soon as I handed her the money she quickly raced off to buy some biscuits and *namkeen* to take with us.

Jaila was certainly savvy enough to use her father's drinking problem as a way of garnering sympathy and financial support from me, as well as from other tourists whom she befriended. However, in sharing these stories, Jaila also seemed to be looking for an audience to validate her indictments. Her complaints about her father often took the form of a question, as though she was uncertain about their very legitimacy, let alone the propriety of voicing them.[15] By sharing such grievances with me and other tourists, Jaila, I think, received the confirmation she was looking for. She also discovered an avenue for expressing feelings and criticisms that she was more reluctant to articulate among her friends, family, and neighbors.

Although Jaila was reluctant to criticize her father when she was with the other children on the ghats, the children did not hesitate to call attention to his shortcomings. For instance, on another occasion, Jaila and I were talking on the ghat when Jay Yadav, a twelve-year-old boy who peddled postcards, came over to join us. He looked at Jaila disapprovingly and shook his head in dismay. "It is wrong that your father always puts you out to work here," he said. "Look how skinny you are becoming, your health is going bad!" Jaila cracked an uncomfortable smile while Jay asked me if young girls like Jaila worked outside the home in America. "Not usually," I replied. Jaila's eyes widened with surprise, "You mean they don't have to work?" she asked. "They just go to school?" I nodded and watched as Jaila retreated into a contemplative silence.

Though I can only speculate here, my sense is that Jaila was not so much surprised by my answer as she was by the experience of momentarily stepping outside of herself and reflecting upon her life from another perspective. Like the other girls on the ghats, Jaila was very aware that there were many children who "just" went to school and who had parents who provided for all of their needs. Again, the differences between children who came from "big" or "good" families and the children who worked on the ghats was a popular topic of conversation, and it often led to a series of "us" versus "them" contrasts. However, what transpired in this exchange was of a different ilk. Jay's penetrating criticisms had the effect of disrupting, or least questioning, the inevitability of this opposition between "us" and "them," and in so doing, I think, he jolted Jaila into a powerful moment of self-reflection. As Jaila sat silently thumbing through her postcards, I sensed that perhaps she was considering what her life would be like if she did not have to sell them.

Priya

Priya Srivastav, age eight, also sold postcards on the ghats, and like Jaila, many of her troubles stemmed from an alcoholic father. At the time of my fieldwork she was one of the most successful postcard peddlers on the ghat. However, unlike some of the other children, her success did not derive from her abilities to charm and endear herself to foreign tourists. In fact, tourists often described her as one of the most "relentless" and "aggravating" children on the riverfront. Priya's success stemmed from the long hours she put in and the strict discipline that was imposed upon her by her father, who also worked on the ghats selling peanuts. Priya would wake up at five in the morning and come to the ghats in order to catch "the sunrise tourists" who were heading out on boating excursions. She would stay on the ghats until nine and then go home to bathe and eat a meal. Around eleven, she would return with a fresh supply of postcards and remain on the ghats for most of the day, returning home with her father after the evening puja. Though she had expressed an interest in school, she told me that her father had forbidden her to attend because he wanted her to sell postcards. "If I don't sell," she frequently reminded me, "then how will we eat?"

Unlike Jaila, who was allowed to save some money for herself, Priya's father kept virtually all of his daughter's earnings, and he kept a close account of how much she made. If he wasn't satisfied with her sales for the day he would openly scold her, and according to Priya, sometimes he would hit her when they went home. If he saw Priya playing with the other girls on the ghat he would often curse at them and order Priya to get back to work. Most of the time, Priya seemed resigned to his overbearing presence, but there were also days when she was clearly fed up, and her eyes would well up with frustration and despair as she reluctantly left playing with her friends to obey her father's orders. When Priya's father would unload his slurred tirades at the children they usually responded with mocking laughter, and many of the young boys would fire back with insults.

One evening in March, I was sitting on the ghat having tea with Pramod Sahani while we waited for the evening puja to begin. Pramod was also twelve years old at the time (about to turn thirteen) and worked as a peddler and guide at Dasashwamedh. Of all the children I came to know, he was definitely the most charismatic and feisty, and it served him very well in business. He never backed down if older boys gave him a difficult time or if young men from outside the neighborhood tried to interfere with his customers As Pramod and I were drinking our tea, Priya and her father were making their way to the crowd that had gathered for the puja. Priya was a few yards ahead and was carrying her postcards while her father stumbled behind her. His hair was disheveled and his button-down shirt and long blue *dhoti* were wrinkled and stained. When Priya's father passed by, Pramod suddenly jumped up and began yelling at him. "You are a drunk, you are no good! You drink your daughter's money! You are ruining her life! You have her out here working on the ghats and you are just a drunk!"

Priya's father was caught off guard but when he finally realized that the remarks were directed at him, he wobbled toward Pramod and stepped out of his *chapal* (sandal), raising it in the air as though he were going to strike. Pramod quickly darted out of his reach and began to skirt around him, wielding more insults. Priya looked back with a nervous smile on her face and watched the banter between them. After a few minutes, Pramod stopped his taunting and sat back down, and Priya's father shuffled off. The onlookers who had gathered to watch the assault departed. "Why did you do that?" I asked. Pramod looked at me as though I were an idiot, and angrily replied, "Because he is a useless drunk, he puts his daughter out to work on the ghats, and spends all of the money she earns on booze. Why should I respect such a man?"

For boys like Pramod and Jay, these fathers were weak and pathetic men who seemed to be sacrificing their daughters to fuel their own addictions, and as such, they were regarded as suitable targets for teasing and abuse even though their seniority should have commanded deference and respect. However, the point I want to emphasize here is that these kinds of public incidents and indictments also, I suggest, affected the way that girls like Priya and Jaila understood their presence on the riverfront. They provided another opportunity, though not necessarily a welcome one, for the girls to compare their own perceptions of their lives and situations against the record of public opinion. Confronted with such forceful criticisms of their parents, and particularly their alcoholic fathers, the girls were, I think, led to ponder why exactly they were working on the riverfront. Was it really about providing food for the family, as Priya so often reminded me? Or, was it about accommodating a father's habitual thirst?

A Play Space

In addition to these kinds of encounters, there were other ways in which the ghats provided the girls with a space for reflecting upon their lives, and even "playing" with their reality (Winnicott 1989). Indeed, often it was through play that the girls experimented with alternative identities and roles for themselves. Notably, these were roles that frequently challenged their subordinate positions as lower-class and lower-caste young female subjects. For instance, one of the games I repeatedly observed was "playing puja." The girls had purchased a small Shiva *lingam*, and sometimes in the late afternoon they would gather at the bottom of the steps and construct a shrine out of mud. They would bring flowers to garland the shrine, light incense, chant "mantras," and then at the conclusion of the ceremony they would distribute *prasad* (food offerings). The girls especially delighted in getting to play the "panditji." One afternoon in October, as I was walking along the ghats, the girls summoned me over to participate in the ceremony. Anita Sahani, who sold diyas, and was well liked by the other girls for her exuberant personality and great sense of humor, was presiding as the priest. "Jenny *Didi*," she said in a commanding voice, "you sit here, and we will give you prasad when we are done." I quickly complied and Anita continued reciting the mantras. The other girls seemed to be listening intently. Before we got to the distribution of the prasad, however, we were interrupted by several people passing by. They all made similar comments. "Anita," they chided, "how can you possibly be the panditji? You eat chicken and fish!"

According to the psychoanalyst Donald Winnicott, who spent much of his career studying and theorizing children's play, these interruptions should have been a deal breaker. For the play space, he argued, cannot "easily admit intrusions" (Winnicott 1989, 51). The play space is maintained by never challenging its reality; by never posing such a question: "How could you possibly be the panditji?" Anita, however, did not seem to be distressed or discouraged by the interruptions. In fact, she responded by closing her eyes and calmly waving her hand in the air, making circular motions as though she were deflecting the remarks away from her and the other girls. Then, after several more minutes of officiating, she finally distributed the prasad.

Through such play, these girls were able to carve out a semi-autonomous space on the ghats where they could escape the demands of everyday life and imaginatively create alternative realities and roles for themselves. However, the fact that their play often involved challenging, if not inverting, established social hierarchies and roles, also suggests that the girls used play as a way to engage and critique their social reality. Moreover, this incident, as well as many others that I witnessed, makes it clear that class and caste were indeed dominating issues on the riverfront. Remarks about "eating chicken and fish," "begging from tourists," or having to work so that they "could earn money and marry early," were not just arbitrary forms of teasing; rather such comments were wielded to remind these girls of their position in society.

Reflecting on Tourists

Whether it was through play or by valorizing their poverty and virtue, the girls found their own ways of challenging established social hierarchies and asserting their monopoly on moral propriety. Another way they did this was by criticizing Western tourists. One of their favorite targets included the foreign women who wandered around "half naked," "showing their bodies." In fact, commenting on the appalling apparel of female tourists seemed to be a favorite pastime for the girls. There were many afternoons when I joined the girls for tea on the ghats, and watched and listened as they sat in groups and berated these visitors. What began as lighthearted ridicule often escalated into expressions of palpable scorn. As Sangeeta remarked one day, "I want to hit those women for wearing those clothes!" The other girls present quickly expressed their agreement, "Yes, look at those foreign women and their dirty clothes! They have no shame! They are showing their bodies!" Such commentary usually led the girls to speculate further about the "sexcapades" of these female visitors and their inappropriate romantic trysts with fellow travelers and older guides and boatmen on the riverfront.

The girls also expressed more general grievances about the "rude" and insulting behavior that tourists exhibited when they were trying to sell their products. As Mona remarked to me one day, "Don't they understand that it is our job to ask? Today an English man knocked my cups out of my hand when I asked him if he wanted some tea and he yelled at me to go away. These tourists are very bad, they have no manners!" Jaila and Priya, who were sitting beside me as Mona recounted the episode also chimed in with their own examples. Priya began talking about all the times tourists had thrown her postcards on the ground when she was trying to sell them, and Jaila began mimicking the way that tourists constantly shooed her away at the evening puja when she approached carrying a basket of diyas.

Finally, some of the girls criticized tourists for overstepping their boundaries. For instance, Malika told me about a French tourist in his late forties named Gilbert whom she had met while she was selling postcards on the ghats. During his stay in Banaras, Gilbert would come to the ghats every day to talk with Malika. As Malika recounted: "One day he came when I was talking with my uncle. When we finished our conversation Gilbert called me over and said 'Malika don't talk to that man! You should not talk to Indian men, they cannot be trusted!' I was thinking to myself, 'What an idiot this man is; I am Indian too! And he doesn't even realize that this is my uncle!'"

In Gilbert's case, Malika's grievances went beyond his rude remarks about India and Indians. Malika told me that when Gilbert returned to France he began sending her "love letters." Initially, I thought Malika was using the term inappropriately, but when she showed me the letters I realized that she did have a good understanding of the genre. Gilbert had decorated the envelopes with magazine pictures of couples kissing and embracing, and one of them featured a woman sitting on a man's lap with her legs wrapped around him. The invitations to "come stay" and Gilbert's repeated declarations of his "love" for Malika definitely diverged from the paternal and maternal sentiments that usually animated tourists' letters. And, even though Malika could not read the letters on her own, she was able to sense this. Upon receiving the letters, Malika actually hid them from her mother, fearing that they would cause her distress and lead her to forbid Malika from continuing her work on the riverfront.

Tourists like Gilbert were an anomaly. With one or two exceptions, I feel confident in saying that most Western tourists were not sexually interested in these children. However, stories about child prostitution in India were pervasive and, as such, tourists often asked me if these children were "at risk" by doing this work. Indeed, one of the things that interested me was the very different ways that Western tourists and people in Banaras perceived these "risks." For many Western tourists, the fact that these girls were children provoked extreme anxiety. Tourists assumed that because they were young they would be more vulnerable, and they repeatedly expressed fears that they would be molested by foreign visitors. However, for many people in Dasashwamedh, it was precisely the opposite. So long as these girls were children it was considered acceptable, even though not desirable, for them to work on the riverfront. Moreover, the potential risks these girls faced were not so much associated with foreign tourists as they were with local boys. As Diraj noted at the outset of this chapter, working on the riverfront became more problematic once these girls got older and the boys on the ghats began looking at them "in the wrong way."

Removed from the Riverfront

By the time the girls reached the ages of twelve or thirteen, therefore, they were usually reeled back into the domestic sphere. At home their bodies, behaviors, and reputations could be carefully monitored and safeguarded, and more time could be devoted to properly training them for their future roles as daughters-in-law. For the girls, then, the passage from childhood to adolescence was marked by a radical withdrawal from public space, thus ensuring that every couple of years a new group of girls would emerge on the ghats to take their place. For the girls whom I knew, this departure from the ghats seemed to be bittersweet. On the one hand, it entailed a significant loss of freedom and mobility. Playtime with friends and access to the fresh air, open spaces, and the excitement of the riverfront were replaced with many more solitary hours of watching TV and doing domestic chores in tight living quarters. For instance, when Anjali was finally forced by her parents to give up working on the ghats because she had begun menstruating, she became frustrated and depressed. When I would visit her at home, she would speak longingly of the freedoms and pleasures she had previously enjoyed.

On the other hand, some of the girls embraced their retirement with a quiet delight. Instead of lamenting the loss of freedom, they seemed excited about moving closer to a new world of womanhood. Malika often told me that she had no desires to return to the ghats, and preferred staying at home and working. Her mother echoed these sentiments. "She is becoming big now," Sharmila said to me one afternoon, "So she should stay at home. On the ghats one encounters all kinds of people (*ghat par har tarik ka log aatta hai*). The atmosphere is not good for girls once they become big."

Indeed, most of the girls seemed to adjust to these new understandings of the ghats quickly. What they once regarded as a relatively friendly place to work and play subsequently emerged as a space of potential danger, where they risked being overexposed to lascivious men and ruthless gossip. One day, for example, I ran into Rita Sahani while she was visiting with her aunt, who owned a bangle stand in the bazaar. A few years before, Rita had been one of the most active girls peddling on the ghats, but by the time I returned to begin my fieldwork she too had retired. Rita had grown considerably, and she broke into a semi-embarrassed smile when I commented on how lovely her blue eye shadow and nail polish looked. I joined Rita and her aunt for a cup of tea and she told me about her new job doing domestic work for a nearby family. "I decided to stop selling on the ghats," she said. "Very dirty things happen there." "Yes," her aunt quickly added, "the people on the ghats are very dirty. It is not a good place for girls like Rita. If you are poor girl like Rita on the ghats the boys will always be propositioning you."[16]

Boys on the Ghats

While the girls were forced into an early retirement in order to safeguard their reputations and thereby "the honor" of their families, the boys were more or less free to participate in this informal economy as long as they wanted—though this was not encouraged. There was definitely pressure on the boys to find more "stable" and "respectable" work, particularly once they neared the age of marriage. Moreover, as the boys themselves often emphasized, once they "got big and they were not as cute anymore," earning money from tourists became more difficult. Many of the older boys who still worked as guides spoke nostalgically of their lucrative "golden years" when their childish charm and appearance rendered them "irresistible" to foreign visitors.

In what follows, I introduce some of the boys who worked at Dasashwamedh Ghat, most of whom were between the ages of eight and fourteen.[17] As will be seen, girls and boys not only had very different work trajectories. They also had very different ways of rendering their work meaningful.

The Importance of Earning: Money Can Buy You Love

Most of the boys I knew at Dasashwamedh Ghat also told me that they began working on the riverfront because of troubles at home. However, in contrast to the girls, the boys did not have to rely upon this narrative to legitimate their participation in this informal economy. In fact, when the boys spoke about why they were working on the riverfront, they focused less on the economic necessities they faced, and much more on the moral compulsion they felt to pull their own weight and contribute to their families. For the boys, the importance of earning was internalized at an early age. Young boys, especially those who were not studying in school (as was the case with many of the boys on the ghats), were repeatedly shamed for "eating without earning" (*sirf baith ke khana khate hain*). Indeed, the threat of this rebuke animated many of our conversations, and on several occasions, I heard this charge being wielded by angry parents. By working with foreign tourists, therefore, the boys found one avenue to assert their sense of masculine responsibility and prove themselves as good and caring family members. The following account of Jay Yadav provides one example.

Jay

I first met Jay when he was ten years old and peddling postcards on the ghats. When I returned in 2000 to begin my fieldwork, he was still selling postcards, but he had also begun actively guiding and doing commission work. Jay was a quiet and relatively shy boy with a slight frame and a serious disposition. Unlike many of the other boys, Jay did not live in the immediate neighborhood, nor did he come from the Mallah caste. His father worked in a printing shop, and his family's home was located near Naya Sarak, about fifteen minutes away. Jay was the second youngest of six children. His mother had died from tuberculosis when he was eight years old, and he was being raised primarily by his older siblings. When his older brother Raj began driving an auto rickshaw near

Dasashwamedh, Jay began accompanying him and eventually he began selling on the ghat. As was the case with Malika and the other children, I primarily got to know Jay through our informal conversations and by spending lots of time with him both on and off the riverfront. However, before my fieldwork concluded, I asked him to sit down with me and tell me about his experiences working on the ghats.

JH: So you've been doing this for two years. How did you start? For instance, did you decide one day, "Okay, I'm going to start selling postcards"?

JY: No, for five or six months I used to come to the ghats every day and I would come every day and watch how the boys would talk to the tourists, so I would just listen. I wouldn't say anything. I would pick up two words and then go tell them to a different tourist. So in this way, for one year I kept asking tourists about the meanings of different words. So the tourists would say, "this means this, this means that." The tourists gave so much knowledge.

As I will discuss in chapter 6, Jay's rather gradual entrance into this informal economy was also linked to the fact that he was an outsider. In order to sell on the ghats, he not only had to learn the right way to speak to tourists but also had to establish himself with the other boys from the neighborhood. Eventually, Jay did manage to befriend several of the boys and develop working relationships with them. I often sensed that some of his chronic seriousness, however, stemmed from his outsider status, which rendered him more susceptible to bullying and abuse. There were several times throughout my fieldwork when such incidents did occur, and though he never followed through, in every instance Jay vowed that he was going to quit selling on the ghats forever. In fact, even in our interview Jay emphasized that he was only doing this work because "he had to." As he explained:

> I will tell you about the troubles at home that require me to do this. No one likes to do business. There is always an unavoidable reason why a man has to do this work, something that forces him to do this work. For those who have nothing better to do they come to the ghats. By talking to English people you end up getting some money and work. A man thinks, "If you sit at home idly then you won't be able to get food." But if you go to the ghat and sit and talk with a tourist then maybe they will help you and give you something.

While both Jay and Malika emphasized that their work on the riverfront was an act of necessity rather than something being pursued for fun or as a hobby, their accounts also differed in interesting ways—particularly in regard to the emphasis that Jay placed on pulling his own weight and keeping his family happy. As he continued:

> My work is selling to tourists so I can make a profit so that I can give money for my school or if there is any problem at home then I can give money to my family, and I stay happy and my family stays happy. Then, at least I am doing something for my family and I'm not just sitting and eating. This way, I earn and don't just eat like I am a useless (*phaltu*) or incapable person. Any man who does business does it for the happiness and progress (*taraqqi*) of his family.

The idea that children would or should earn money to keep their families happy is unsettling for many people in Western capitalist society, and it certainly disturbed many of the tourists whom I interviewed. Not only did this conjure up fears of callous caretakers and exploited or exploitable children. It also violated tourists' cherished belief that familial love, and perhaps love more generally, should be unconditional and not something that is given or withheld because of fluctuations in one's income.[18] For sure, similar ideas may be found within India as well, and certainly, the image of the overindulged Indian son and his doting, altruistic, symbiotic mother, has been commented upon in anthropological, psychoanalytic, and popular discourses (Copeman 2009, 47; Kakar 1981).

The boys who worked on the riverfront, however, frequently offered a very different version or rather, vision, of the parent-child relationship—one that was far less altruistic. There were times when these boys clearly felt that their family relationships and attachments, and even their own sense of worth, were being constructed and calculated in explicitly instrumental terms. In fact, they often suggested that money did buy them love at home, or at least, extra affection, praise, and attention from their parents. As Keshwar Pandey remarked to me one day, "I get headaches when a few days pass and I don't sell any postcards and I have no money to give at home. My parents get angry, they call me a loafer. They threaten not to give me food." Pramod, whom I introduced earlier and who sold fans and colors on the ghat, had similar experiences. Pramod's parents had died several years before, and his primary caretaker was his aunt. When I would see him running to and fro on the ghat with his supplies in hand, he often greeted me by saying, "Hi Jenny, I have to go. Remember, as long as I am making money I will have an aunt (*jab tak paisa rahega tab tak chachi rahegi*). If that ends, so will the love between us."[19]

Of Debts and Distinctions

Although the boys often drew attention to the instrumental nature of their relationships with their family members, and suggested that there was indeed a correlation between the amount of money they earned and gave at home and the amount of affection they received, they also interpreted the significance of their earnings through a more devotional register. What was interesting was the way these boys reevaluated their earnings as part of a domestic devotional economy. Many of the boys emphasized that they had an obligation to "repay" their parents, and particularly their mothers, for all of the sacrifices they had made on their behalf. From the boys' perspectives, one of the most helpful and convenient ways for them to do this was by earning money and easing the financial burden at home. "Mothers," I was frequently told by the boys, "give us life, so we must also give to them" (*Ma to janam dete hain, to ham ko bhi dena hai*).[20] Thus, instead of diametrically opposing instrumentality versus sentimentality, or economic versus cultural and moral concerns, these boys (and girls) also seemed quite capable of conjoining these different registers of value, and rendering them "interoperable" (Copeman 2009, 4).[21]

The boys were also very eager to emphasize that they were in fact earning their money and not getting it by other disreputable means. I will discuss this in greater detail in chapter 6, but one example occurred on a late March afternoon. A Korean filmmaking team was in town, and some of the children and I were invited to watch the shooting on the other side of the river. While we boated over, I was talking with Jaggu Mukherjee. Jaggu was eleven years old and had been selling colors on the ghat for almost two years. His older brother Mohan was about to turn thirteen, and he was also involved in peddling and guiding. Seated beside us was another boy named Ravi, whom I regularly encountered in tattered clothes, begging on the ghats. After speaking with Jaggu for a while, I turned and asked Ravi if he ever sold postcards, diyas, or colors. Before he could reply, Jaggu excitedly interrupted. He began cupping his hands to his mouth saying, "Oh no! This helpless fellow is poor, he can't sell like we do, he begs."

Jaggu's reaction again made me realize just how concerned these children were with distinguishing themselves from the poorer children who came to Dasashwamedh to beg. The children who worked on the ghats often displayed compassion for the children who begged, and they even spoke of how "auspicious" their blessings were. But, it was very clear that they did not want to be lumped into the same category. This was particularly interesting in light of the fact that children like Jaggu and Mohan often played "the poverty card" in their attempts to earn more money from Western tourists. However, from their perspective, this was part of an earning strategy that required the mastery of certain skills and knowledge, or in Bourdieu's terms, a certain amount of "cultural capital" that these less fortunate children did not possess (Bourdieu 1984, 1993).

Seeking Fun, Freedom, Fortune, and Fame

Although the boys felt a moral obligation to earn, in contrast to the girls, their narratives also placed much more emphasis on the fun and "fantastic" elements of working with foreign tourists. The boys were much more imaginatively invested in this informal tourist economy. For them, working with foreign tourists led to fantasies of striking it rich, of consuming new pleasures, and of achieving fame by having one's name and reputation, if not oneself, travel to distant lands. Many of the boys also said that they liked working with foreign tourists because foreign people treated them with respect and did not care about caste distinctions the way Indian customers did. Finally, the boys often said that they chose this work because they liked the freedom of being their own bosses. Instead of having to be beholden to someone else's schedule and demands, they could work when they wanted to, spend time with their friends, enjoy the fresh air (*hawa pani*) of the riverfront, and actually have fun while they were making money. The following examples demonstrate how the pursuit of fun, freedom, fortune, and fame animated the boys' experiences and the way they rendered their work meaningful.

Pramod

Of all the young boys on the ghat, Pramod Sahani was one of the most popular with foreign tourists, and by most people's account, one of the most financially successful. I first met him when he was ten years old and I had recently arrived in Banaras to study Hindi. I was sitting on the steps at Dasashwamedh when Pramod approached me with a fast-talking, joke-cracking sales pitch. Later, I came to recognize this as one of his signature sales moves. Despite his pitching me a fireball of charm, I declined to buy the fans he was peddling that morning, but explained to him that there would be many more opportunities for him to try his luck with me.

When I came to know Pramod better, we often spoke about why he was doing this work and what he liked and disliked about it. As I mentioned earlier, his parents had died several years before and although they had left him a small shop and a residential property to inherit upon turning eighteen, he was living with his aunt and felt compelled to contribute to the household expenses. Pramod was a very bold and a self-proclaimed "stubborn" young boy. He told me that he worked on the ghats because he did not like having to obey anybody else's orders. He also said that the money he made by selling to foreign tourists far exceeded what he would make if he sold to Indian customers or if he worked for a salary in a shop or factory. Several of the other boys on the ghats had experimented with such options, but they quit because they found the work too boring, dirty, physically demanding, or underpaid. "When you work with tourists," Pramod said, "they take you to movies, they take you to eat in restaurants, you get to see all of the city! Why would a boy want to sit in a shop all day, getting tea for a boss? We make money and we have fun, no one tells us what to do, what could be better?"

By the time I had returned to Banaras, Pramod's success had reached legendary proportions. Stories and rumors circulated that he had sold paper fans to tourists for as much as $100 apiece, and that he regularly earned three or four hundred rupees a day just by peddling on the ghats. While the money was undoubtedly important to Pramod, it seemed that he enjoyed the stories of his success as much as the actual earnings (the amount of which he never did disclose to me). He often spoke proudly of the fact that he had achieved this level of fame, not only among people on the ghats but also among foreign tourists who continued to write to him, send him money and presents, and even recommend him to subsequent customers who were visiting Banaras. Nor was Pramod alone in this respect. Many of the boys told me that one of the things they liked most about this work was that it gave them a chance to "make a name" for themselves. I often heard the boys say things like, "I am famous in Spain, all of the Spanish tourists who come here ask for me." Or, as Mohan remarked one day, "I think by doing this work I will develop a name, and people in all the corners of the world will remember me." In fact, it took me a while to realize that this desire for fame and recognition was also frequently expressed through recurring complaints of how "selfish" foreign tourists could be, how they went away and "forgot" about the people whom they met in Banaras.

At first, I dismissed these comments as generic criticisms that the boys unloaded when they were having bad days. However, over time, I began to realize that having one's name celebrated, remembered, and circulated not only enhanced the boys' self-esteem and sense of importance; in their minds, it also brought possibilities for greater earnings in the future. For as they had observed, there were many instances when new tourists did come asking for a particular boy on the ghats. Indeed, the boys' recurring emphasis on fame and forgetting raise some interesting parallels with Nancy Munn's study of value creation and transformation in the island society of Gawa. In *The Fame of Gawa*, Munn develops the notion of "spacetime as the relevant potency and value parameter" within Gawan society (1992). Munn argues that in the Gawan case, "value may be characterized in terms of an act's relative capacity to extend or expand . . . *intersubjective spacetime*—a spacetime of self-other relationships formed in and through acts and practices" (Munn 1992, 9). For the Gawa, such practices often include the reciprocal giving of food, kula shells, or building canoes, but Munn also cites remembering as a "subjective act" that is regarded as having a formidable "productive capacity." For the Gawa, she writes, "one's gifts' are the means of moving the mind of the other . . . they emphasize the importance of remembering as the means by which acts occurring at a given time (or spatiotemporal locus) may be projected forward and their capacities retained so that they may yield desired outcomes at a later time" (9–10). One of the ways these boys tried to increase their chances of being remembered, and thus increase the likelihood of yielding desired outcomes in the future, was by sending gifts and writing letters to tourists which, not surprisingly, often ended with the refrain, "please don't forget me."

At the Center of the World

In *Suitably Modern: Making Middle-Class Culture in a New Consumer Society*, Mark Liechty writes of the "anxiety" and "peripheral consciousness" that configures the self-understanding of young middle-class males in Kathmandu, many of whom work in the foreign tourist trade. He finds that these young men experience themselves as caught between "the dream of modernity" and the "lived" realities of growing up on the global "periphery." According to Liechty, "The entire discourse of modernization, progress, and development fuse with the image worlds of media" to give these young men "an acute sense of marginality" (Liechty 2003, 238–239). These males frequently fashion themselves after foreign film actors and lifestyles, and in the process, he argues, they "have trouble identifying a place for identity." In many ways, they end up cultivating an inferiority complex and come to feel that Kathmandu offers an inadequate substitute for real life, which they perceive as existing elsewhere (240).

Liechty's study provides a productive foil for thinking about the boys who worked at Dasashwamedh. Although their fear of being forgotten may suggest that these boys harbored deep anxieties about being peripheral, in many respects, their consciousness would be more aptly characterized as centripetal. The boys I knew often seemed to imagine themselves as being and working at the very center of the world. They would proudly exclaim. "Why do we need to go anywhere else when everyone comes to us?" "Every kind of person comes to Dasashwamedh. Tourists and pilgrims, criminals and scholars, famous holy men and politicians, even Indian and international movie stars!" In terms of geography, the boys lived a very parochial existence, perhaps even more so than the young men Liechty describes. Most of their time was spent moving back and forth between the ghats and the tea stalls that were nestled at the end of the main road above the riverfront. In many ways, however, they experienced this space as a central artery through which people from all over the world, and from every walk of life, passed. Thus, if the girls sought to safeguard their reputations by domesticating the ghats and rendering them a virtual extension of the home, the boys sought to enhance theirs by casting Dasashwamedh as a virtual microcosm of the planet.[22]

Moreover, when these boys did articulate feelings of being on the periphery, it was expressed in more local rather than global coordinates. In terms of their media consumption, Bollywood, not Hollywood, provided the preferred imaginary Other and model of the good life. If they spoke of being marginalized in society, their grievances were usually framed in terms of local caste and class inequalities or in relation to their illegal and quasi-persecuted status as unlicensed guides and commission agents. Finally, when they discussed their aspirations for the future, the boys of Dasashwamedh did not usually talk about wanting to travel abroad, or live like foreigners do, or even move to another city. As I will discuss shortly, what these boys hoped for and aspired to was the possibility of moving up from the rough and tough world of the ghats, where one was perpetually chasing customers and subject to police harassment, to a more "respectable" and "established" life in the bazaar or, as they often put it, "in the world above."

Spaces of Surveillance

For the boys at Dasashwamedh, the riverfront served numerous functions. In addition to being a place to earn money, it provided the primary space for these boys to play. This often included swimming, boating, playing cricket, cards, marbles, dice games, gambling, or just palling around with friends. In fact, many of the boys spent more time on the ghats than they did at home. As Dipesh (age ten) explained: "Home is a place to eat and sleep but we don't like to stay there, it is better to be on the ghats, we are free here, we can do what we want." This was true, to an extent. Most of the boys who worked on the ghat lived in small one- or two-room homes where there was little opportunity to escape a parent's gaze or family presence. In certain respects, therefore, they had more "privacy" and freedom when they were in public. Like the girls, the boys found opportunities to sequester play spaces for themselves. However, they were also aware of three major forms of surveillance that threatened to hinder both their recreation and business: kin relations, neighbors, and the police.

The boys were highly cognizant of the presence of relatives and neighbors when they were playing and working on the ghats, and this became significant for two main reasons. First, there was the fear that these onlookers would report any misdeeds to their parents. For instance, every Saturday afternoon I would go to Jaggu and Mohan Mukherhjee's house to eat lunch with their older sister Bharati and mother Devika. On one occasion, the ladies and I were knuckle deep in rice and lentils (*kitchari*) when Mohan arrived home for his afternoon meal. When Mohan had barely stepped inside the door, his mother exploded at him, "You bastard! I heard from Malika's mother that you are wandering around with a bunch of bad boys on the ghats and that you have been smoking cigarettes! Don't come here for food! I am not feeding you today!" Mohan immediately protested, saying that it was a lie, but Devika just continued to berate him as he slumped into the corner and watched us finish our meal.

Second, as is more generally the case in India, juniors are expected to show deference to their elders, whether they be significantly older, such as a parent or grandparent, or even just an older sibling. Showing deference not only involves using the appropriate forms of address. It also often involves affecting a more demure and discreet manner before one's elders. In some cases, it may entail avoiding them altogether, for in mixed company the presence of a junior can become an interactional burden for the elder, as well. In terms of both play and work, this deference code helped maintain a certain kind of order on the ghats, but it also created some interactional challenges for the boys. For instance, although Mohan and Jaggu were just two years apart, and both of them were friends with Pramod, the three boys never played all together. I realized this one day when Pramod was happily telling me about a picnic that he, Mohan and some other boys were planning on the other side of the river. "What about Jaggu I asked? Isn't he going? He's your friend?" "Of course not," Pramod replied. "He can't go, we will be joking and having fun and enjoying ourselves and if Jaggu went then Mohan would not be able to enjoy himself freely. Jaggu knows this. He is respecting his older brother." Alternatively, when the boys were trying to "woo" and impress their customers (*grahak ko patana*) they often said that they felt encumbered by the presence of older relatives. "We get embarrassed if we are joking around with a tourist and an elder is nearby. It doesn't feel right to us." Jay explained.

The biggest encumbrance, however, was the chronic threat of the police. Unlicensed guiding was and still is illegal in Banaras, and all the boys I knew had stories about being harassed and even beaten by the police. In fact, at the time of my research, a special Tourism Police Task Force was being developed to help put an end to the practice, and the crackdown on unlicensed tourism workers escalated considerably.[23] As Jay explained, "If the police see you talking to a tourist for a long time, or walking around with one, then they call you over and demand money. Sometimes if I am with a tourist and I see the police I walk away from my customer." Or, as Ramesh told me one day, "They know how to beat us so that we don't get any bruises, then they take our money. I started hiding my money in my shoes but if they demand it and you don't give it to them things just become worse." Raju (age eleven), who also sold postcards, said, "The number-one rule on the ghats is that you have to give the police 30 percent of everything you make. Otherwise, they will trouble you constantly." Indeed, a number of the boys did pay off the police on a weekly (*hafta*), or monthly (*mahina*) basis, but many of them, as Pramod explained, regarded this as a self-defeating strategy. "Some of the boys pay them *hafta* but once you start doing that you can never stop. So I have never done it."

In Search of Respect

For the boys on the riverfront, police harassment certainly posed aggravating and practical challenges to their attempts to earn a living. The boys also resented their interventions, however, because they found them deeply humiliating. "They beat us with their sticks like dogs. They can do what they want to us." "There is no respect in this line," the boys would often say. "The police can catch you and beat you at any time." Thus, while the informal tourist economy provided these boys with a chance to pursue fun, freedom, fortune, and fame, it also made them feel as though they had to constantly struggle for respect and survival. As will be seen, this struggle was experienced and articulated in different ways.

Many of the boys told me that peddling and guiding were disrespected not only because they were readily subject to humiliating police harassment but also because both were forms of "wandering work" (*ghumney wale kam*).[24] When the boys talked about what they hoped for in the future they almost always spoke of "establishing their own place" (*apna sthan*) where customers would come to them. As was the case with the girls, the boys also felt frustrated and sometimes insulted when tourists would shoo them away or rudely refuse the items they were selling. As Raju said when I interviewed him, "It would be much better to have a shop in the bazaar, where you sit in your own place and customers come to you. I don't like it when the customers wave me away or tell me to stop bothering them." Certainly, it was possible to have a "fixed" place on the ghats, as well. There were garland sellers like Malika's mother, who set up their shop in the same place every day, as well tea stalls and cold drink stands that were more or less permanent fixtures on the ghats. However, moving up into the bazaar was significant for these boys, because it was also seen as a qualitatively different, and in many ways socially more respectable, space. The boys often referred to the bazaar as "the world above" where important contacts could be made and where people behaved with a greater degree of civility. "The people who work above meet important people, good people, and become acquainted with them" (*jo log uppar kam karte hain, ve bare logo se milte hain, acche logo se milte hain, aur un ki parichit ban jati hain*). "They speak nicely with each other, they have a good manner about them" (*ve log qaayde se bat karte hain, unka vyavhar bahut acche hote hain*).

In contrast, the ghats were described as "the world below" (*nitchi wali duniya*) or as a "separate world" (*ghat to alag duniya*) that was distinguished by its rough and tough atmosphere and déclassé inhabitants. As Raju explained, "To survive on the ghats you must learn how to insult others. Otherwise people there will think you are straight and they will abuse you." Jay agreed. In our interview he remarked:

JY: As is the environment so is the intelligence that comes to one. This is a very dirty environment, there is much filth here (*jaisa mahaul wasi buddhi ayegi, yeh mahaul bahut ganda hai. Yahan pe bahut gandagi hoti hain*). If you have to live on the ghats then you have to become a mongrel/deceitful person (*dogla*), if you are straight (*sidha*) then all the boys will bother you. If you are a mongrel and some boy speaks rudely to you then you will also speak rudely and he will go away. If you are straight and you're sitting and talking, if you have money he will take your money by force. But if you're a mongrel and he even asks you for five rupees then you will say, "Get lost, I don't have any money." If you talk like that he will go away. But if you are straight, on the ghats, you shouldn't be straight with anyone. You should be straight with those who are straight.

JH: So you are not straight?

JY: I am both straight and crooked.

Jay's remarks are interesting for a number of reasons. First, his perspective on the corrosive elements of tourism work differed significantly from the perspective offered by many local adults. As I will discuss in chapter 5, many of the adults I knew in Dasashwamedh tended to blame Western tourists, and more specifically Western money, for corrupting the children who worked in this informal economy. Jay suggested, however, that the real problem was domestic "filth." He proposed that the boys on the ghats were forced to become deceitful and "crooked" in order to survive in this tough and often violent atmosphere. Second, Jay's remarks are noteworthy because they also reflect a set of culturally pervasive ideas regarding the relationship between places, persons, and the (in)compatibility of different substances. The idea that people are "substantially" transformed in and through their transactions with others has been noted by many anthropologists working in South Asia (E. V. Daniel 1984; Lamb 2000; Marriott 1976, 1990). Here, Jay's invocation of the term *dogla*, which literally translates as a person or animal of mixed blood and figuratively connotes the idea of someone who is cunning and deceitful, captures this concept succinctly. This concern with mixing and contamination also surfaced later in the interview, when I asked Jay how Western tourists perceived the boys on the ghats. He replied: "They think we are dirty because we drink dirty Ganga water. They would not want to marry Indian boys."

If the boys sometimes saw themselves as "dirty" when they looked through the eyes of their foreign Other, they also inverted the charge by repeatedly emphasizing how unclean Western tourists were. Indeed, some of the boys cited their exposure to these polluted people as one of the reasons why their work was regarded with such little respect. For example, Gappa Sahani (age seventeen and a guide at Dasashwamedh), explained:

GS: There is no respect in this work because everyone thinks that we just chase after Angreze [Westerners] like dogs. People think, "Oh, this motherfucker always keeps tagging behind foreigners, he must be a beggar." That's why people think this is dog's work, what's the use? It is worthless. If you do your own real work then there is some respect in that.

JH: Suppose you don't chase after Angreze but work with Indian people?

GS: There is respect in that.

JH: Really? So if you work with foreigners then it is dishonorable but if you work with Indians it's okay? Why is it like that?

GS: Because they are Indians and foreigners live in a very dirty way. They don't keep their bodies clean. They wipe their noses with paper and keep it in their pockets, they don't wash their hands, that's why. People think Angreze are dirty.

Gappa's remarks actually bring together a number of different issues. He was certainly concerned with the stigmatized nature of "wandering work" and the perception that working with foreign tourists might be regarded as potentially polluting. However, his response also returns us to the fear these boys had of being perceived as "beggars" who merely tagged after tourists looking for handouts, rather than earning their money through respectable means. Finally, even if the boys were not worried about being perceived as "beggars," they were still aware that many people did not regard guiding as a form of "real" work. Shop owners, for instance, frequently told me that there was "no hard work involved in guiding" (*is kam me koi mehnat nahin hai*).

When I would share such opinions with the boys, they often responded with outrage, and they would go into great detail about the amount of physical exertion that guiding required. For instance, as Mohan remarked:

> Look, in the hot season a boy goes to the ghats to find customers, if he meets a customer he has to take him around by walking, and if he gets caught by the police he has to give them money. If he doesn't get caught then he has to wander around in the hot sun. When he has to walk far that's a lot of work. If a customer says, "Take me walking from Raj Ghat to Assi," so isn't there hard work involved in that? Then he has to take him to the shopkeepers. How can anyone say that there isn't hard work involved? If I go from here to Godolia to look for customers, isn't that work? These men sit in shops and think that we just fleece the Angrez (*Angrez ko mus lete hain*). "Cheat" them. We do cheat people but we also work hard.

Or as Jay interjected with great enthusiasm: "No, listen! You should have said this to the shopkeeper. 'First, in such strong sun, if any man comes to the ghats to do business and stays for ten hours then it is certain that his health will have to become bad!' You tell the man who said this that, you tell him that, 'Saying is very easy and doing is very difficult!' We people take postcards and look for customers and wander far in the hot sun, from here to there so that we can get some benefit and be able to buy some things."

In their ongoing "search for respect" (Bourgois 1996), the boys did more than emphasize the physical demands of guiding. For instance, Jay went on to talk about how much intelligence, diplomatic skill, and bravery it required to survive on the ghats:

JH: Do you think that a boy should have certain kinds of qualities to do this work? For example should he be funny or serious? How should he be?

JY: Look, a boy should have three minds for this. First strength (*dam*), he should have power in him (*us me bal rahena chahiye, jaise koi taaqat hai*). Second, he should have brains (*dimag*) and intelligence (*buddhi*). He should know how to keep a man under his influence and spell (*kis prakar se admi ko vash mein kar sakta hai*). He should know in what way he will earn his money. And third, if there is anyone who is doing any kind of fighting, then he should be able to mediate and ask, "Why are you fighting? Please don't fight, this isn't good for you." He should be able to explain things so that it will be settled.

JH: So you shouldn't fight?

JY: No.

JH: Is there a lot of fighting on the ghats?

JY: It happens . . . there are some men who insult others in order to earn their money. For instance if I have a customer they will say bad things about me in order to woo the customer for himself. My habit is that I should earn and I should also let him earn his living. This way I may be happy and he may be happy. This doesn't mean that you should go ahead and steal my livelihood (*pet ka roti china chahiye*) and eat for yourself.

Jay was not the only boy who lived and worked by a moral "code." In fact, in chapter 6, I examine the rules that regulated the children's earning practices, and I discuss how they were and were not reflective of a larger moral economy that was premised upon the idea that "everyone should have a chance to earn." However, here I want to point out that although the boys frequently complained about the "dirty," violent, and uncouth atmosphere on the ghats, they also incorporated these grievances into more valorizing representations and understandings of themselves. As Pramod said to me one day with a gleam of pride in his eyes, "Look, Jenny, not just any boy can do this work. It takes a special kind."

Concluding Considerations: Class, Caste, and Neighborhood

In her preliminary study of "the structure and imagining of space in the lives of children," Nita Kumar rightly notes that within the city of Banaras gender plays a fundamental role in shaping children's experiences. She makes some pivotal observations about the ways adults use space to socialize children along gendered lines, and she raises important questions about how children "reappropriate space" and use tactics, both overt and clandestine, "to escape the nets of disciplining." Finally, she suggests that greater attention must be paid to the ways children "participate in their own socialization" (Kumar 2007, 246).

In many ways, the examples I have presented reinforce Kumar's findings. Gender not only influenced the children's access to difference spaces in the city but it also shaped the way they experienced and negotiated these spaces. Girls were limited to selling postcards, diyas, and tea on the riverfront (where their behavior and actions could be more closely monitored), whereas boys were free to roam about the city and participate in the more lucrative enterprise of guiding and commission work. Although both girls and boys frequently alluded to the rough and "dirty" atmosphere on the ghats, they emphasized different strategies for surviving in such an environment. The boys thought it was crucial to learn how "to insult others" and become "crooked" and "tough." The girls, by contrast, continually tried to demonstrate how "straight" and virtuous they were. In fact, the very ways in which they narrated their involvement in this informal economy were geared toward maintaining such an image. This included: continually emphasizing their necessity to work and rejecting any suggestions that they were earning money to indulge their own interests or pleasures; domesticating the ghats and casting it as a safer place to work; and disciplining each other through forms of ridicule that were meant to ensure proper feminine behavior and decorum.

So long as the girls were considered children, the riverfront was regarded as a fairly innocuous space for them to work in, and their presence on the ghats was socially tolerated, even if it was not deemed socially desirable. It was once these girls "got big" and neared the age of sexual maturity that working on the riverfront became problematic. In order to safeguard their reputations, the girls were removed from the riverfront and placed under much closer supervision in the home. For girls, therefore, the passage from childhood to adolescence was much more clearly and abruptly marked than it was for boys, and it involved a radical withdrawal from the public sphere. The boys, on the other hand, were more or less free to continue doing this work as long as they wanted, and they were also much more imaginatively invested in it than the girls. Boys often spoke of the fun, freedom, and fame that came from working with foreign tourists, and they associated it with possibilities for better futures.

Clearly, therefore, gender played a pivotal role. However, the children's experiences, both spatially and otherwise, were also considerably shaped by their class, caste, and neighborhood affiliations. If we want to grasp the complexity and diversity of children's lives, these aspects of identity warrant much closer attention. Kumar herself alludes to this when she says, "of course, class is important," but she then goes on to say that "class socialization is much weaker than gender socialization. Unlike with gender where both parents are simultaneously present for comparison, there is no other model before the child except the home she is born into" (Kumar 2007, 259).

What I observed in and through my interactions with the children on the ghats suggests otherwise. The children themselves were often concerned with discussing and analyzing the differences between the "rich" and the "poor," and they were they extremely sensitive to class- and caste-based insults; indeed, these were frequently used by the children as means to discipline and humiliate each other. Moreover, as I mentioned earlier, working on the ghats often provided these children with significant opportunities for self-reflection. By interacting with tourists and local people, the children did have the chance to confront alternative models outside of the home and reevaluate their lives through the eyes of Others.

Kumar is correct when she notes that there are significant contrasts between the spatial freedoms afforded to boys and the spatial restrictions placed on girls: "Apart from traveling to and from school, mobility is not a structural characteristic for girls. They do not go out for pleasure, for hanging out, or to pass the time. There would be nowhere to go. A street side, pan shop, tea shop, or any open urban space is not the provenance of the female of any age, unless they are professionals or otherwise have work" (Kumar 2007, 262). This observation, however, again needs to be qualified by the examples presented in this chapter. In many regards, the lower-class girls who worked on the ghats had much more mobility and freedom from the home than middle-class girls their age. Moreover, under the cover of work, they were able to sequester play spaces for themselves on the riverfront and escape, at least for a little while, the nets of adult disciplining.

Alternatively, although the boys I knew were free to "wander," their experiences of space and city were also significantly mediated by their class positions and aspirations, as well as by their caste and neighborhood affiliations. As I will discuss further in chapter 6, boys who did not come from the immediate neighborhood of Manmandir and who did not have a set of elder kinsmen with territorial rights on the ghats had a much more difficult time establishing themselves on the riverfront. Finally, for many of these boys, the difference between the riverfront and the "the world above" was not just a strictly spatial issue, but a social one. They were regarded as qualitatively different spaces that both required and reflected different kinds of social and cultural capital and different kinds of hopes for the future. In the next two chapters, I explore how Western tourists and local adults assessed the children on the riverfront and again, I consider how these assessments were linked to particular spatial experiences and imaginings.

4

Innocent Children or Little Adults?

Throughout my fieldwork I was continually intrigued by the responses that Western tourists had to the children on the riverfront. Not only did tourists' reactions display a surprising emotional intensity but in many cases they were diametrically opposed. Some tourists praised these young workers for their "charm" and "innocence," and suggested that they were "more pure" and "playful" than "children at home." Other tourists castigated them for their "corruption." As I was told, "These aren't children! They're just little adults in kids' bodies! All they're interested in is business and money, they're ruined!" However, there were also tourists who were very impressed with the budding "entrepreneurial skills" of these young peddlers and guides, and saw their developing "business acumen" as something to encourage and celebrate. Finally, for other tourists, the children did not appear to be savvy, business-minded youngsters with bright futures, but rather, they seemed more akin to "street urchins" and "beggars" who, as many tourists suggested, "were being exploited by despotic masters." How are we to understand these varied yet patterned reactions?

In this chapter, I pursue this question by drawing upon some earlier attempts to analyze the complex and contradictory ways that children are defined and valued within the global sphere. For instance, in studying "the cultural politics of childhood," Nancy Scheper-Hughes and Carolyn Sargent have drawn attention to two pervasive, yet opposing trends. On the one hand, they observe that within the context of an integrated global political economy, the category of the child is currently at risk of "disappearing."[1] They conclude, "Thoroughly postmodern children—reminiscent of Philippe Ariès's (1962) premodern child—are increasingly represented as miniature adults, endowed with quasi-adult rights and responsibilities" (Scheper-Hughes and Sargent 1998, 13). On the other hand, they observe that even though middle-class and upper-class children may possess little instrumental value, their sentimental and "expressive value" continues to render them precious subjects. "In the late-modern world the instrumental value of children has been largely replaced by their expressive value. *Children have become relatively worthless economically to their parents, but priceless in terms of their psychological worth*" (12; italics in original).

As Scheper-Hughes and Sargent rightly argue, understanding these trends requires interrogating how conceptions of childhood are influenced by a complex conjuncture of social forces and relations, including: global political-economic structures, ideological agendas, discourses that constitute and represent children as particular kinds of subjects, and "the everyday practices embedded in the micro-level interactions of local cultures" (1998, 2). In what follows, I attend to these multiple determinations. I consider how they influenced the ways that Western tourists conceived of the children on the riverfront and transacted with them. Drawing upon some concepts from psychoanalytic theory, however, I also argue that tourists' assessments of the youngsters on the ghat and their recurring tendencies to cast them as "innocent children" or corrupt "little adults" were also linked to a set of psychodynamics that involved processes of splitting, projection, idealization, and denial (Klein 1975, [1946] 1987, [1948] 1975, [1955] 1987). That is, I propose that the classification and treatment of children should not be reduced to an exclusively social phenomenon.

Innocent Children

Anthropologists and historians have repeatedly demonstrated that children are not universally regarded as innocent beings. However, for many of the Western tourists I encountered, innocence was the defining characteristic and even essence of childhood. Echoing what James, Jenks, and Prout describe as "the presociological" model of the child, which views children as "essentially pure in heart and uncorrupted by the world they have entered into" (1998, 10), Western tourists often told me, "children are by *nature* innocent creatures!" "They have no bad intentions." Or as Scott, a twenty-three-year-old American tourist, remarked: "Children are innocent, they are not going to try and cheat you like the adults do here, so I prefer to do business with them." And yet, as will be seen, even though presumptions of childhood innocence were widespread, this did not mean that tourists operated with the same understanding of what this innocence entailed, of how it could be detected, or even why it was deemed such a desirable quality for the children on the riverfront to possess.

Sincerity and Trustworthiness

Innocence often conjured up notions of a child who was sincere and trustworthy. The desire for trust and the perpetual disappointments that tourists experienced in trying to achieve it, were central preoccupations for the travelers I interviewed. As Peter began to articulate in chapter 2, tourists often found that when dealing with local people they were afflicted by a chronic sense of "suspicion," "second-guessing," and even "paranoia." "You have to constantly be on your guard here," I was repeatedly told, "everyone is going to try and cheat you."

In fact, many tourists told me that they began "bracing" themselves for "the assault of India" even before departing from home. As Mark, a twenty-four-year-old traveler from the United States, noted: "I sought out guidebooks, films, advice from other travelers. I wanted to be as prepared as possible to deal with all the difficulties. I mean I had heard and read so much about the people who will cheat you, the contaminated food and water, parasites, malaria, the depressing poverty, the heat, the crowds the lawless roads, I just wanted to try to be as prepared as possible." Indeed, many tourists seemed to travel to India because of these "dangers" rather than in spite of them. However, once they arrived, the allure of such threats was also offset by the profound sense of ontological insecurity that they engendered. For instance, Kevin, a twenty-six-year-old traveler from the United States, described the feeling of helplessness and suspicion that afflicted many of the tourists whom I met: "You're helpless here, and they make you helpless. Everyone here tells you, 'don't trust that guy,' you talk to one guy and then behind that guy there is someone else saying, 'he's bad, he's bad, be careful!' They all pit you against everyone else."

Although tourists expected this kind of behavior from adults, they were often far less suspicious of children. As Alex, a thirty-year-old traveler from Austria, remarked: "I think there is a big difference between these children touts and the adults. Because I make fair business with the children but these adults they are really cheating you so you have to pay attention. But I haven't met any children in Varanasi who have been lying." In such cases, therefore, tourists interpreted innocence as a resilient force that enabled children to participate in this informal economy without falling prey to the more "corrosive" elements of commerce. Thus, it took on significance because it both reaffirmed tourists' preconceived notions of children, and because it resonated with their desires to enter into "fair" and honest exchanges.[2]

The Noble Savage

The presumed innocence of the children on the ghats also took on significance as a marker of difference between the East and the West. Following the legacy of Rousseau, Western tourists frequently configured the children on the ghats as "noble savages" whom they regarded as uncorrupted by the "ills" and "excesses" of Western civilization, and who were perceived as living both closer to nature and closer to a moral "paradise of goodness and reciprocity" (James, Jenks, and Prout 1998, 15). In such cases, the innocence attributed to the children clearly resonated with tourists' desires to encounter a more authentic Other. But it also provided tourists with an opportunity to critique the artifice and stultifying effects of childhood at home. Peter, the middle-aged appliance repairman from England, again provides one of many vivid examples.

I officially met Peter on a chilly January morning. He was sitting on the ghats, wrapped in a paisley shawl, having tea with several of the girls who sold diyas. Anita Sahani was among them, and with her usual good cheer and perky disposition she called me over to arrange an introduction: "Jenny *Didi*, come meet our friend from England! He is good man, you interview him." I happily complied with Anita's instructions and made my way over to say hello. I had been observing Peter for a couple of days and was interested in the rapport he had established with some of the children on the riverfront. In fact, the day before, Anita had told me that Peter had treated her and another girl and boy to samosas at a nearby restaurant. I sat down on the ghat and Peter and I began chatting while the girls fluttered around us making fun of his long, gray wavy hair, "like an old woman," they laughed.[3] Peter smiled, and although he looked a bit embarrassed, he also seemed pleased by the attention. He informed me that he was on his way to the Kumbh Mela in Allahabhad but was planning to return to Banaras in a few weeks, and that he would be happy to speak more with me then.

A few days after Peter's return we met for an interview, and he shared some of his impressions of the children on the ghats. As he began:

P: One thing I would say about the children on the ghats, and I had this experience in the last couple of days, I get up very early in the morning and I go to one of the chai shops on the ghats and one of the girls who sells the puja candles was standing by so I bought her a chai. Later in the day she came running over to me and opened her hand and she had some sweets that a Korean girl had given her and she said, "Here, take two sweets!" I said, "No, no just one is enough, you can have the rest." And then there was another instance of a little boy whose father works in the market, one morning he was standing by the chai stand and he had two rupees in his hand and I said, "Oh go on, take this chai." And like a Western child would probably stick those two rupees in his pocket and think, "I'll keep it a big secret," and then nip out during the day and buy some sweets. But he actually put the two rupees on the counter and asked for four biscuits and he gave me one biscuit, he had one biscuit himself, he passed one up to a monkey that was on the roof, and then he was going to eat the fourth one and he saw some puppies and he just broke it up and threw it to the puppies and I thought that was really nice, unlike a Western kid.

From Peter's perspective, the honesty, compassion, and generosity of the children on the ghats clearly set them apart from the spoiled Western kids whom he usually encountered at home. As he went on to say:

> Well I haven't got children me-self but I do come in contact with a lot of children through my work in England. I go into people's houses. This isn't on any social level, it's for installing central heating and fixing kitchens. And when you see a kid in his house in his bedroom with like 500 pounds worth of toys and the kid is whingeing all the time cause he's bored, "I'm bored and I've got all this." And then you see the kids in India they seem to make the best out of a dreadful situation. That's the biggest contrast between Western children and the ones I meet in India.

Peter's remarks are interesting for a number of reasons. First, they give voice to what Scheper-Hughes and Sargent refer to as the highly "ambivalent and declining social value" of children in advanced industrial societies which, as they note, has led to an increase in criticisms of children as parasitic, "lazy and 'greedy' offspring" (Scheper-Hughes and Sargent 1998, 10). Peter, who was from a self-described working-class background, critiqued the overindulgent and stultifying effects of Western middle-class childhood by casting the Western child as an ungrateful economic siphon who was no longer capable of imaginative play. His comments also reveal how tourists' assessments of the children were animated by a good deal of guesswork and assumption. Like Peter, many tourists readily assumed that the children on riverfront were growing up in a "dreadful situation," or, as tourists frequently put it, in "the school of hard knocks." This perception of deprivation and struggle, in turn, rendered the children's knowledge and cheerfulness all the more "remarkable" to tourists. For instance, in recounting his excursion to the restaurant with Anita and the other children, Peter said:

> When the change was brought up, a ten rupee note, one of them held the note up to see if there was a watermark and she said, "Oh that's a good note," and on the ten rupee note she pointed to Gandhi and she said, "Do you know this man?" And I said, "Yes, yes, of course I know him." And she said, "Oh he's Gandhiji, he's a very good man for India." And I was amazed that a kid who was nine, whereas if you showed a nine-year-old kid in England a picture of Winston Churchill they wouldn't have a clue of who he was and these are supposedly uneducated kids who haven't been to school! But they know so much from doing this work.

Most nine-year-old children in England probably would be able to identify Winston Churchill, and perhaps, if Peter had had children of his own he would have considered this likely. However, the point here is that for Peter, "these supposedly uneducated kids" should not have been able to recognize one of the founding fathers of their nation. Thus, what most people would consider ordinary for a nine-year-old child at home was often regarded as extraordinary for the children on the ghats. In many cases, tourists conveyed how impressed they were by lavishing the children with special treats, or by purchasing more of their goods and services. As Brian, a twenty-five-year-old American tourist, explained when recounting his interaction with Diraj Pandey, "I was really impressed with how much this kid knew about my country. He was rattling off all the names of the cities, so I bought some of his postcards."

Nor was it only "children from home" who provided the foil against which Western tourists celebrated the special qualities of the children on the ghats. Many tourists also drew contrasts between these children and the "upper-class" Indian children whom they encountered on their travels. For instance, further along in our interview, Peter remarked:

> These street children they talk, they're very free, they talk very freely to you. I remember a couple of weeks ago when I was in Allahabad, I met a family there from Calcutta, a very well-off family and there was a child there, a boy, who was about eleven or twelve, who obviously had private school by the way he was dressed, so he probably spoke absolutely fluent English and the only thing he could think of to say to me was, "You've got white skin, I've got dark skin," and then giggled and ran away because he wasn't used to talking to Westerners. And I thought, what a contrast, this kid goes to a private school and I can't have a conversation with this eleven-year-old and with the street kids or whatever you want to call these kids on the ghat, you can have a conversation with them.

Here again, Peter's remarks display the kind of guesswork that animated tourists' assessments of the children. As I will discuss later, like Peter, many tourists assumed that the children on the riverfront fell into the category of "street children" who had no homes or support from their families. Second, in valorizing the uninhibited natures of the children on the ghats, Peter again alluded to the corrosive effects that wealth has on children, this time suggesting that affluence actually renders children *too* childlike.[4] Thus, what tourists like Peter seemed to yearn for was a child who was simultaneously innocent and uninhibited, yet also mature and worldly enough to relate to them—a child who could accommodate their desires for recognition and make tourists feel acknowledged as unique human beings rather than just "white skin."

And yet, at the same time that tourists wanted to be seen as more than "white skin," many of them also desired children who would dutifully fulfill their roles as "traditional" and "authentic" Indian subjects. Sharon Stephens has noted that such demands are increasingly common "in a world of shifting values and challenged boundaries," and that when children fail to live up to these expectations they frequently generate anger (Stephens 1995, 11). For example, Etty "Mama" was a forty-eight-year-old Israeli tourist who had been coming to Banaras for over ten years. During her first visit she had befriended Bali Sahani, one of the young guides on the ghats, who eventually became her "adopted son." In addition to visiting him bi-annually, she also sent him money every few months, and over the years her support had enabled him to finance the construction of a new home for his family. Among the children on the ghats, Etty Mama was regarded as the paradigmatic "lucky catch," the tourist who keeps on giving.

I interviewed Etty toward the end of her two-week stay in the city, and we spoke at length about her relationship with Bali, her experiences with the children on the ghats, and her overall impressions of what it is like to grow up in India. Prior to coming to Banaras, she had spent a week staying with her "wealthy Indian friends" in New Delhi but, as she told me in the interview, she had come away from the visit "very disappointed":

> The rich children here are very different and I think what they are very sorry about is that their skin is dark and not white because they are trying to assimilate the Western way of living, at least what they think is the Western way of living. They don't even like Indian music. Because I like Indian classical music so I've asked them, "What music do you like?" For me it's like kind of a way to click with them. They like Western pop, not even Indian pop, for them that's lowly. They don't relate to that at all, everything they want in their life is being Western, their dream is to go to the States to study there, to live there, and many of them probably will, they have enough money . . . there is none of this like traditional respect relationship, I think it is very Western but with an Indian color and I don't like it. I don't like it because they are not connected with what their country is and what their tradition is and where they come from basically.

Etty's comments provide a clear example of the dynamic Stephens points to and the hostility that can arise when children fail to fulfill their "traditional" roles. However, I also suspect that Etty was disturbed by more than just the children's alleged culture loss and neocolonial "mimicry" (Bhabha 1997).[5] Like Peter, Etty was also upset by her inability to relate to these children. Much to her dismay, her love of Indian music had not laid the ground for a positive identification, or as she put it, an opportunity "to click with them." As such, in a rather paradoxical twist, the children's apparent rejection of Indian tradition and culture became, for Etty, a personal one.

The Purity of Play

Innocence was also intimately linked to play. Perhaps more than anything else, playfulness was taken to be *the* sign of an intact child; that is, a child who, despite being introduced to an adult world of work and responsibility, was still perceived as being spontaneous, free, creative, and who possessed an almost kinetic appeal.[6] Moreover, when tourists encountered such children on the riverfront, they often expressed a sense of relief, as though it represented a triumph of nature over nurture. As Charlotte, an Irish traveler in her early twenties, remarked, "Well at least you know that no matter how bad it is children are going to be children wherever you go. They're going to play around, have fun, and just be kids." Or as Sara, a twenty-nine-year-old Canadian tourist, noted in our interview, "It makes me happy when I see that these kids will suddenly drop their work and start playing with each other and become totally absorbed in it. They're not obsessed with selling like most of the adults are. There is still something pure about them." Nusan, an Israeli-American tourist, remarked: "A child is innocent in America and at the same time ignorant, here a child is innocent but not ignorant, you know, the innocence of the child is still there, like if you try to play with the child, or you want to make friends with the child, you still can. They are going to run around and play and be like a child—innocent." Finally, as Charles, a forty-year-old American tourist, noted when describing the children on the riverfront: "They don't look like children because they learn the business strategy so well, they are good at business these children, they are really good. But after that you see them play, you see them run one after the other and laughing, this attractive energy they have, these children, they're funny!" However, beyond indexing an innocent, intact, or pure child, what else did playfulness signify for tourists? And, why was this quality deemed so precious?

As Charles's and Sara's remarks begin to suggest, the children's playfulness took on significance, in part, because it stood in opposition to what tourists perceived as the coercive, instrumental, and even "dehumanizing" realm of adult work and commerce. This was rendered particularly clear in cases where tourists critiqued the children for not being playful enough. For example, Kirsten was a twenty-one-year-old tourist from Germany whom I interviewed at a rooftop restaurant one afternoon in February. Our interview got off to an explosive start when I mentioned that Western tourists often found the children on the ghats "charming and cute." As soon the words were spoken, Kirsten, who initially seemed uninterested in having the conversation, turned her eyes up from the cup of milky tea that she had been staring into and looked at me with an incredulous and outraged expression. As her face flushed red under a heavy tangle of blond dreadlocks that were beginning to quiver with rage, she replied:

> Uggh! I think that these kids on the ghats are some of the worst kids that I've met in India! They don't even treat you like you are human! They can't jump out of their roles. They don't get it. The first day I came here I went to the ghats to watch the puja. I was thinking that it would be a nice religious experience, I was trying to sit there and watch something that was a part of their fucking culture and every five minutes I had a kid

come up to me to try and sell me something! There was one young girl who was trying to sell me puja [she meant diyas]. The first time she came up to me I said "No," then she came back again and I said "No!" And the third time when she approached me I got so upset that I ended up knocking over her entire basket of flowers and they ended up on the ground. I didn't mean for it to happen but it did and she glared at me and I glared back at her. Of course the Indians who were there didn't know my side of the story. They just thought "Here is another fucking crazy tourist!" The kids will follow you around, they won't leave you alone! I just expect to be treated like a human but they can't do this . . . [voice becoming calmer] I feel sorry for them because I know there is probably a lot of love inside them but they are ruined. They have to work, but still.

For Kirsten, the children were far from playful or spontaneous, and their inability to "jump out of their roles" bespoke the devastating effects of commerce. Moreover, for Kirsten, it was not just the children who were being dehumanized in and through these transactions, but also tourists like herself. Laurien, a middle-aged traveler from the United States, expressed similar sentiments when describing some of her interactions with the children on the ghats and some of the child peddlers she had encountered in Goa:

It's like they lost their childhood, you know, because they're . . . the pressure to sell when you're five! I think they're like adults, they just have to grow up so fast, I think they're totally different from kids in the States. They've been forced to become commercial people at age five or six and that changes their nature. I saw kids in Goa who were you know with all the necklaces hanging and with scarves and shawls around their arms and you know they've got this whole sales pitch and they're just [emphatically] *twisted, distorted* . . . in fact it is the *distortion* of children, watching that, you know, and you couldn't penetrate beyond it. I mean, it doesn't bother me that they're selling stuff, I think it's just part of what goes on, it's just part of what is here. There's just. . . . there's a point of twist to me, and I know for me what that point is, and it's very subjective, it's the point where *I'm* uncomfortable, for my comfort level they're going too far and then I wonder what is it that doesn't receive back from me, for instance with this little girl Priya I think, "What is it in this little tiny girl that doesn't . . ." I look her right in the eye and I say, "I really don't want a candle, I'm talking to my friend." And then she won't stop. You know what I mean? It's just [emphatically]—it's a *human* thing! That could be a thirty-year-old person that I would be dealing with and I would be thinking the same thing. But I think, what's driving this five-year-old to be so . . . so *heavy*? You know? That's the question!

Thus, in contrast to the "heavy" and "hardened" children that Laurien and many other tourists complained about, playful children reassured tourists that even though these youngsters "had to earn," their spirits had not been totally dominated by the imperatives of profit. Indeed, for some tourists, the playful children on the ghats seemed to embody the very essence of "the Romantic child" which, as historian Anne Higonnet argues, first became a dominant ideal in Western society during the eighteenth century (Higonnet 1998). As Higonnet writes, the Romantic child "is desirable precisely to the extent that it does not understand desire." It is a child that "does not connect with adults, one that seems unaware of adults," one who is "presented to be looked at . . . but not for us to make any psychological connection with." The allure of this child is that it "cannot" be reached (28).

And yet, while some tourists celebrated the impenetrable revelry of the children on the ghats, many more wanted to actually join in the fun. As the remarks above already begin to suggest, tourists wanted children with whom they could "click." Often, tourists expressed these yearnings in very physical ways. Some tourists even commented on fellow travelers who were seen as "desperately clinging" to the children on the ghats. For instance, in recounting his experiences at the evening puja, Charles exclaimed:

> Oh God! I saw a woman sitting right next to the Pepsi stand with like a baby at the breast, and another one just hanging on her knee and she was feeding them and very just, having a great time, everybody was loving it! I mean come on, I've seen so many like her. They come to India thinking they're going to [making quote gestures with his fingers] "Save the Children," become Mother Theresa or Patrick Swazye from *The City of Joy*. Give me a break!

For Charles, these were comical spectacles that revealed tourists' own fantasies to establish themselves as benevolent benefactors, even it if was only for a few days. And, as I will discuss later, in many ways Charles's interpretation was astute. However, when I observed these scenes, I sensed that there was something more at stake. Like good teddy bears, the children also provided these tourists with an enhanced sense of comfort and security which, in many cases, enabled them to negotiate the riverfront with greater ease, joy, and confidence.[7]

For instance, Ross was a twenty-five-year-old American tourist who had come to Banaras for several weeks to study *tabla*. I interviewed him toward the end of his stay, and as he began talking his face lit up with a smile. "I'm happy because I've been here a while now and I've finally reached the point with the kids where they actually say hi to me instead of just 'You buy postcard?' You know, sometimes we even play!" Indeed, there were several occasions when I discovered Ross "playing" with the children on the riverfront. For instance, one afternoon he was sitting on the ghats with Jaggu, Diraj, and Pramod. The boys were shooting marbles and as the game proceeded they began to quarrel over whose turn it was. Pramod began hitting Jaggu with a few lackluster strikes to the head, as though he were trying to swat a fly away rather than inflict any kind of real injury. In a sudden movement, Ross leaned over, whisked Pramod up from the ground, and then placed him squarely over his knee so that his rear faced the sky. In an exaggerated motion, with a wide-open palm, Ross began to slap Pramod on his bottom and in a playful holler cried, "That is not nice! Bad boy! Bad boy!" This made all three of the boys, as well as Ross, reel with laughter.

Ross's response again suggests that there was a good deal of role playing going on in these interactions, and when I witnessed these kinds of exchanges I often wondered if tourists would have taken such liberties with children at home. However, the point I want to emphasize here is that, for tourists like Ross, playfulness not only emerged as a sign of an innate and incorruptible childish essence but it also came to index an affirming *interaction* between the tourist and child. In fact, in many cases, this was precisely the criterion that tourists used to assess whether a child was playful or not. As Ross insightfully noted later in the interview, "A lot of tourists meet these kids on the riverfront and complain that they are only interested in business, but that's like going to someone's place of work and asking why they aren't playful. You have to see them on their own."

Deficient but Desirable

Although tourists frequently linked innocence to a playful "essence" that children "possessed" or were innately endowed with, they also configured it in terms of a generalized *lack*; that is, as the byproduct of children's "immaturity" and limited exposure to particular forms of knowledge and experience. Following the legacy of Locke rather than Rousseau, tourists often cast the children on the ghats as veritable "blank slates," who were desirable precisely because they could be more easily influenced and controlled.[8] For instance, in explaining why he preferred to be guided by a child, Casey, a twenty-four-year-old American tourist, remarked: "I feel better going with these kids. With their mentality you can still guide them. I still don't think their minds are fully formed even if they're ten years old. Even if they want money, even if they're doing a job out there, take them away from that, they're still kids."

Jorgen, a thirty-one-year-old Dutch tourist, provides another example. Jorgen arrived in Banaras in May of 2000. I was introduced to him by Mohan who, on the first day of Jorgen's arrival, had managed to secure a position as his guide. Initially, Jorgen had planned to stay in Banaras for only three days, but after getting to know Mohan, he decided to extend his visit to over a week. For reasons I will discuss in chapter 7, Jorgen was one of the more memorable tourists or, rather, "case studies" that I came across during my fieldwork. Like Casey, Jorgen also expressed his explicit preference for "a child guide."[9] As he explained in our interview:

> I much rather be taken around by a young boy like Mohan, I think it makes a big difference. Um, when I meet an adult here and he is providing me a guide service, I expect a reasonable level of professionality and I doubt whether the Indians whom I've met so far would be able to provide me with that level of professionality. And it would upset me. But when I'm walking around with a boy like Mohan it is more easy for me to accept that some things he doesn't know, and at the same time, and I think this is a very important one, it is much more easy for me to control him in doing what I want than it would be for me to control an adult Indian to do what I want.

Jorgen's complaints about the inadequacies of professional guides in India recall those put forth by W. S. Caine in his 1890 guidebook, and they reinstate a larger set of colonial discourses about the inferiority of "the natives." This kind of discourse was extremely common among Western tourists, and it often provided a narrative frame for endless hours of conversation and complaining. However, as Jorgen's remarks also reveal, these critiques frequently betrayed tourists' own anxieties about being at the mercy of local people and not being able to "control" them or their intentions. Amid such fears, many tourists did find it preferable to employ children as guides, even if it meant that they would be primarily relying upon their guidebooks to get detailed information about the sites they were visiting. This was especially the case for women travelers. For instance, as Alexandra, a twenty-six-year-old tourist from Switzerland, remarked:

A: I like to have more contact with kids because you can see them from here, you can look down. But most men you have to treat them also as kids but they are taller than you, so it's a bit difficult.

JH: Why do you have to treat most men as kids?

A: Well, they act like kids, I mean, I have the feeling sometimes I am either a one rupee bank note, or it's written here, "Fuckable and enjoy me," yeah that's it. But with kids, no, they prefer to play with you, and they are more pure in a way.

In Alexandra's remarks, the category of the child was used to critique an immature male subject, and again to valorize a more pure and playful one. Indeed, many of the women I met during my fieldwork spoke of Indian men as "children" who, on the one hand, were perceived as being incredibly inept when it came to dealing with the opposite sex, but also potentially dangerous. Most Western women traveling in India were well acquainted with stories and experiences of sexual harassment, and a fear of being abused was a common theme in women's travel narratives. As such, children became desirable to interact with not only because of their seemingly innocent natures, but also, as Alexandra remarked, because of their less intimidating size.

Little Adults

Although some tourists embraced the children on the riverfront for their innocent natures and playful resiliency, other tourists had a very difficult time reconciling these young peddlers and guides as children. In fact, they often denied them the status altogether. Variously expressing feelings of outrage, remorse, and admiration, tourists repeatedly exclaimed: "These aren't children. They're just little adults in kids' bodies!" "These kids have the minds of forty-year-olds and the bodies of ten-year-olds" (Alicia, a thirty-one-year old tourist from England). "The children on the ghats are so clever, they really are little adults so you have to be careful doing business with them" (Tanya, thirty-two-year-old tourist from the United States).

Such statements could be downplayed as "mere" figures of speech; following Lakoff and Johnson (1980), however, I want to consider how the metaphor of the little adult structured the way Western tourists both perceived the children on the ghats and actually related to them. Here again, I demonstrate that although this metaphor was widely invoked by Western tourists, it also took on different meanings and reflected different kinds of discourses and assumptions about children and childhood.

Pathologically Precocious

For many Western tourists, the metaphor of the little adult was invoked as a way to critique and lament the precociousness of the children on the ghats. Unlike those tourists who operated with a "presociological" model of the child, these tourists were very attuned to the impact of the environment and the role it played in "distorting" children's natures. Again, as Laurien expressed, "It's like they've lost their childhood . . . it's the very distortion of children . . . they're like adults, they just have to grow up so fast." Or as Joyce, a twenty-five-year-old tourist from the United States, remarked when describing her encounter with Priya: "My friend and I met a little girl on the ghats this morning who was selling postcards and she was hardened. Usually the kids in India love it when we take pictures, they say, 'Photo, photo,' but when my friend got out his video camera she wanted no part of it, she said 'No photo' and was just waiting patiently for her money. She was hardened like an adult." Or finally as Kimberley, a twenty-four-year-old traveler from Canada, commented: "They are just little adults in kid's bodies; all they are interested in is business and money, they are ruined now!"

In such commentaries, tourists went beyond mourning the apparent loss of childhood. They also suggested that the entire developmental trajectory of these young salespeople was at risk. From their perspective, the children's early exposure to commerce would ultimately turn them into "stunted adults" who would never fully mature or flourish in the future. Robin Rawlins refers to this as a theory of "hot house development" and she has traced its presence in late nineteenth- and early twentieth-century middle-class discourses about poor working children. As Rawlins argues, one of the ways the emerging bourgeois sought to distinguish themselves from the working class was by upholding a sentimental conception of childhood that viewed children as fundamentally innocent, closer to nature, and in need of protection. "Precocious children who failed to conform to the middle-class ideal of dependent childhood were considered deviant, pathological, and sometimes criminal" (Rawlins 2002, 100–101). Alternatively, in his writings on aging and modernity in India, the anthropologist Lawrence Cohen has observed that ideas about "an all-too ephemeral precocity" also played a central role in colonial pedagogic and medical discourses. Whether attributed to the intensity of life in the tropics, or the particulars of the Indian brain, native minds where often depicted as "flowering early and luxuriantly" but putrefying and rotting just as quickly (Cohen 1998, 22).

In tourists' accounts of the children on the riverfront, both kinds of discourses manifested themselves, albeit with various twists. For instance, when I asked Etty Mama for her impressions of the children working on the riverfront, she depicted a disheartening situation in which children could no longer be children and adults could never fully mature. As she explained:

> Well, I think these kids really do not have the chance of being children and they do not have the chance of learning the basic things in life like a child, like how do we grow up? I don't say that the Western education is the best, I really don't think so. Childhood is a time for like, acquiring all kinds of values and all kinds of abilities, like simple things, like sharing or dealing with your aggression, or dealing with authority, like basic things not writing and . . . that's not so important but *basic human things*, you learn them being in a child's society, yeah, that's why children are in nursery school and that's why they play with peers. Here they don't have that so much because what I see over on the ghats, like sitting there, the moment these children start to play or interact the adults throw them apart, they, they . . . "Go do your work." I see it with this Priya, I am watching her, she is walking with her postcards, then she finds a girl, they are playing, they are happy, here comes her father "WRAGH, WRAGH, GO!" There she goes, they don't even allow her a little bit of fun like playing with her friend, and it's important because that's the way kids acquire their skills as adults. So it's not surprising that these kids grow up to be adults who are pushy and unpleasant and cheating, so many of them are, sorry, that's the way it is.

In this account, the children on the ghats were clearly cast as deviant subjects who were barred from acquiring "basic human skills." Though Etty decried the way wealthy Indian children seemed to mimic Western culture and society, here, she reinstated the West as the norm against which all others models of childhood socialization should be judged. Moreover, for Etty the children were doomed to become "pushy," "unpleasant," and "cheating" adults because they were denied the opportunity to play. Here again, therefore, play emerged as crucial category in defining children and childhood. However, instead of indexing a realm of authentic, spontaneous, and carefree behavior, Etty conceived of play as a critical stage in the developmental process.[10]

How did this perception of the precocious little adult affect the ways that tourists actually related to the children? For as Lakoff and Johnson remind us, metaphors have "entailments" or consequences not only at the level of conceptual systems, but also in the practice of our everyday lives. Metaphors "structure what we perceive, how we get around in this world, and how we relate to other people" (Lakoff and Johnson 1980, 3).

In some cases, tourists felt sympathy for these seemingly "ruined" children, and this actually prompted them to purchase more than they might otherwise have. For instance, when discussing his encounter with Priya, Max, an Australian tourist, explained: "This girl really disturbs me, she's like a little adult, the only thing she has on her mind is selling and she doesn't stop. But I bought postcards from her because I can tell she has a tough life and a really mean father." However, in other cases, when tourists perceived the children as "heavy," "hardened," or even "aggressive" "little adults," they themselves became more callous. There was less hesitation to shoo a child away, to shout at them, or even as Priya, Mona, and Jaila occasionally complained, to throw their postcards or tea cups on the ground. Although some Western tourists clung to the children like teddy bears, I observed many more who looked as though they were preparing to do battle with the children on the ghats. In fact, often this was precisely the kind of language they used to describe their interactions.

Erin, for instance, was a thirty-eight-year-old carpenter from the United States and was traveling through India with Charles. In contrast to Charles, who seemed utterly delighted with his trip thus far, Erin found it very difficult to be a tourist in India. As he told me at the outset of our interview, "I knew it was going to be intense, but not this intense, after two hours of being in this country I was like, can I get back on the plane now?" During their week-long stay in the city, I had the chance to observe and chat with Charles and Erin on the ghats. However, after a couple of days, Erin's presence became less frequent, and Charles informed me that he had decided "to hole up" in the guest house where he could enjoy a scenic view of the riverfront without being "hassled." It was then that I paid Erin a visit and asked if I could interview him.

We sat down to a rooftop lunch of tomato soup, cheese toast, and fries, or as Erin put it, "a bevy of comfort food," and he began to tell me about why he had wanted to come to India and his experiences thus far. About twenty minutes into our conversation I mentioned that I had seen some of the kids approach him on the ghats and try to sell him postcards. Erin responded quickly and excitedly:

> These kids, they're very good at one thing that has been taught to them by probably somebody who beats them if they don't do it. I don't know, I mean I don't know how it's enforced, and I've seen enough kids fighting amongst themselves, and there's a certain base level of aggression that uh, it's not beyond their character to get a little rise out of getting a little rise out of you. It's a little bit kind of fun to see what this tourist freak is going to do. The other day I met a kid and he was trying to sell me some postcards and I waved him off and he was trying to evoke a guilty feeling from me for waving him off. Or some will say, "hello" and try to sell you something and you'll say, [in a very stern voice] "NO!" and then they'll say [again in a soft voice] "Why?" It's like, like you hurt them, the subtlety with which they know. I mean I feel like consciously they know how to play on Western guilt. It's psychological warfare out here!

Erin did not explicitly invoke the metaphor of the little adult, but like many tourists, he did view these children as precocious subjects who were aggressive and manipulative beyond their years and who needed to be dealt with accordingly. In fact, many of the tourists I observed and spoke with actively experimented with different strategies for dealing with these children. As Nicholas, a twenty-two-year-old tourist from Seattle, remarked, "At first I was very polite, and I said no thank you I don't want your candles—but after being *bombarded* by these kids again and again, I've become much nastier, I even give them mean looks to try and scare them away."

The Little Professional

If some tourists invoked the metaphor of the little adult to criticize the children, other tourists invoked the metaphor as a form of praise. From their perspective, the children were not so much developmentally skewed as developmentally savvy. Their budding business acumen was something to encourage and celebrate, for it bespoke their ability to adapt to the exigencies of their environment and keep pace with changing times and opportunities. In fact, often, tourists referred to the children admiringly (particularly the boys), as "little businessmen," "little entrepreneurs," or "little professionals," and they speculated that the boys would have very promising futures as a result of honing their sales skills with tourists. As Jorgen noted when commenting on Mohan's future, "I wouldn't be surprised if the work he is doing now helps him get a good job in the future, he is developing very useful skills by working with tourists, maybe a company will hire him to work with foreigners." Or, alternatively, as Phillip, a Canadian tourist, commented after purchasing a stack of postcards from Pramod, "I bet within twenty years this kid becomes CEO of a company! He is a natural businessman!"

While Phillip suggested that Pramod's business acumen was a reflection of his "natural" talents and charismatic personality, other tourists proposed that the children's business prowess was a product of their environment. The metaphor of the little businessman was often invoked to contrast the very different social contexts and pressures that children in India and children in the West had to contend with. As Peter's remarks suggested earlier, in many instances, the children on the ghats elicited admiration from tourists precisely because their lives seemed "so different" from the pampered, "spoiled," and sheltered existences of children at home. And yet there were also tourists who recognized similarities between the "professional" lives and responsibilities of the children on the ghats and children at home. Mike, for instance, was a thirty-two-year-old environmental engineer who lived in California and came from a self-described "upper-middle-class family." In our interview, I asked him what he thought of the children whom he had encountered on the riverfront, and his response began with the following comparison:

> In the States parents are thinking about what professional summer camp to send their kids to. But I think that kids who sell things on the ghats are just like kids in the United States, kids that are more, are more, some of them might be more driven, you know just like an overachiever but overachieving is not like getting an A-plus in school, or acing all your math classes, it's being a little salesman and developing relationships with people. I don't think that kids here are that different from kids in the United States, they can go between their professional and not professional lives just as much as kids in developing worlds, it just so happens that they have different ideas about what it means to be professional. I mean, being a professional here means you're able to make money on a daily basis. To be a professional in the United States, means to become educated which then allows you to have that career, our economy is more fueled by ideas than it is by labor and making things.

For Mike, overachieving, whether it be in terms of "earning an A" or becoming the best "little businessman" was a common and necessary part of childhood socialization, or rather, to use his language, "professionalization," which was fundamentally concerned with grooming children for success in the future. Thus, while Peter's reactions reflected a larger critique of children as parasitic, "lazy and 'greedy' offspring" (Scheper-Hughes and Sargent 1998, 10), Mike's response points to another prevalent discourse which views and values children in terms of their potential as future producers: through the proper summer camps, schools, and experiences selling, Mike suggested that in today's world children can, and perhaps should, be programmed early on for a life of productivity.[11]

Beggars, Street Kids, and Pestilence

Tourists like Mike were able to reconcile the differences between the children on the ghats and children at home by projecting their Western middle-class conceptions of childhood onto these young peddlers and guides and viewing them as little businessmen with potentially bright futures. However, for other tourists, these youngsters more closely resembled "beggars" or "street urchins," and their presence on the riverfront seemed to evidence the harsh realities of neglect, poverty, and exploitation. Therefore, instead of evoking praise and admiration from tourists, when perceived in this light, the children could variously arouse feelings of pity, anger, frustration, and guilt. For instance, Jay was a thirty-four-year-old tourist from the United States who came to Banaras at the end of January. I had seen him on the ghats several times and was struck by his hostile demeanor toward the children. When they approached, he would wave them away gruffly, and on one occasion, he began shouting at Priya and Jaila when they tried to sell him postcards and diyas during the evening puja. After witnessing this behavior, I was not eager to arrange an interview with Jay, but I decided to do so for the sake of my research.

To my surprise, when I approached Jay on the ghats the next afternoon he welcomed my request and said he was relieved to meet someone from his "own country." We went to a rooftop restaurant and I broke out my tape recorder as he ordered a drink. After listening to Jay recount his "extensive travels" in Southeast Asia, and some of his experiences in India, I directed the conversation to Banaras. I asked him what he thought about the children who were selling on the riverfront. His reply quickly erupted into an impassioned diatribe against the government of India:

> Well that's fine because I've realized that the opportunity or the luxury to stay in school until you are eighteen years old and have your parents cater to your every whim is not in this culture. I would like to see it that way but it isn't. In a broader standpoint it makes me angry against the government. "Um, yeah we've got a billion people, yeah we know how to fuck, yeah we have a bomb that we can blow away our neighbors with, we're people with power but we can't keep our kids in school, we can't have decent conditions for our country. We have open sewers everywhere, we

have disease and pestilence, but we have a bomb, we've really achieved a lot, we think we're a world superpower." No! In my opinion it takes a lot more to be superpower. Your people have to live to a certain standard to be a superpower. Otherwise you've just got a big stick and you're an idiot. Well India's got a big stick and they're idiots cause if they think they're a superpower with the open sewers, with the kids not going to school, with the disease, polio, leprosy, all these diseases that have come from Western society, but "we're a superpower." Bullshit! I beg to differ with you!

Jay's rant continued for several more minutes as he proceeded to criticize the "stupidity" of the Indian government; the "pathetic" subway system that had been developed in Calcutta, the "arrogance and national pride" that prevented India from "truly utilizing global knowledge" to improve life for Indian citizens. "Give me a break!" he exclaimed, as though he were speaking directly to a government official, "you have centuries to go before you reach what it means to be a superpower, you have centuries to go until you can provide your people with a decent standard of living, and until you do don't bastardize the word superpower because it doesn't take a brain surgeon to have a look at the comparison!"

Jay's response did startle me, and I was struck by the anger in his voice. However, as I listened to Jay unload this litany of accusations and criticisms, part of what I heard him suggesting was that the children on the riverfront were also, like open sewers, disease, broken subways, and pestilence, disturbing indexes of India's larger order problems and "crimes." His response, therefore, was less a reflection on his encounters with the actual children on the ghats than a reaction to what they represented. When Jay's tirade was finished and he paused to take a sip of his drink, I tried to steer our conversation back to the children on the riverfront by asking him if he had bought any postcards or diyas. This elicited another irate, yet revealing response:

> When kids come up to me with postcards and say "Rupee, rupee, give me two rupees." "No, you know, you're not my mistake, I didn't do it, you know, I didn't make you." I would not leave my child on the streets. If a woman comes up to me with a baby in arms and begs for food, "I didn't have the fifteen minutes of fun, you did, don't look at me like I should owe you anything, you know, no, you made the mistake, live with it! Unfortunately your child is going to have to suffer more than you are, the child is the one who's going to suffer, you had your fun!" I look at these God-awful dirty and homeless and disgusting women and I'm like, "Who in their right mind did this? Where did you find the luxury when you're starving in the street, where do you find the luxury to have sex, yeah, and where did you find the stupidity to keep it? You should have used something that wasn't going to get you knocked up." You know,

that's stupidity and I will not pay for them enjoying their stupidity. I don't reward that, I don't reward the lady with the babies who had fifteen minutes of fun and I'm not going to take the responsibility from the government for their responsibility. It's the society. It's India's responsibility to take care of those people!

Here again, Jay's anger flared up as he quickly moved from answering a question about the children who peddled postcards on the ghats to offering another incensed critique of the Indian government and the "unethical" and "irresponsible" practices of the nation's homeless population. Indeed, Jay suggested that although the children on the ghats sold postcards, diyas, and trinkets, and although most of them were not garbed in "filthy" clothes, they were really no different than the other "beggars" in India who were "born out of poverty and ignorance." As Jay emphasized, it was not his "responsibility" to pay for these "mistakes." In fact, he even suggest that to do so, would render him complicit in this cycle of oppression. As he remarked further along in the interview: "There is no way I am going to contribute to these problems by buying postcards from these kids; all that does is send the message that I support this!"

This kind of rationale was echoed by other tourists who viewed the children as "neglected street kids," or who suspected that the children were being required to work against their will; an idea that was commonly perpetuated by guidebooks as well as travel lore. As Rakhel, an Israeli tourist, noted, "I've heard that these kids are all forced to work on the ghats and are not allowed to keep their money, they have to give it to some boss who makes them come here every day." Or as Diane, a tourist from England, remarked, "I'm sure they have some master who they have to give their earnings to so I don't want to buy anything from them." Finally Chris, a twenty-six-year-old tourist from Montreal, also presumed that these children were being exploited. As he remarked in our interview:

C: I have bought many postcards and also one floating lamp because these children are working and they sell something not too expensive, but what I don't like is the master who organizes it. I don't like this so I thought afterward that maybe I should not buy because I just contribute.
JH: So, you think there is a person who takes the money from the kids?
C: I am quite sure of it, so maybe it is not good to contribute.

For these tourists, travelers like Mike, who were able to draw similarities between "the professionalization" of children in the West and the working lives of children on the ghats, seemed absurd. Whereas Mike envisioned profit potentials for these entrepreneurial "little salesmen" and was willing to support their endeavors through buying their goods, tourists like Jay, Chris, Diane, and Rakhel saw exploitation, and were very reluctant to participate in business transactions with these children. Of course, such "explanations" may also be interpreted as rationalizations which, on the one hand, enabled tourists to recuse themselves from having to take "responsibility" for these children, and on the other, enabled tourists to portray themselves as responsible and compassionate people even if they were not going to comply with the children's appeals. However, in either case, it is clear that representations of street children, which again, were widely circulated in both guidebooks and travel lore, did come to configure the way tourists responded to the children on the ghats.

The Psychodynamics of Classification

Tourists' reactions to the children on the riverfront were both informed by and reflective of the tropes and themes through which they came to know India, the ways they read and interpreted the space of the ghats, and by different discourses regarding children and childhood. I want shift to another level of analysis, however, and consider how tourists' responses were also linked to a set of *psychodynamics*.[12] Following the psychoanalyst Melanie Klein, I argue that in many cases, these reactions reflected unconscious "defence mechanisms" that enabled tourists to better cope with the feelings of guilt and "persecutory anxiety" that the children, and the surrounding environment, so frequently aroused in them (Klein 1975, [1946] 1987, [1948] 1975, [1955] 1987).[13]

Idealization and Denial

The examples we have encountered so far already demonstrate that tourists' reactions were both emotionally charged and highly polarized. In many cases, tourists either idealized the children as being more pure, playful, or even mature and savvy than children at home. Or alternatively, they denied them the status of children altogether and lamented, as well as criticized, their apparent corruption. In other words, to borrow Klein's terminology, tourists had a very difficult time accepting these children as "whole objects" with both "good" and "bad" attributes.[14] Instead, their reactions indicated processes of splitting, projection, idealization, and denial which, as Klein argued, often operate as unconscious defense mechanisms that enable people to cope with feelings of anxiety and guilt. The following case, taken from my interview with Usha, provides a particularly vivid example.

Usha was a twenty-three-year-old traveler from Germany who had come to India in search of "spiritual enlightenment." She had planned to travel in India for several months before returning home to begin a nursing program. I came to know her when she began renting one of the rooms across from me at the Laxmi guest house. When she first arrived in the city, Usha had sought accommodations near Assi Ghat, but after a few days roaming the riverfront, she met a local *sadhu* named Babaji who lived and meditated near Dasashwamedh. After a series of "amazing conversations" (which were all the more amazing considering that Babaji spoke almost no English and Usha no Hindi), Usha was convinced that Babaji would provide her with invaluable spiritual mentoring. As such, she decided to relocate to Dasashwamedh so that she could be closer to him. To express her gratitude, she had also promised Babaji that she would stay in the city and help him recover from a broken foot he had recently suffered. As it turned out, this took over a month, and although Usha was ready to move on after a couple of weeks, she made good on her promise and waited until Babaji was fully bipedal again.

Because of the length of her stay, and because she was living right across the hall from me, Usha and I had the chance to get to know each other through a number of informal conversations. However, as Usha seemed primarily fixated on her relationship with Babaji, and as I rarely saw her spending time on the ghats without him, it never occurred to me to talk to her about her interactions with the children. One night, however, we had gathered in my office for tea. Usha was in a particularly chatty mood, and my tape recorder was laid out on my desk. She started inquiring about how my work was progressing, noting that she had seen many tourists coming and going from my room over the last few weeks. "Why haven't you interviewed me?" she asked. "I have met these kids, and I am right here across from you!"

I took the cue and set up my recorder. I had barely finished articulating my first question when Usha began launching into a detailed discussion of the various scams and disappointments that she had been subjected to upon her arrival in New Delhi. After some time, she moved on to Banaras, and it was then that I asked her about her interactions with the children on the ghats. "So, tell me about your experiences with these kids," I prompted her. She took a deep breath and exhaled purposively before responding:

> Oh yes, the first time I came to the ghats, I thought, "Oh no what can I do? There are so many children around me, oohh they are taking away my peace. Oh this is not nice," and then I walk straight and I don't look anywhere, and sometimes I put on my Walkman, then I cannot listen and people see "Oh she cannot hear," and then they do not come to you. They come and then they go.... But then you learn to say, "Hey, go away, quick, *chalo,*" and then they are going. At first you think, oh, this is a small boy, I cannot say so harshly, "Hey go away," oh this is a sweet, small boy and he asks you [making her voice soft and cute], "Oh would you like to buy postcards?" And in one way it's sweet, it's nice and you cannot say like this, [in a deep stern voice] "Hey go!" But then when it's getting too much because it's not only one, then you learn to be, to . . . and sometimes

> I take their neck like here [making the sweeping and grabbing gesture with her hand] and I push them away, and say, "GO!" Not hard, but like if you're swimming and you make some rubbish . . . rubbish . . . [making clearing away movements with her arms] very gentle but "go."[15]

Regrettably, I cannot play the audio tape here or capture all of the gestures and expressions that animated Usha's dramatic reenactment of her experiences on the ghats. Yet, as this brief, transcribed excerpt begins to make clear, it was indeed a reenactment, and a dramatic one at that. Usha began waving her arms, and mimicking the various voices of the children on the ghats, thereby creating the sense that there were several interlocutors in the room with us. As was the case with Jay, Usha also appeared to be on an emotional rollercoaster where feelings of frustration, guilt, or sympathy could quickly give way to expressions of anger, and then revert once again. For instance, when I proceeded to ask Usha, "What do you think it is like for these kids who work on the ghats? What do you think they think of tourists?" She exploded with the following reply, again mimicking the voices of the children:

> I think they are very . . . [in an explosive voice] I think they *hate* tourists! I think that they hate tourists and need them and they hate. . . . and they think also that tourists are very stupid people, very stupid, and fat, and big money, and tourists are only good for making money, because they are stupid and you can get on their nerves and no problem, they are not the same human being as Indians, they are more polite also and so you can step on them, you can go one step more with them. You cannot go to an Indian and say, "Oohhh" and pull their clothes and say, "Please buy colors," and "Buy me a chocolate and this and this and this," it's not possible but with the tourist they think, "Oh yeah, they have enough, they are fat with big cameras and they are only good to give money, and only good to buy my stuff and they'll take it, why not? They have enough, so I have the full right to go there and get on their nerves and they are all stupid."

The semiotician Jonathan Culler has noted that tourists are often afflicted by powerful feelings of "self-loathing" (Culler 1981), and this may be even more pronounced in places like India, where Western tourists frequently experience feelings of guilt due to their comparatively rich status. For example, as Erin remarked in our interview, "When I arrive here and I'm a wealthy person in a very poor place I feel a base level of guilt that I have the means to just traipse through their struggle, through their scrapping out a life, and I can just breeze through with my four-hundred-dollar camera snapping snappies, so there is a certain level of guilt I feel." To a certain extent, therefore, one could interpret Usha's response to my question as a projection of such disdain for both herself and her fellow tourists who were able to "traipse through people's suffering" with their big cameras.[16] However, although projection may indeed have played a role in shaping her reactions, and although Klein herself wrote quite a bit about how projection operates in such emotionally tense situations, it is also clear that Usha did have moments when she experienced these children as real external threats with a persecutory presence.

Indeed, part of what fascinated me about Usha was the way her dramatic emotional oscillations also corresponded to her varying classifications of these children. There were sympathetic moments when she was able to idealize these young peddlers as "sweet" innocent children who deserved considerate treatment, and then there were moments when she herself became more animated and aggressive and cast the children as predatory pests who, as Erin had also pointed out, warranted much "harsher" tactics. For instance, as she commented later in the interview:

U: I think, I think after some time you forget that children are . . . children are trying to sell you something. It's like uh. . . . for me they are often like flies and because if there are only a few, maybe one or two or three, you can try and be very honest and very kind to them, because it's not too much, but when they are all hanging around you then you want take, take your body and go away, you want only that they go away, you don't think about their personality, about their family or their money, you only think, "I'm coming here, I want to walk this way and I don't ask you for postcards, I don't ask you for colors so please don't hang on my body."

JH: It bothers you if they touch you?

U: Yeah. Yeah, and then also when they don't touch me they come so close that you have the feeling that they are hanging on you. But you come with this idea, "I'm coming for a walk," but when there are ten people around you then you cannot enjoy your walk anymore, then you try to push them away, "Go, let me . . ." and this is mixed feelings of being afraid and angriness and then you, then you forget, "Oh they're children, or maybe they have poor families." You think this when the first one is coming, but not when there are so many around. You only want to have your peace. These ghat kids bother you so much with their postcards and candles and make you so mad that you forget they are children and you don't speak kindly to them, you just want them to go away [her voice softening] and then after you yell at them and shoo them off you feel bad and think "Oh this is just a poor child I shouldn't be like this."

Here again, Usha's reply evidenced processes of splitting and denial. By casting these young peddlers as irritating "flies" she was able to psychically and physically defend herself against the children on the ghats and the feelings of persecutory anxiety that they aroused in her. However, Usha also struggled with more reflective, or what Klein describes as "depressive," moments in which she was able to acknowledge the children as "whole objects" with both good and bad attributes. When this occurred, her feelings of guilt resurfaced and she expressed a felt need to "make reparations" (Klein 1987, 189). Indeed, as Usha continued to narrate her experiences with the children on the ghats, she cycled through several more emotional upheavals in which she oscillated back and forth between feelings of extreme guilt and anger.

My interview with Usha was one of the more memorable interviews I conducted in Banaras. As I listened to her work through these experiences and feelings, and then watched as she collapsed like a jellyfish on my office floor after two hours of talking, I felt as if I had been participating in a therapeutic encounter. However, part of what made Usha's interview memorable was precisely the fact that it vividly highlighted the kinds of feelings that so many other tourists expressed and attempted to defend against.

Conclusion: The Appearance and Disappearance of Childhood

What ultimately determined tourists' assessments of the children on the riverfront? How are we to make sense of their varied yet patterned reactions? How did tourists' evaluations of the children as innocent subjects, little adults, or victimized street kids affect their decisions to do business with them? And finally, how might these examples speak to a larger set of issues regarding the ways children are variously classified and valued within the global sphere?

Clearly, tourists' assessments of the children on the riverfront were shaped by multiple determinations. As I will discuss in later chapters, the actual children that tourists encountered, and their varying abilities to perform different presentations of self, played a considerable role in influencing how tourists responded to them. Some children were very adept at manipulating the sales pitch and endearing themselves to these visitors, whereas others were decried for their "relentless" sales tactics and "whiny beggar voices."

Although the children's performances were significant, however, in this chapter I have primarily focused on the way their encounters with tourists were mediated by other factors. First, tourists engaged in a significant amount of guesswork when assessing the children, and their assumptions were frequently shaped by the broader discursive and thematic frames through which they came to know India. Second, to use the language of the symbolic interactionists, tourists' evaluations were also influenced by the different ways they "defined the situation" and interpreted the space of the riverfront. While the children themselves drew sharp distinctions between "the world of the ghats" and "the world above," tourists often conflated the two. They viewed these young peddlers and guides as operating in a space of potential "stranger danger," and frequently failed to recognize the ways the children were surrounded by the watchful eyes of kinsmen and neighbors.

Moreover, in defining the situation, tourists drew upon different discourses regarding the nature of children and childhood. In fact, the reactions that Western tourists exhibited are interesting, in part, precisely because they provide a condensed view of some of the conflicting ways that children are defined within the global sphere. For instance, notions of "the postmodern" and "premodern" child as "miniature adult" "imbued with adult rights and responsibilities" (Scheper-Hughes and Sargent 1998, 13) were readily invoked by some travelers. For other tourists, the concept of the child was still fundamentally linked to Modernist and Romantic ideas about the innocence, goodness, and the playfulness of youth; when tourists failed to discover these attributes in the youngsters who worked on the riverfront, they failed to encounter children. These assessments, in turn, affected how tourists actually transacted with these children. In many cases, those who appeared playful and innocent had greater success selling their goods, thereby suggesting that within this informal economy the production and pursuit of value was intimately linked to tourists' desires for particular kinds of children.

The examples discussed in this chapter thus provide an opportunity to enhance our understanding of the way children are affirmed and denied in different contexts. Much of the existing scholarship emphasizes how conceptions of childhood are influenced by a complex conjuncture of social forces and relations, and throughout this chapter, I have tried to attend to this conjuncture. However, I have also proposed that there are other kinds of forces and relations that can and should be considered. To return to Usha's comment: "These ghat kids bother you so much with their postcards and candles and make you so mad that you forget they are children and you don't speak kindly to them, you just want them to go away and then after you yell at them and shoo them off you feel bad and think [softening her voice], 'Oh this is just a poor child I shouldn't be like this.'" In such cases it was not a "category mistake" that prompted tourists to disavow these youngsters the status of children. Rather, it was the very act of denial that made it more comfortable for tourists to turn these children away, and if the situation called for it, treat them harshly. That is, on the riverfront of Banaras, the classification and treatment of children was determined as much by psychodynamics as by social ones.

In the next chapter I examine how people in Dasashwamedh assessed the children on the ghats, and I again consider the multiple determinations that shaped their reactions. Like the tourists I have discussed here, locals' responses were also frequently linked to a set of deeper anxieties. However, for people in Dasashwamedh these anxieties stemmed more from concerns about the social and cultural impact of foreign tourism than from the feelings of guilt and "persecution" that so frequently plagued tourists.

5

The Minds and Hearts of Children

Initially, I assumed that people in Dasashwamedh would have much more measured reactions to the children who worked on the riverfront than Western tourists. Over time, however, I discovered that their responses were also emotionally charged and frequently conflicting. Some locals praised the children for their maturity and compassion, whereas others vehemently decried their precociousness and corruption. "Children go bad from doing this work!" I was told. "They become impulsive!" "They become arrogant (*ghamandi*) and bold (*tez*)!" "They stop listening to their parents!" Indeed, part of what interested me was the way people in the neighborhood both discursively and conceptually linked the minds (*man*), hearts (*dil*), and behavior (*vyavhar*) of the children to the reproduction of a larger social and moral order.[1] Whether praising their capacity for empathy or criticizing the children's arrogance and lack of fear, locals almost always articulated the children's individual qualities in terms of their social consequences.[2]

In this chapter, I explore how people in Dasashwamedh variously assessed the children on the riverfront, and I pay particular attention to the way they interpreted the impact of foreign tourism through discourses about their minds and hearts. My discussion departs from Lawrence Cohen's insightful study of the ways that old minds, voices, and bodies signify across caste and class lines in the city of Banaras. Working between several neighborhoods, including the predominantly upper-middle-class neighborhood of Ravindrapuri Colony and the Nagwa slum, which is home to the "untouchable" caste of Chamars, Cohen contrasts the ways residents of the city invoke different "villains" when articulating the dilemmas of old age.[3]

For upper-middle-class colony dwellers, Cohen notes that the senility of elders is frequently expressed through a narrative of "the Fall," which underscores the corrosive impacts of Western modernity, especially the disintegration of the joint family and the ensuing loss of respect for elders. In these narratives, he argues, disturbed or "unmatched" old voices and bodies signal a breakdown in the moral coherence and transactional economy of the Indian family.[4] Among the lower-class and lower-caste residents of Nagwa, however, Cohen argues that narratives about "the bad family" and the ills of Western modernity are far less influential in people's constructions and explanations of the dilemmas of old age. Instead, he observes that these people draw upon the "encompassing" themes of caste oppression, social weakness, and poverty, thereby mitigating "the need for intrafamilial accountability" (Cohen 1998, 230).

Although Cohen's work focuses on the elderly, it provides a useful departure point for considering the following questions: What did the minds, hearts, and behavior of the children on the ghat signify to different people in Dasashwamedh? When did they invoke admiration, and when were they regarded as problematic or pathological? Was the behavior of these lower-class and lower-caste subjects "encompassed" by the themes of poverty and weakness? Or, did they signal the presence of "bad families" who were also seen as corrupted by Western influences, and more specifically, by Western cash? Finally, how were locals' reactions to these children both similar to and different from those of Western tourists? For although both tourists and locals variously praised these youngsters for their admirable qualities and criticized them for their apparent corruption, their responses, I argue, ultimately reflected very different understandings and concerns.

The Goodness and Godliness of Children

Among people in Dasashwamedh, discourses about the innocence of children were also pervasive and polyvalent, traversing a range of ideas about the ignorance, purity, and playfulness of youth. Children, I was frequently told, are "innocent" and "ignorant" (*masoom, nadan, nasamajh, anjan*). They "lack the power to discriminate between right and wrong" (*vivek karne ka kshamta nahin hoti hai*). "They are incapable of sin or deceit." For instance, after singing the following line, "children are pure of heart!" (*bache man ke sache*), from an old Hindi film song, Diraj Sahani went on to explain: "children do not have any cunningness (*chal ka pat*) in them. Their hearts are clean (*dil saf*). They can neither think nor comprehend, so whatever they do is deemed to be an act of ignorance. This is why they are the form of god (*bhagwan ka rup*).God plays with children. It is god who makes them laugh and smile."

In certain respects, therefore, locals also operated with a "presociological" model of the child, which viewed children as "essentially pure in heart and uncorrupted by the world they have entered into" (James, Jenks, and Prout 1998, 10).[5] However, in contrast to Western tourists, whose conceptions of childhood innocence were often influenced by Rousseauian notions of the noble savage or by Lockeian conceptions of the child as a blank slate, people in Dasashwamedh elaborated the innocence of children through a religious discourse that emphasized not just the goodness of children but also, as Diraj alluded to at the end of his remarks, their godliness. Throughout my fieldwork, I encountered a range of expressions that metaphorically and metonymically linked children with gods: "children are gods," "children are like gods," "children live in god's shadow," or "children contain a portion (*ansh*) of god within them."

Clearly, these expressions took on different meanings in different contexts. However, as Steven Parish has also observed among the Hindu Newar community in Nepal, in many instances people invoked these expressions to foreground children's status as morally neutral, rather than morally innocent subjects. As Parish writes: "Children, in general, are said to be 'like gods,' and this comparison acknowledges their relative freedom from obligations and constraints, a result of their inability to conform to the moral code. Since children are 'like gods,' their many minor transgressions are supposed to be forgiven" (Parish 1994, 87).

Among people in Dasashwamedh, this idea was commonly articulated through the recurring refrain "Oh, forget it, they are only children!" (*arey rahene do, bache to hain!*) But it was also communicated in other ways. Most of the people I spoke with agreed that, unlike adults, children do not have to endure any karmic retribution for their wrongdoings. "As a child sows he does not reap" (*jaise karega waisa nahin payega*), I was often told.[6] Thus, instead of describing children as living closer to a moral "paradise of goodness and reciprocity" (James, Jenks, and Prout 1998, 15), as some Western tourists tended to do, in their everyday speech people in Dasashwamedh deployed discourses about the godliness of children to emphasize the ways that children were viewed as existing outside the realm of human morality and reciprocity.

Yet, as I soon discovered, there was a big difference between the way locals talked about children in general and the way they talked about the children on the riverfront in particular. When people in Dasashwamedh assessed the children who worked on the riverfront, what came to the fore was a conflicting set of narratives that explicitly highlighted the moral and immoral behavior of these children. Moreover, as the examples below begin to illustrate, these assessments also reaffirmed a shared, yet at times contested, set of ideas about the differences between girls and boys and the differences between rich and poor children and families.

Compassion and Understanding

It was a late September morning. Sharmila and I sat on the ghat sorting through a bunch of garlands when Malika arrived with a tiffin of puris and *subzi* (vegetables) for her mother. "Mummy, if you do not eat your health will become bad," she said as she took the basket of garlands away from her mother and placed the tiffin in her lap. Sharmila's eyes sparkled with pride. "Do you see how she takes care of me? Do you see what a thoughtful daughter I have? A son would never think of me this way."

While it was rare for Sharmila to praise her daughters in front of them, it was not the first time that I had heard her compliment Malika. When business was slow, I often visited Sharmila at her garland stand on the ghat, and she would talk about how grateful she was to have a daughter as mature and understanding as Malika. "If it hadn't been for Malika," she frequently reminded me, "our entire family would have been doomed after my husband broke his leg." One afternoon in March, I sat with Sharmila while she tearfully narrated the story:

SS: You see, when Malika's father broke his leg our life really changed and things became really bad. In the proper course of things I should never have had to come to this ghat. I should never have stepped out of my home. I used to do household chores and I used to do sewing at home and I raised my children with that money but when his leg broke I thought to myself, "What is left in my life that is worth living for?" I was at a total loss as to what to do. My Malika was still very young, she was only seven or eight years old at the time and I thought to myself, "She is still a child, what can she do to help?" But I was wrong. I don't know where she got the inspiration from, but I am swearing to you right here, sitting next to Mother Ganga, that Malika suddenly became so mature overnight that . . . [starts crying]. We did have some hard times during that period when her father was in the hospital. It was then that I began sitting on the ghat, and I used to sit there with such a long *ghunghat* [veil] covering my face. And the very first day that I came down onto the ghats to sell garlands I was crying the whole way. I thought "Oh God, I think I should die along with my children." And yet, on the other hand, I said to myself, "I will see right to the end what God will do with me, whether it will be good or bad." I put down my bundle of garlands and it was Malika who set up the shop, who put out the garlands on display. She consoled me by saying, "Mummy, don't cry, everything will turn out fine, I will do what needs to be done." Malika used to come to the shop with me in the morning and explain everything to me about how to run the shop. And after coming to the shop with me she used to leave to sell diyas. And then, after she helped me close the shop for the day, she used to go out again to sell these lamps and I would leave for the hospital to look after her father. I used to run the shop the whole day and I didn't eat anything here. I only used to drink tea and even that was only when someone would urge me to do so. But to make a long story short, all I will say is that Malika did far more than a son could ever have done. Malika began to work with foreigners by selling postcards and from that time onward we began to rise in life. And it was after this that she stopped wearing girls' clothes and she began to dress like a boy.

JH: Why?

SS: Because she had to mold herself into that atmosphere, she had to do work that boys normally do. She had to talk with foreigners to sell colors and postcards and girls don't do this work. She was the first girl.

JH: So did people give her any problems?

SS: No. She actually won people's love. She received love from her environment because of her behavior. People were impressed by the fact that here was such a young girl who had such a feeling for her mother and such brains, she was so wise (*samajhdar*). You rarely come across children like that. People say that a son could never have endured the extent to which I have suffered and the extent to which Malika has suffered with me. A son could never do that. And Jenny, I probably would have died if I had a son instead of Malika because he would surely have been only interested in fashion, he would only have been interested in his own petty scams.

In many respects, Sharmila's narrative recalls Benedicte Grima's discussion of the "aesthetics of *gham*" (misfortune). Along with shame and modesty, Grima argues that suffering plays a central role in structuring rural Paxtun women's presentations of self and notions of feminine honor (Grima 1994, 86).[7] However, among Paxtun women, "*gham* and *taklif*" (misfortune and hardship) are usually believed to begin with marriage. As Grima writes, "Before that," a girl "is not expected to know anything about life, or to share in *gham*. She neither considers herself, nor is she considered by the community, to have begun living or to have any kind of story to tell. She is frequently referred to, in this regard, as *kam-'aqla*, or ignorant" (84–85).

As I discussed in chapter 3, the girls who worked on the riverfront clearly invoked stories of hardship to assert and defend their feminine honor and legitimate their presence on the ghat. And here too, Sharmila suggested that despite being a child, Malika was no stranger to suffering. In fact, although Sharmila was proud and grateful that Malika's earnings had saved the family from economic ruin, when we spoke, she often cast Malika's financial contributions to the household as less significant than her ability to gracefully endure hardships and shoulder the pain of others.[8]

Discourses about the feminine capacity to suffer and empathize surfaced in many conversations that I had. Anjali's mother Madhuri provides another example. It was toward the end of my fieldwork and I had gone to visit Anjali at her home, since she was no longer permitted to sell tea on the ghats with her two younger sisters Mona and Gulab. With a bag of warm *jalebis* in hand, I climbed the dark narrow stairs that led to their rooftop apartment. It consisted of two small rooms with concrete walls that opened onto a patio that had been partially covered with a tarp awning. When I arrived, Anjali was washing dishes from the evening meal the night before. Her younger sister Mona was vigorously massaging her mother's legs as she leaned against a wooden charpoy. Gulab and Dinku (Madhuri's youngest son), were playing marbles in the corner.

At the sight of the jalebis, the children lit up with a smile, and Anjali instructed me to sit down and talk to her mother while she prepared tea. Madhuri and I began chatting and I asked her how her oldest son Maneesh was doing with his cleaning job at the photo lab. She threw her hands in the air as if to express her frustration and disgust. "Oh that one, he is useless. Yes, he is working, but he doesn't think of me, he thinks of himself. My daughters, they understand my suffering. They know my husband is no good. They know how many hardships I have endured. You see, it is good to have girls. Girls are very straight (*sidhi*) but boys! My son is useless, he understands nothing!"

Although both Sharmila and Madhuri clearly viewed gender as a decisive factor in shaping children's emotional capacities, they also suggested that class played a significant role. Like the girls who worked on the ghats, both Sharmila and Madhuri drew sharp contrasts between their own children and children who came from "big families." For instance, after criticizing some of the boys from Dasashwamedh for their bad behavior, Sharmila remarked: "But the children from rich people behave in an even more uncouth manner. The children of poor people work hard, not all children are the same, of course. Some do begin to throw money around, loaf around. But the children from rich families, they will never think about their parents, they will just say, 'Do this for me, do that for me!'" Or as Madhuri proposed, "My children have to work because my husband is no good, what can we do? But I have seen that children who come from rich families they do not behave nicely with their parents. They want their money. When the parents don't give them money then the love between them is finished. I used to work for such a family. I saw this happen." Or as Bali Sahani commented when reflecting upon his own childhood experiences working on the ghats, "Since I was a kid I knew I had to work to keep my family going. Those children who just study, they remain aloof from the struggles and sorrows of their families and just think about themselves and about enjoying life, but those children who earn they know about everything."

Certainly, there were boys on the riverfront who were also commended for trying to understand and ameliorate their families' struggles. However, by and large, girls were most often the recipients of such praise. By working hard, by subordinating their individual desires to the needs of others, and by demonstrating their capacity to empathize with their mothers' pain, the girls on the ghats established themselves as morally responsible and virtuous subjects. Although these attributes clearly challenged everyday assumptions about the innocence and ignorance of children, they in no way marked the girls as corrupt. Indeed, for mothers like Sharmila and Madhuri, having a mature and compassionate daughter far outweighed the benefits or charms of having a child who understood nothing of their plight.

Without Fear or Shame

Through their displays of empathy and obedience the girls on the riverfront usually, though not always, evaded being cast as corrupt or wayward children. The boys, however, often had a much more difficult time dispelling such charges. Many people insisted that their work in the informal tourist economy was having deleterious effects on their behavior. One recurring complaint was that the boys had lost their sense of fear and shame. In his study *Culture in Action: Family Life, Emotion, and Male Dominance in Banaras, India*, Steve Derné observes that among upper-middle-class men a sense of social fear is regarded as an "exemplary emotion" precisely because it subordinates the will of the individual to the larger social collective, thereby prompting "moral" and "correct behavior" (Derné 1995, 80). Other anthropologists working in South Asia have made similar observations, noting that the perceived absence of fear in individuals often evokes anxiety and criticism (Lamb 2000; Parish 1994; Vatuk 1990). As the following examples demonstrate, throughout my fieldwork, I repeatedly encountered such ideas and concerns.

Demanding Children

Lalu Chacha also came from the Mallah caste and was reputedly one of the first and most famous guides ever to work with foreign tourists in the Dasashwamedh area. He had begun guiding as a young man during the late 1970s. At the time of my research, he was in his early fifties, and was struggling with serious financial and health problems that had been exacerbated by his battle with drug and alcohol addiction. Among the young guides and children who worked on the ghat he evoked both admiration and ridicule. The legendary successes and stories from his youth seemed a far cry from the thin, wasted-looking man who stood before them then. In fact, I often sensed that Lalu Chacha's downward spiral had prompted some of the boys to question their own futures, for he was frequently held up as an ominous example of what could happen if one continued working with tourists for too long.

Lalu Chacha himself was ambivalent about the new generation of boys who were guiding on the ghats. On the one hand, he sympathized with these "arrogant" and "impulsive children" whom he regarded as the products of poverty and disadvantage. On the other hand, however, he accused the boys of exacerbating tensions in the home by failing to subordinate themselves to "the normative hierarchy of parents over children" (Cohen 1998, 178). For instance, one afternoon, I invited Lalu Chacha over for an interview. After listening to him talk about his own experiences working in the tourist economy, I asked him what he thought about the boys who were currently guiding at Dasashwamedh. He replied:

> You see, our children work. But rich people send their children to school and they make sure that there is someone from the family or their staff who will escort the child safely back home from school. Then after coming back from school the child gets to eat and the child is given whatever he wants to eat, and then made to study again. So this really sharpens their children's [in English] "mentality." But our children are sent out to earn on the ghats, to earn money from foreigners so they become impulsive and whimsical. If children are earning, then they will inevitably be impulsive and do what they want (*apne man ka karte hain*). Then they will leave their parents behind, they will completely ignore them and then demand food the minute they enter the house simply because they are earning and giving money at home. This has happened in my house. These boys are earning from tourists, so when they go home they say instantly, "Give me food because I am earning." They become very proud and arrogant. They want everyone to move the moment they enter the house, parents rush to serve them with eagerness.

In contrast to Sharmila and Madhuri, Lalu Chacha did not provide a narrative that extolled the moral virtues and emotional sensitivities of poor children. Rather, although sympathetic to a degree, his remarks read more like a moral indictment of these lower-class boys and their arrogant and disruptive behaviors. Although he certainly invoked poverty and poor food as a causal explanation, this did not preclude Lalu Chacha from simultaneously generating a discourse about "intrafamilial" accountability (Cohen 1998, 230).[9] For Lalu Chacha, the problem was not just parents who were weak and poor but also children who were too powerful. By virtue of their earnings from foreign tourists, the boys had attained a position of centrality in the transactional nexus of the family (Lamb 2000) that enabled them "to demand" food and service on the spot.[10]

Again, such criticisms stand in marked contrast to the ways that girls were usually regarded. Granted, most girls earned far less money than the boys who participated in guiding and commission work. However, even in cases where girls did attain similar positions of centrality vis-à-vis their earnings from foreign tourists (as was the case with Malika and Priya), they were usually praised for their "performative deference" (Cohen 1998, 180) rather than criticized for their excessive demands.

The Foot Massage

Observers in the neighborhood also complained that this lack of fear and shame could be detected in the boys' dealings with tourists. For instance, one day I stopped in to say hello to my friend Ganesh Sahani. Ganesh was in his mid-twenties, had grown up in the neighborhood, and by most accounts was among the first generation of children to guide foreign tourists at Dasashwamedh Ghat. Though perceptions of him varied, for many of the younger boys working on the ghats he represented a success story. Through guiding, he had earned and saved enough money over the years to convert the downstairs room of his family home into a modest silk shop. Moreover, due to a subsequent year-long romance with a Japanese tourist that almost ended in marriage, his shop had made it into a number of Japanese guidebooks, thereby providing him with a slight advantage over some of the local competition.

However, despite the publicity afforded by the guidebooks, like many other shops Ganesh's store was not located on the main road. It was tucked away in the winding galis of the old city, and this rendered him more dependent upon the boys who worked on the riverfront to bring him customers. He courted their favor by giving them commissions, but also by finessing a role that fell somewhere between friendly confidant, patron, and elder brother. On this particular afternoon, Ganesh was in the shop with Jay, Mohan, and Sara, the twenty-nine-year-old Canadian tourist whom Mohan and Jay had been guiding for several days. Mohan and Sara were sitting next to each other on the thin padded mattress that covered the shop floor while Jay was perched in the doorway. Ganesh had assumed the responsibilities of DJ, and sat across from them near the stereo. I took off my *chapals* (sandals), entered the shop, and strategically positioned myself as far away as possible from the blaring boom box. Ganesh promptly ordered Jay to go out and get chai and samosas while the rest of us waited and listened to Ganesh proudly showcase his newest Bollywood cassette tape. Mohan reclined on the mattress and stretched his feet out across Sara's lap. She began cracking his toes, massaging his feet, and cooing over him almost as though he were a baby. When Ganesh saw this, his face turned sour and in a quiet yet explosive voice he reprimanded Mohan in Hindi, "Hey, don't behave shamelessly here! This is not appropriate. This is a home!" Mohan quickly withdrew his feet from Sara's lap and sat upright against the wall looking embarrassed.

Though seemingly innocent from Sara's perspective, the foot massage marked a transgression on several counts. First, it violated notions of domestic propriety by suggesting an inappropriate intimacy between unrelated members of the opposite sex. It also defied proscriptions regarding purity and pollution by exposing Sara to one of the most defiled parts of the Hindu body, the feet.[11] However, what disturbed Ganesh the most about this quasi-lewd, quasi-polluting display of intimacy was that it indicated to Ganesh that Mohan was not paying him the respect and deference he deserved. When Sara and the boys left the shop after having their tea and samosas, I asked Ganesh why he had become so upset. "Jenny," he replied, "If you are with boys your own age you might behave in such an unrestrained manner, you might be so bold. But never in front of your elders! I would be ashamed to act like that before one of my elders! It would make me very uncomfortable! But these boys don't think that way!"

The Behavioral Conundrum

The boys who pursued foreign tourists on the riverfront were, therefore, often confronted with a behavioral conundrum. On the one hand, they had to contend with local criticisms that their "shameless" and "brazen" behavior was spoiling their character and undermining traditional age-based hierarchies that required them to monitor and modulate their behaviors in front of elders.[12] For instance, Titu owned a sari and silk shop in Dasashwamedh. Although most of his business was geared toward an Indian clientele, he had recently begun diversifying his product line with the hopes of attracting more foreign tourists. Like Ganesh, he also had an interest in persuading the boys to guide tourists to his shop, and he had been trying to entice them with handsome commissions. One morning, I went to his shop to interview him, and he shared his impressions of the boys on the ghats with me: "These children working as guides get spoiled (*bigar jatey hain*). Earlier, as far as I know, children did not work as guides, a few did, but even they used to work within a certain limit. First, they used to earn a very modest amount of money; second, they were always under the watchful eyes of everyone so they were afraid of doing anything wrong. Today these children are very bold (*tez*), their fear isn't there anymore. You should see the way they behave with these foreigners on the ghats."[13]

Whereas Titu suggested that the boys had become bold and fearless because they were earning too much money and were no longer adequately supervised, the boys, on the other hand, often complained that one of their biggest challenges came precisely from having to pursue foreign tourists under "the watchful eyes" of elders and kinsmen. The ghats were littered with relatives and close social relations who also used the riverfront as a place to earn their living, and this could put the boys who worked with foreign tourists in rather awkward situations. Narratives about the bold/sharp (*tez*) minds and fearless dispositions of ghat children, therefore, both concealed and revealed deeper anxieties about fundamental transformations in the organization of social roles and space. While "the problem" was repeatedly articulated as an emotional deficiency on the part of the boys, it often stemmed from the transactional demands that tourism work placed on the children and the challenges that came with having to maneuver themselves and their customers through a diverse and uncertain social topography. For instance, was Ganesh's silk shop "a home" where certain forms of decorum needed to be maintained, or was it a place of commerce where the ultimate goal was keeping the customer happy?

The Virtues of Being Bold

As Derné has pointed out, in Banaras, a sense of social fear is particularly valued among males within the context of upper-middle-class family life, as it ensures that individuals will subordinate themselves to the established domestic hierarchy and thereby contribute to the harmonious functioning of the household.[14] In other contexts, however, such fear may be regarded as a debilitating attribute. Indeed, the boys repeatedly emphasized that in order to win over customers and maintain respect amid the rough-and-tumble world of the ghats they had to be bold, brave, and sometimes outspoken. Of all the boys working on the ghat during the time of my research, Pramod most vividly embodied these virtues. Known for his tremendous wit, charisma, and feisty personality, he would challenge older boys and men on the ghats when they interfered with his business dealings or when they offended his sense of moral propriety. As I noted in chapter 3, one such example occurred when he publicly reprimanded Priya's alcoholic father for drinking his daughter's earnings.

One afternoon, Pramod and I were sitting on the ghat talking when two young men, claiming to be students from Banaras Hindu University (B.H.U.), approached us. With little regard for our conversation, they interrupted and introduced themselves to me, though noticeably not to Pramod. An onslaught of questions quickly followed: "Where are from?" "How do you know Hindi?" "What are you doing in Banaras?" Though I found them incredibly irritating and deeply resented the sense of entitlement that these male intruders exhibited, I had become used to such interruptions. On numerous occasions, my conversations with the children on the ghats were derailed by nosey young men from outside the neighborhood who seemed to assume that I would find conversing with them far more gratifying than talking to "uneducated" children. On this occasion, I told the intruders that I had come to Banaras to write a book about boys like Pramod who worked with foreign tourists. Then, I pointed out that we were in the middle of a conversation and I politely asked them to go away. Apparently, both my response and request fell on deaf ears, for the two young men remained in our presence and immediately began issuing me a warning. Switching into broken English (perhaps assuming that Pramod would not be able to understand them), they cautioned: "Do not trust the boys on the ghats. They cheat you. They want your money. If you want to learn about Banaras, you come to our university. These are uneducated people. They cannot tell you about the city."

Before I had the chance to respond, Pramod, who had been surprisingly quiet up until this point, stood up to berate the two young men. Waving his hands in the air, he shouted back in Hindi, "You bastards, I earn my money through hard work! Don't come here and insult me! Leave us alone, motherfuckers! Go away! She doesn't want to talk to you!" The two students were taken aback by Pramod's slew of profanities, but they quickly countered with insults and threats of their own. Switching back to Hindi, they exclaimed, "See how this little boy behaves! Look at the dirty things he says! This is a public place; we can be here if we want! You have no right to tell us where to go! We are going to report you to the police for guiding!"

As the tensions between Pramod and the two young men escalated, Kaushal, who was in his mid-twenties and who sold garlands on the ghat, came over to intervene. Though they shared no actual kinship ties, from the time Pramod had begun selling on the ghats Kaushal had taken him under his wing. The two had developed a very close friendship, and Kaushal was constantly looking out for Pramod to make sure that he did not get into trouble. Pramod lovingly referred to Kauhshal as his Guruji and Kaushal, in turn, referred to Pramod as his *chela* or disciple/pupil.

When Kaushal approached, he was joined by some of the older guides who happened to be sitting nearby. Forming a somewhat menacing circle around the B.H.U. students, Kaushal and the others took over the verbal assault and warned the two young men that it would be best for them to leave immediately and not show their faces at Dasashwamedh Ghat again. Looking rather nervous, the young men bitterly retreated. After they left, Pramod was still incensed by the incident, but as he and the others began to bask in their post-showdown glory, his mood quickly improved. "We won't see those two again," Kaushal said. "They know they do not want to have trouble with the boys from Dasashwamedh. Everyone knows our reputation in the city. They know we are not afraid of anyone!" Pramod smiled and nodded in agreement while Kaushal put his arm around him as if to congratulate him on the victory. "Do you see my chela, Jenny? He is not afraid of anyone! He is a very special boy!"

Thus, when directed at the appropriate targets, such as insulting and meddlesome outsiders, the boys' lack of social fear was seen as a virtue rather than a vice. Through such run-ins, boys like Pramod not only demonstrated their abilities to stand their own ground, protect their business interests, and prove themselves among their peers and elders on the ghats; they also "spoke back" to the everyday injustices and insults that were heaped upon them as lower-caste and lower-class subjects. In so doing, they rendered the ghats a contested space, where social hierarchies were actively challenged as well as reproduced.

And yet, while boys like Pramod could be pardoned and even praised for their lack of social fear, their assertiveness on the ghats, and their willingness to challenge social hierarchies, girls were usually criticized if they were perceived as displaying such qualities. Anjali, for instance, had a personality that was every bit as extroverted and fiery as Pramod's. Indeed, it was part of the reason she derived so much pleasure from working on the ghats and was so despondent when she was forced into her post-pubescent retirement. However, in contrast to Pramod, her displays of wit and her attempts to assert herself among males who frequently harangued her did not win her praise or approval.

For example, Suriya Sahani worked as a boatman at Dasashwamedh and was in his early twenties. He was a gentle and serious young man who had achieved his own measure of local celebrity as a competitive swimmer. Although most of his business stemmed from catering to Indian pilgrims, he did occasionally take foreign tourists out for boat rides, and sometimes he would ask me to accompany him. It was through these outings that we became friendly with each other. One Sunday morning, he invited me to his home for a midday meal. After polishing off a delectable lunch of curried jackfruit, we retreated to the roof to digest, and I asked him if I could interview him. When our conversation turned to the children who work on the ghats, I asked him what he thought of the girls who sold postcards, diyas, and tea. He shook his head, and immediately cited Anjali as an example of why girls should not be allowed to do this work:

> She sells tea but look at her behavior. She doesn't know how to talk properly. She thinks that because she sells tea she has become very important. She talks the way that we do, that's why I don't talk to her very much. Sometimes she jokes with me but I never joke with her. I have seen that there are some people on the ghats who misbehave with her and say "Do this with me, do that with me," they shouldn't do this. But this girl is also very wicked (*harami*). When she first started coming to the ghats she spoke nicely with people (*prem se*) and did good work. But when she started to make a lot of money her audacity increased. It is okay for one's wealth to increase, but their pride shouldn't. She misbehaves and uses curses. People talk carelessly with Anjali so this has become her daily habit. She doesn't think, "I am a girl." She thinks, "I am a boy." I think that maybe if I were in her position I would also behave like this, but so many times I've told her, "Your head has gotten very big, I'm going to hit you today, you misbehave a lot, you sell tea okay but don't trouble anyone." Sometimes she calls me brother, sometimes she calls me baldy (*takla*), she speaks rudely.

Suriya was able to concede that Anjali's "tough" and "boylike" behavior might be an adaptive, or perhaps, even contagious response to her working environment: to recall Jay Yadav's comments, "as is the environment so is the intelligence that comes to one." However, from his perspective, girls like Anjali, who talked "tough" instead of lovingly and who tried to act like boys instead of girls, signified a disheartening deterioration of the normative codes of conduct that were supposed to regulate interactions between men and women, the young and old, and people who were either familiar or strange. Thus, although working on the ghats could provide the girls with avenues to prove their dedication and service (*seva*) to their parents (as "good daughters" are taught to do from a very early age), their presence in this public space also evoked anxiety from people in the community. This anxiety, moreover, was exacerbated by girls like Anjali who seemed incapable or unwilling to adequately perform feminine presentations of self. Malika's younger sister Jaila was often cited as another example. Whereas Malika "won people's love" with her compassionate and demure demeanor, Jaila was routinely ridiculed and scolded for her temperamental outbursts and for speaking rudely to other children and elders on the ghats. "With that temper and tongue, what kind of daughter-in-law will you be?" her mother often admonished her, "Look at how you behave!"

Making Them Bold: Bad Families, Greedy Parents, and Foreign Money

Although critical of their behaviors, people in Dasashwamedh also exhibited sympathy towards the "bold," "arrogant," and "demanding" children who worked on the ghats. They not only viewed them as victims of poverty but, in many cases, they also viewed them as victims of bad families and more specifically, greedy parents who were willing to "ruin" their children's lives in exchange for foreign money.

Rani Goswami, for instance, was the mother of four. She and her husband earned their living by selling necklaces and beads at a small kiosk on the road above Dasashwamedh Ghat. Over the years, the couple had established a number of enduring relationships with foreign tourists who had helped them finance the construction of their new home. Our friendship developed when Rani and her husband began recruiting me to write letters on their behalf. I would be making my way along the main road to the ghat, and Rani would summon me over with an enthusiastic wave and smile. "Jenny, we got another letter, I have some work for you! Come! Come!"

At the time of my fieldwork, Rani's children ranged in age from two to ten years old and they spent most of their time with their parents, either playing in front of the kiosk or nearby on the side of the road. Often, their beautiful faces and bright personalities attracted the attention of foreigners who were passing by. However, unlike many of the other children in the neighborhood, Rani's children were forbidden from selling postcards or pursuing any other kind of business venture with tourists. From what I observed, they were never encouraged to try to sell anything from their parent's shop, either. Both Rani and her husband hoped that their children would pursue a different line of work in the future, and they often spoke proudly and optimistically about the academic success that their older daughter and son were already achieving in elementary school. When I finally sat down with Rani for a taped interview, we talked about the children who worked with foreign tourists, and Rani contrasted them with her own:

RG: These children who work on the ghats are very bold and their parents make them bold in their childhood. They make them bold enough to go out, that is why girls are not afraid to do so, they do this work right from their childhood. For example, my daughter, I do not allow her to go into the business line to begin with, even if a customer were to come to the shop and if she is there alone she simply cannot sell because she is not used to it. She will be busy either playing or studying, she will not enjoy tending to the shop.

JH: Why?

RG: Because if I had made a practice of scolding her or beating her or asking her to look after the shop and to sell stuff to the customers when they come and to call out to customers when they are passing by then this practice would have become instilled in her brain but it is just the opposite. Today, even if she wants to sell at the shop I tell her, "No, come with me," so she has no sense as to how to do business.

Rani attributed the children's behavioral problems to pushy parents who were interested in producing offspring who earned rather than playing or studying. Echoing sentiments expressed by Etty (see chapter 4), she also suggested that the children's early exposure to commercial life had eclipsed the development of other important skills and attributes. She went on to say, "What kind of future will these children have? They have no education, their parents are always yelling at them, scolding them, they do not learn how to behave properly! They will do the same with their children. It is like this with these people from the Mallah caste. It is their way" (*yeh to unka rahen sahen hai*).

By emphasizing the way that certain practices could become instilled in the brains of children, Rani seemed to invoke a Lockeian model of the child as a blank slate. However, her remarks also allude to a culturally pervasive Hindu discourse, which posits "substantial" differences between people of different castes. The idea that people of different castes develop different temperaments and characters because of their environment or the "substance codes" they transact has been duly noted within ethnosociological models of the Hindu person (Daniel 1984; Marriott 1968, 1976, 1990). However, among residents in Dasashwamedh, this "fluid" conception of the individual actor who is made and remade through transactions with others was also qualified by the idea that people's dispositions are, in part, determined by the bio-moral substance codes they inherit as members of a particular caste, and as such are, to a certain extent, immutable.[15]

Caste differences were often invoked as a way to distinguish one's self and one's family from others in the neighborhood. For instance, even though Rani and others self-identified as "poor people" (and in some cases were less financially secure than the Mallah families who worked on the ghat), in private conversations, they rarely let an opportunity pass to make note of their comparatively higher-caste status. Mohan and Jaggu's mother's Devika provides another example. She was particularly fond of reminding me that although both of her sons worked as guides, and although they too came from a poor family, there was a world of difference between them and, as she put it, "those uneducated Mallah boys who cheat tourists on the ghats." "They are low-caste people," she would remark, "This is their habit." Similarly, on more than one occasion I was reprimanded by Mallah children and elders for eating at the home of a young boy named Raju who came from the Dome caste and who sold postcards near Manikarnika Ghat. "You shouldn't go there and eat their food, Jenny! The people from that caste are very dirty! Chi, chi, chi!"[16] And yet, although caste played a pivotal role in people's attempts to achieve "distinction" (Bourdieu 1984) and jockey for bio-moral superiority,[17] I also discovered that even among families of the same caste, this kind of moral one-upsmanship and "othering" was very common. With fingers wagging, I was often told, "Our children work because we have no choice, but in *that* family, the parents make their children sell on the ghats because they are greedy!"[18]

In other cases, however, foreign tourists, rather than greedy parents, were held accountable for corrupting the minds and behaviors of these children. Vinod Pandey, for example, was twenty-six years old and had grown up guiding foreign tourists on the ghats.[19] We first became friendly when I was living in Banaras studying Hindi, and I gifted him a bright orange-and-yellow Hawaiian shirt, which, I insisted, would help him attract more customers. When I returned to Banaras for my fieldwork, Vinod had just come back from an extended stay abroad and was recovering from a bitter breakup with his Norwegian girlfriend, with whom he had fathered a son. As Vinod frequently reminded me, he was at a low point in his life, and sometimes he drank in order to quell his pain and anxiety. I interviewed him one evening at my guest house when he was in a particularly irritable mood and clearly had been drinking. "You grew up guiding foreign tourists" I began. "What do you think this work is like for these kids?" His response was vehement:

VP: [In English] This is the worst, and I think, and I want to abuse at that moment, to the tourist who gives them money. I feel that sometimes I should abuse them or go up and hit them, I don't care but what I am giving you is the real answer, I feel that I should abuse the tourist. [Then switching to Hindi] I want to curse them when they give money to kids.

JH: Why?

VP: [Back in English] Because this is the worst thing they are doing, because this happened in my life, because this happened in my life, how I came in this business, so if they give them money it means that they are going in the same direction, and always when the tourists are with me I explain to them, "You don't have to give a single penny to children."

JH: [In Hindi] So what about when the tourists buy postcards from these kids?

VP: [In English] That's also wrong. That's also wrong, because they are not looking, what is in the future, they are looking at the present and that present it makes them die in the future, like what happened with me now, I am uneducated, I am only educated till high school and that makes me sad because I am educated until high school and that's not enough to do any work in this world. So I want them to study and do something, and get out of my face and do something. I don't want to see them all their lives selling postcards, or do something worse.

Vinod was not alone in his opinions, nor did I suspect they were merely the embellished product of a few stiff drinks. Many others in Dasashwamedh shared his anger and resentment, and they too, claimed that Western tourists were the real problem in the children's lives. As Avi Sahani, a former guide from Dasashwamedh, remarked, "The situation is such that these children have already become brazen (*unka man bara hua hai*) because of the money they get from tourists. Before, they did not used to be like this, and then if tomorrow they do not get this money, they will start stealing at home because they will need money regardless of how they get it." Or as Sudesh, a middle-aged commission man who worked on the main road above Dasashwamedh, noted: "It is because of the coming of tourists that these children have become bad, this was not the case earlier. When tourists began coming here they saw these children and out of pity for their poverty they began giving them large amounts of money, and now you go see what the children do with this!" Finally, Rahul Sahani, who also grew up doing commission work, asserted, "The only way things will improve for these kids will be when tourists stop coming to Banaras!"[20]

Precocious Children, the Ills of Modernity, and Degenerate Times

While Vinod and Rahul fantasized about the demise of foreign tourism in Banaras, many people working in Dasashwamedh feared this possibility. Indeed, throughout my fieldwork locals expressed profound concerns about the future of the industry. In some cases, they even suggested that the children on the ghats, particularly the "clever" (*chalak*) and "cunning" (*chalu*) young boys who worked as guides and commission agents, were partially to blame for its anticipated decline. "Tourists in Banaras must be careful," I was constantly told, "These boys are very cunning!" Or as Rohan, an older commission man who mostly trafficked in drugs, remarked, "These boys can make a fool (*murk*) of anyone! They can make anyone an idiot (*chutiya*)! With their cheating and swindling tourists will not want to come here! These boys give the city a very bad name!" Indeed, in January of 2000, when I interviewed the information officer at the U.P. Tourism Office in the Cantonment District, he echoed Rohan's sentiments and noted that one of the primary reasons a tourist police task force was being developed in Banaras was precisely to make sure that foreign tourists did not fall prey to the chicanery of these young "touts." Thus, instead of being interpreted as a promising sign of their budding business acumen, the boys' cleverness and cunning was often cast as morally, socially, and economically problematic.

Moreover, people in Dasashawamedh explained the boys' cunning in varying ways. Some reiterated the idea that it was a product of their lower-caste and lower-class habitus. Others interpreted it as an impact of foreign tourism. Vishnu, for instance, had started off working as a silk shop commission man in Godolia. Over the years his entrepreneurial interests had shifted, and at the time of my fieldwork he was making most of his money selling drugs. In our interview he reflected upon how the tourism industry in Banaras had changed and the effect it was having on these children:

VK: Since I started selling there are less tourists now. And in the future if tourists do come then they will be cunning. Before none of them were. If you just talked a little bit then they would believe you and go with you, give money, or go to buy something. They would buy with their eyes closed. And now, if you have something that is ten rupees and you say it is ten rupees then they will say "I'll give three, four rupees." There isn't any profit in that, no commission.

JH: So how did tourists become cunning?

VK: From each other, they made each other cunning. For instance I talked to you, [in English] "Take care on the ghat, many boys talk to you." What happens from this is that the tourist becomes wise and then if another boy comes he will say, "Go away!" [Back in Hindi] Five or eight years before there weren't as many commission boys. Now there are a lot of boys doing commission work. Now since five years there has been bargaining and tourists have come to know what bargaining is. Before they didn't know. Also now, from the minute they step off the plane in Delhi to the minute they get here they are approached by so many commission men that they don't trust anyone. So now, in order for these children to make money from the tourists they have to be very cunning.

While Vishnu attributed these changes to an over-saturated labor market, others suggested that the boys' precociousness was a more general consequence of "modern times." The ills of modernity were a very popular topic among people in Dasashwamedh. In fact, discussions about the children who worked on the riverfront usually provided a launching point for broaching this larger issue. As Avi remarked further along in our interview:

> The environment today is very different from the environment before. Now, these young kids, they are no longer kids—that's the first thing. You will see this small kid and you would love him like a mother or a sister would love a kid brother, you would view him in that light, but his way of looking at things would be something else, he will look at you with the wrong kind of love. Later on he will tell his friends "I kissed that girl. I touched her here and there." Even small kids do that. You have no idea what these small boys are up to, what tricks they are up to. You have no idea where these small kids will take you. Because nowadays it is not possible to trust anyone anymore.

In many cases, the perceived changes in the social environment were explicitly attributed to the greater forces of modernization. However, as Sarah Lamb has noted in her study of aging in West Bengal, the ills of modernity are also frequently viewed as the "devolutionary" product of cosmic time (Lamb 2000, 94).[21] Many of my informants insisted that it was not just Westernization or modernization or even foreign tourism that was wreaking havoc on the order of things. Rather, it was the degenerative age of the Kali Yuga itself, which is widely believed to erode the social and moral or *dharmic* order of society.[22] As Diraj Sahani further observed:

> Tourists see a young kid and they think that he is just a kid and he knows nothing. But the fact is that that kid is even more knowledgeable than we are. These small boys who are doing commission work they are our fathers (*veh humare bap hain*). These days you find ten-year-old boys in Banaras who can give you and me a lesson in how to do things and they talk like fifty-year-olds, so sharp are they in talking. Boys today are really very sharp. But also remember it is the Kali Yuga and within the next 100–200 years you will find small kids becoming even sharper (*aur tez*). The time will come when all sons will teach their fathers how to go about life.

As was the case elsewhere, Diraj also cast the boys' intellectual precocity as a problem rather than a boon, and its deleterious effects were again registered in social rather than individual terms. In this case, sharp and savvy young boys led to apocalyptic visions of a world where sons (or juniors) prematurely displaced their fathers (elders). Indeed, in certain respects, this vision had already become a reality for Diraj and many of the older guides who were trying to hang on to their business. These fast-talking young boys were, after all, their competition and, like many of the other commission men I knew, for Diraj this engendered both concern and resentment. As he put it: "These kids have a big advantage over us, they are cute. The tourists love them and trust them, but when you get older like me, and are not so cute anymore it is much harder to get money from tourists."

The Stages of Life, the Division of Labor, and the Value of Knowledge

In addition to indexing the ills of modernity and the foreboding onset of the Kali Yuga, the children's precocity was also elaborated through discourses regarding the stages of life. As many scholars have pointed out, the idea of "doing the right thing at the right time" has deep roots in Hindu cultural understandings of the life-course.[23] According to Sylvia Vatuk, for instance: "the notion that life is made up of distinctive developmental stages, each with its own appropriate normative code for conduct, immediate and long-term goals, and suitable rewards, guides the thinking of Indians about how they ought to live and shapes their aspirations" (Vatuk 1990, 70). When people in Dasashwamedh assessed the children who worked with foreign tourists, such understandings of the life-course often provided an interpretive frame.

Arjun Pandey, for example, was a university student from a lower-middle-class Brahmin family and was working toward a degree in computer science. He ran the e-mail and Internet shop that was located beneath my guest house in Dasashwamedh. At the time of my research, the Internet revolution was still in its infancy in Banaras, and the shop was one of a handful that was offering Internet access in the city. As such, it was actively sought out by foreign tourists and by local young men who were just beginning to "surf the wave" of Internet porn. This particular mix of clientele and Internet usage rendered the shop an extremely interesting, though at times, profoundly awkward social space.

Because many of the boys brought their customers to the shop, Arjun had become familiar with the young guides working at Dasashwamedh, and for the most, part he was on very friendly terms with them. However, when it came to divulging his private thoughts about the boys and their futures, he was more critical. In a tone that mixed genuine concern with obvious snobbery, he observed:

> Look, if a person does any work without any education and before the proper time in his life for that work then he cannot succeed in that work. The boys who work as guides with tourists, they use the English language without having been properly educated into it. It is not a real education and when these kids speak English they do not speak flawless English, whenever they speak they will speak broken, flawed English. So they keep working as long as they find work, but in future they remain good only for guiding work, nothing more. They will remain stuck in that groove. But, if you study and get an education at the right time and you acquire

some degree like high school or intermediate, then you will have a certain tone, way of speaking, you will have a proper manner of speaking, you will know which word to use when and this will be instrumental in your success in later life. But suppose I try my hand at the computer without learning how to use it, simply by watching others use it for some time, then it is quite possible that I may ruin the machine. One should do the right thing at the right time.

As was the case with some of the Western tourists whom I interviewed, here again, charges of mimicry and the trope of "ephemeral precocity" (Cohen 1998, 22) emerged. By failing to follow the "proper" sequence and do the right thing at the right time, Arjun was sure that the children would inevitably find themselves "stuck" in a juvenile line of work and behavior. Moreover, in Arjun's narrative, the developmental trajectory of the children was perceived as both temporally and topically skewed. The implication of his remarks was that speaking English, like operating computers, was not what "uneducated" people are supposed to do, and when they try, it leads to bad copies, or worse, to ruin. Arjun thus suggested that the "appropriate normative code for conduct" varies not only according to distinct life-cycle stages, as Vatuk has noted, but according to class. This notion was also expressed by middle-class residents who were both surprised and impressed by "how much English these uneducated children" knew. As one of my friends remarked, after attending the evening puja with me, "I can't believe it, I am a university student at B.H.U. and these kids on the ghats speak much better English than I do!"

The idea that different sorts of conduct and education are regarded as appropriate for different classes of people, has been richly explored in Myron Weiner's book *The Child and the State in India*. Weiner attempts to explain why the Indian government, unlike so many others, has failed to remove children from the labor force and establish compulsory education. In surveying other developed and developing nations, Weiner concludes that in India's case, it is not a lack of resources that has prevented the state from developing better education and employment policies for poor children. Rather, he attributes this systematic and institutionalized neglect to a set of widely shared cultural beliefs that ultimately create a middle-class and upper-class public who are "remarkably indifferent" to the plights of the poor. As he writes:

> At the core of these beliefs are the Indian view of the social order, notions concerning the respective roles of upper and lower social strata, the role of education as a means of maintaining differentiations among social classes, and concerns that "excessive" and "inappropriate" education for the poor would disrupt existing social arrangements. . . . The Indian position rests on deeply held beliefs that there is a division between people

who work with their minds and rule and people who work with their hands and are ruled, and that education should reinforce rather than break down the division. (Weiner 1991, 5–6)

At first glance, it may seem that Arjun's comments are at odds with Weiner's findings, for he was genuinely concerned about the boys' futures and their lack of "real education." However, part of what troubled Arjun, and many others with whom I spoke, was precisely the fact that these boys challenged the categories of "people who work with their minds and people who work with their hands." Their broken English also bespoke an uncomfortable proximity to middle-class aspirations and life styles.

Alternatively, for others, the children's lack of education was disturbing precisely because it suggested forms of institutional neglect that reproduced the vast distance between the rich and the poor. For instance, as Raj Yadav (the elder brother of Jay), commented:

Over here the government takes absolutely no interest in what happens to a kid, here the government does not give any money to the poor people to educate their children or to set up a small business to pay for their livelihoods. And what can you expect from kids who have never been to school? Kids who have never been to school are like a crazy man on the street who doesn't know what he is doing, they live their lives exactly in the same fashion. They will do whatever would seem right to them and would quit whenever they feel like quitting.

Like Arjun and Vinod, Raj also suggested that the knowledge that children accrued by working with foreign tourists was in a sense counterfeit. It would not "provide the key to many other exchanges" and make a better future possible (Willis 1977, 64). And yet the children themselves, as well as their family members, often challenged this idea. They emphasized that in terms of getting a good job, a formal degree was useless unless one had the right connections, or was able to muster enough money to pay exorbitant bribes.[24] Thus, in this regard, some people in Dasashwamedh suggested that working with foreign tourists could provide a more expedient and realistic way of moving up from the world of the ghats.

Conclusion: The Ways Children Matter

Lawrence Cohen's work provided a departure point for exploring how people in Dasashwamedh assessed the children on the riverfront and articulated the impacts of foreign tourism through discourses about their minds, hearts, and behavior. As we have seen, locals' reactions to the children were by no means univocal, and they reflected the different perspectives and experiences of a varied "community of listeners and their interrelationships" (Cohen 1998, 179). Depending on the situation, the children could be praised for their compassion and obedience, criticized for their arrogance and lack of fear, or even admired for their outspokenness.

These assessments not only reflected the specific viewpoints of people in the neighborhood and their particular relationships with particular children. They also reflected a more pervasive, though by no means uniform, set of understandings about different kinds of persons. Gender norms and expectations clearly influenced the way the children were assessed and the ways their cognitive and emotional states were evaluated. Moreover, as Cohen noted in his research among the elderly, caste and class also figured prominently in narratives about the children on the riverfront, though they by no means fully "encompassed" them. In some cases, these "bold" and "demanding" children were viewed as the victims of poverty and oppression. In other cases, they bespoke the presence of greedy families who had been seduced by the influx of tourist wealth and were seen as willing to "sacrifice" their children in exchange for foreign money. Within the neighborhood of Dasashwamedh, therefore, the West did emerge as "a villain" and for many locals it was precisely the children who worked on the riverfront, especially the boys, who most vividly embodied this fraught encounter between the East and West.

This is also to say that although the children elicited powerful reactions from both tourists and locals, they did so in different ways and for different reasons. As I discussed in chapter 4, tourists' reactions were in large part motivated by the powerful fantasies and persecutory anxieties that came with being a foreign tourist in India. In Gananath Obeyesekere's terms, we might say that tourists related to the children not just as social or cultural symbols but as "personal" ones (Obeyesekere 1981).[25] Their reactions were as much determined by "intrapsychic" conflicts and defense mechanisms as they were by the social and cultural significance these children took on. By contrast, and perhaps paradoxically, locals' reactions were far less "personal" in this sense. For people in Dasashwamedh, the children had become public symbols of a rapidly changing and uncertain world, and what their narratives most forcefully communicated were anxieties regarding social roles, reproduction, and change. And yet, as will be seen in the following chapter, these anxieties were not always commensurate with the actions and behavior of the children themselves: for when it came to doing business, the children also reproduced traditional understandings and expectations. In many respects, the informal tourist economy was a moral economy that was "submerged" in sociocultural relations (Polanyi 1957, 48) and regulated by long-standing expectations of everybody's "right to earn."

PART 3

Conceptions of Value

6

Earning, Spending, Saving

Although the children on the ghats were definitely interested in making as much money as they could from foreign tourists, the pursuit of profit was far from unbridled. As Sangeeta Sahani, an eleven-year-old diya seller, remarked: "You should do only one kind of work, whether it is selling diyas or postcards or colors. If you switch and do someone else's, that is wrong. Everyone comes here to earn. Everyone has a right (*haq*) to earn. You shouldn't steal anyone's livelihood." Indeed, in many ways this informal tourist economy reflected features of "the moral economy" that regulates work relations among boatmen on the riverfront.[1] In his ethnography of the boatmen of Banaras, Assa Doron investigates "the social values and practices underlying the boatmen's informal work system." As he observes: "this work system reveals a unique set of social, technical and economic arrangements underpinned by subjective notions of social justice and moral expectations, largely designed to protect the community from the potential threats of market economy and state intervention. At the most basic level this means that all boatmen, regardless of socio-economic status, are entitled to a living from the river economy" (Doron 2008, 82).

Doron offers a detailed account of the rules and practices that boatmen rely upon in their efforts to ensure everybody's "right to earn," and his analysis provides the departure point for the ensuing discussion. In what follows, however, I also want to consider the ways the children spent and saved their earnings. For as numerous scholars have noted, processes of distribution and consumption are also influenced by cultural understandings and expectations, and they are central to the ways that social actors attempt to *produce themselves* as valued members of their communities.[2] In this chapter, therefore, I examine how the children on the riverfront earned, spent, and saved the money they made from foreign tourists. Once again, I consider how gender norms configured these practices.

Rights and Rules among Boatmen on the Ghats

Most of the children who worked at Dasashwamedh during the time of my fieldwork came from Mallah families. As such, they were exposed to, if not explicitly knowledgeable about, the rules that determined the boatmen's work system. Among the boatmen of Banaras, the distribution of passengers is regulated around territorial boundaries and recognized ancestral rights. The ghats have boundaries called *hads*, which "indicate the precise place where each individual ghat territory begins and ends" (Doron 2008, 86). Though invisible to the outsider observer, these territorial markers provide "the basis for the system of passenger distribution across the riverfront," and boatmen are only allowed to pursue customers at the ghat they are affiliated with. According to Doron, "disputes and conflicts between ghats are a rarity on the riverfront" but, should a breach occur, those belonging to a particular ghat will unite and "exhibit group solidarity" to ward off any outside "infringement on their rights and territory" (91).

Moreover, within the boundaries of each ghat, a distinction is made between resident boatmen and nonresident boatmen. The resident boatmen, or *ghatwars*, have "sole jurisdiction over their defined space" and are "entitled to park their boats" on their ghat by virtue of their patrilineal descent, which is seen as the "ultimate source of legitimacy" (Doron 2008, 91). The nonresident boatmen, or *mallahis*, work as hired oarsmen for the ghatwars, have no residential rights on the ghat, and receive a percentage of the ghatwars' earnings (85).

In order to prevent customer disputes on the ghat, the ghatwars rely upon the *boli* system.[3] The central premise here is that as soon as a ghatwar spots a potential passenger he can claim the passenger by "calling out," or verbally identifying him, such as "the person with the red hat." This establishes his right to approach the customer himself, or he can send a mallahi on his behalf. However, once this verbal identification has been made, other ghatwars are not supposed to try to compete for the passenger's business.

Both Doron and his informants are sensitive to how these "customary laws and traditional practices" "mask power and inequality" (Doron 2008, 90). Indeed, one of the strengths of Doron's analysis is that he avoids romanticizing the boatmen and reminds us that within subaltern communities, contests for power and privilege are a part of everyday life. For the most part, however, his informants maintain that this informal work system is rarely transgressed. Adherence is "not forced through any single coercive authority imposing its will on the weaker members of the community." Rather, it is the product of shared traditional values and customary practices (85). Finally, Doron observes that despite some internal conflicts, the sense of a riverfront Mallah community also acts as a crucial deterrent to outsiders who might be interested in entering the boating business: "Although state law allows anyone with a license, regardless of caste or status, to operate a boating business, the work system, integrated by local norms and customs, prevents outsiders from entering the boating business" (85). As will be seen, when it came to organizing their own work system, the children drew upon many of these principles and rules.

Rights and Rules among the Children on the Ghats

For the children on the ghats, "the right to earn" was supposed to be safeguarded through an informal division of labor. This division of labor first entailed rules about where the children could sell. As Doron points out, what is usually referred to as the Main Ghat of Dasashwamedh actually consists of four distinct ghats that together span a distance of several hundred yards. To the tourists whom I met, it felt like a unified hub of activity, heavily populated with tourist and pilgrimage traffic. Like the boatmen, however, the children recognized boundaries or hads that were invisible to these outside observers. The children who sold diyas were particularly cognizant of these territorial markers. For instance, early on in my fieldwork, I naively suggested to Rehka and Sangeeta that they expand their zone of operation by about twenty yards and sell diyas closer to the evening puja since it usually attracted so many tourists. They refused, explaining, "We only sell on our ghat, we have been doing this since we were little and we can't sell anywhere else. If other girls come here and try to sell we will beat them, and if we go over there, they will try to beat us."[4]

The second rule pertained to the items the children could sell. The children repeatedly told me "you can sell only one item at a time. If you are selling diyas, then do not sell postcards or colors. That is wrong." In deciding which item to sell, the children took account of several factors: these included what others on the ghat were already selling, what they had the easiest access to, and what they thought would be most profitable. It also included a consideration of what they felt was most appropriate for them to sell. For instance, several of the girls told me that they sold diyas because it was something that girls from the Mallah caste had been doing for generations and was thus part of a traditional caste occupation. On another occasion, when Sangeeta was complaining about how few diyas she had sold, I suggested that she begin selling postcards to make some extra money. She snapped back at me and with visceral disgust exclaimed, "Jenny *Didi*, look, I sell diyas because there are some troubles in my home and this work is okay because it is work related to worship (*yeh to puja ka kam*), but I would rather die than sell postcards!" Alternatively, although there were Mallah boys as young as five and six selling diyas on the ghats, those boys who had reached the ages of eight, nine, ten, or older told me that it would be embarrassing for them to sell diyas. As Pradeep (age eleven) explained, "That is something that only girls and very small children do. I cannot do that work now. It would not feel right."

While most of the children paid lip-service to the one-item rule, in practice it was rendered more flexible. Many boys maintained that there was a progression involved in working on the ghats and that over time, a boy could earn the right to expand his product repertoire. As Keshwar Pandey explained:

KP: The rule is that one boy is allowed to sell one thing at first and then two things, not more than two things otherwise they will take those things away from him. For example, I keep postcards and colors.

JH: But if you go there with postcards, colors, and beads then people will complain?

KP: Yes. Yes, there will be a complaint against me, there will be a fight. The guys selling the other things will think, "Why is he selling my things?" and they will begin to beat me.

This idea of progressing in the business also applied to the shift from peddling to guiding. As Harsha Sahani (age fifteen) commented, "At first you start by selling one thing, and then you can move onto two, and then only after you have sold on the ghats for a few years can you begin doing commission work *dalali*."

Although boys were supposed to "earn their stripes" before beginning commission work, in most cases, the allure of extra money proved too much to resist. For instance, Jay observed:

There are some people on the ghats who think you should just do one business, you either sell postcards, or colors or you do guiding. But every single boy on the ghat does all of this business. People do business according to the tourists they see. Some know that this person is interested in silk so they will speak to him accordingly and say, "Here you will get good stuff, there you will get good stuff." Tourists believe the kids in Banaras. They go all around Banaras with them. So the kids think, "Why shouldn't I sell something to this tourist?"

These rules, therefore, were not only perceived as limiting "conflict and competition." As Doron has pointed out, they could also be perceived as masking or perpetuating "power relations and inequalities" (Doron 2008, 90). What Jay and others implied was that the rules really favored older boys on the ghats who wanted to try and secure their advantage over their younger and cuter rivals.

Finally, the children on the ghats also had a set of informal rules about staking claims on customers that bore a resemblance to the boatmen's boli system. The standard protocol was that once a boy began talking to a tourist and was in the process of trying to "woo" him or her, his efforts should not be interfered with by others. As Jay explained:

It's like this, if you approach someone else's customer and he's talking to him or her and you say "Can I also to talk to him?" then he won't like it. He will say, "This is my customer; this isn't your customer." So I will say, "Your name is not written on this customer." So he will say, "Yes it is. This is my customer you go away or I will hit you. After I leave the customer you can say whatever you want to me." So that way if I have any business with the customer, like selling silk, it won't get messed up. If I say anything else that's inappropriate, for instance if I talk about silk, or say that "this is available there, or there," then he won't like it and he will say "You are selling, you're messing things up for me, you're doing all of this kind of stuff, if you do this then I can't hook you up with this customer later."

In many cases it took threats of physical violence or promises of reciprocal "hookups" to deter others from meddling in one's business. Indeed, managing the other boys on the ghats was a perpetual struggle. The boys had to balance their individual desires to profit with a social imperative that demanded that everyone "get a little something." This meant that even when a customer was claimed by a particular boy, he still acknowledged an obligation to see it to it that others earned from him as well. "You see," Jay continued, "everyone should earn a little something from the customer. My friends will say, 'Hook me up with this customer, Tell him that I am your brother.' So I think, 'what kind of mind should I use so that these boys will go away from me and then meet me afterward?' If a boy asks me for money then I give it to him. Or, if some boy comes to me and says 'Hook me up, hook me up,' if I do this for him today, then tomorrow, he will hook me up with his customer."

These examples demonstrate that there were some striking similarities between the organization of the children's informal work system and the boatmen's. However, they also reveal that the children neither unanimously agreed upon the rules governing their work system nor unequivocally obeyed them. In fact, in contrast to what Doron has described among the boatmen, in this informal tourist economy, "transgressions" and disputes were extremely common, and as I will discuss below, adherence to the rules was often the result of stronger boys or girls actively imposing their wills on weaker ones.

Tyranny, Diplomacy, and Respect

Sanju and Keshwar

I first met Sanju Srivastav when he was a slight child of twelve roaming the ghats with a handful of postcards. By the time I returned to begin my fieldwork, he had gone through a rather startling growth spurt and had become one of the tallest and strongest boys peddling on the ghat. Although he was not from a Mallah family, his size, strength, and connections in the neighborhood enabled Sanju to wield considerable power over the younger boys who worked at Dasashwamedh. Most of these boys viewed Sanju as a run-of-the-mill bully, but Sanju preferred to see himself a valuable enforcer of ghat laws and justice. When a boy was caught selling more than one item at a time, or participating in commission work "prematurely," or was perceived as trespassing on the highly coveted sales territory at Dasashwamedh, Sanju was usually one of the first to intervene. His methods for addressing these transgressions varied. Depending on the situation, he might resort to verbal harassment, seize children's products, deploy outright physical violence, or a combination of all three.

Such was the case in his dealings with Keshwar Pandey. Keshwar was fourteen, a year younger than Sanju, and he lived about a mile away from Dasashwamedh. He had been selling at the Main Ghat for three years, but he was still being routinely harassed by Sanju and some of the other boys from the neighborhood who resented his intruding on their business prospects. Indeed, the boys often complained that their sales territory was being invaded by boys "from the outside." As Sanju told me one afternoon, "Before, it was only boys from our neighborhood who did this work. But now boys from all over Banaras want to come here. They think that they if they come to Dasashwamedh they will make a lot of money from foreign tourists. They are trying to ruin our business so we have to chase them away."[5] At the time of my research, Keshwar had become one of the more visible targets of this effort to rid the ghats of outside competition. In our interview, he talked about his run-ins with the tyrannical Sanju, the challenges he faced as an outsider, and some of the ways that he tried to cope with the labor politics and disputes on the ghats:

KP: If I want to sell something on the ghats, I have to take permission, because suppose someone threatens me or tries to beat me. In order to prevent that, I have to make a relationship with them first (*un se vyavhar banana*). I never think of going there to sell something new without first having made a relationship with the people who are already selling that stuff, because only after making a relationship can I make any changes in the items that I am selling. For example, I was not allowed to sell colors and even today people fight with me about this.

JH: Who does?

KP: There is Sanju, he says to me "Don't sell your stuff here."

JH: You mean Sanju, the nephew of Apu?

KP: Yes, yes. His nephew. So one day I went to Apu and I said to him, "Apu Bhai, Sanju always says to me 'Don't sell this or don't sell that otherwise I will take it away from you and beat you, and don't sell your stuff here.'" I often go and complain to Apu about this, I have already complained to him twice. Now if this happens with me a third time then I will complain again and after that, if he does not discourage his nephew from doing this to me then I also will fight. Suppose he slaps me ten times, I will also slap him at least once and then what will happen? He will lose face among the people there, because I am younger and he is older. Since he is older I try to avoid a fight. He thinks he is the boss of this area but I'm not afraid of him; I will sell my things anyway.

To succeed on the ghats, therefore, it was not enough for boys to know how to insult and abuse others. Boys like Keshwar also had to learn how to use diplomacy as a way of securing a space for themselves within this economy. In fact, in his initial efforts to settle his conflicts with Sanju, Keshwar tried to pursue a diplomatic strategy that was in close keeping with traditional conceptions of age-based hierarchies and respect. He avoided a direct confrontation with Sanju and instead appealed to one of Sanju's elders to intervene. Perhaps if Keshwar had been from the neighborhood, his appeals would have been taken more seriously, and he would not have felt compelled to supplement diplomacy with a show of physical force and bravery. However, based on his prior experiences with Sanju and some of the other boys from Dasashwamedh, Keshwar felt that he had reached a crossroads. As he went on to explain:

I don't enjoy fighting, but I will fight with those who fight with me. I am ready to hit and to be hit. Before, these boys used to intimidate me a lot. They used to say to me, "Don't sell this, don't sell that," and when I would sell something they would want me to spend my money on them. They used to beat me to make me comply. At first, I used to do whatever I was told but then I thought to myself, "If I bring things for them one day then they will want me to do that again the next day." So one day I swore to myself that I wasn't going to do anything for anyone anymore. I wasn't going to be anyone's servant. They would always say, "Hey motherfucker, come here! Go get this, go get that!" I don't like swear words, that's why now I fight back. Earlier there was a boy who used to beat me a lot by twisting my arm behind my back. One day he hit me in the stomach after twisting my arm and when he let go of my arm I hit him with all of my strength and he doubled up in pain. Since then, he doesn't fight with me anymore. When I hit him I was crying because I was hurting very badly where he hit me but I hit him with two punches with all of my strength. Everyone around pulled us apart and they asked the boy, "Since you are older than him, why are you beating someone younger than you?" And then everyone asked me, "Why did the fight break out?" I said, "He was beating me, he was ordering me around, telling me to bring this and that and I said that I wouldn't. And every day he tells me to bring things for him and one day is fine but I won't do it every day." So all the men said that I was right and that it wasn't my fault, it was the other guy's fault. Now, I never think of anyone as being stronger than me anymore. I killed my fear that day.

Keshwar did not convince me that he had "killed" his fear that day but he did make me realize that fear and violence were central preoccupations for the boys who worked on the ghats. While girls also spoke of giving and getting beatings, or engaging in hair-pulling scuffles (*jhonta jhonti karna*), their relationship to violence seemed more pragmatic. As Sangeeta suggested, it was an expedient way of protecting one's territory. For the boys on the ghats, however, violence was about more than just ensuring one's business interests. Fighting also provided the boys with an embodied idiom for asserting highly valued masculine attributes like autonomy, bravery, and strength.[6] In so doing, it became a primary means of preserving or accruing one of the most coveted forms of symbolic capital, respect (*izzat*).

Sanju and the Yadav Brothers

This deep concern with respect also emerged in another incident that involved Sanju and Jay Yadav. Like Keshwar, Jay was a target for harassment because of his outsider status, and there were many occasions when Sanju would tease Jay and scold him for working on "his" ghat. However, unlike Keshwar, Jay did have some backing in the neighborhood. Not only had he managed to make friends with some of the boys at Dasashwamedh, but two of his older brothers, Raj (age twenty-two) and Pradeep (age nineteen), also worked near the ghat. Raj, as I noted in chapter 3, drove an auto rickshaw and was often parked nearby at the top of the main road. Pradeep worked in a lassi shop in the bazaar. One day, Jay felt that Sanju had taken his taunting too far and he went to Pradeep to complain. Pradeep tracked Sanju down, slapped him across the face, and issued him a stern warning about "messing" with his brother. When Raj found out about Pradeep's intervention, he was extremely angry and scolded Pradeep, telling him that he should not have interfered with the boys' business on the ghats. In an attempt to right the situation, Raj went to Sanju and apologized on his younger brothers' behalf. It seemed, then, that the matter was resolved.

The next evening, I was sitting with Raj and Jay at the top of the road, as they waited for Pradeep near the rickshaw. Jay was exhausted and discouraged after a long and very slow day of business, and Raj was explaining to me why he felt it was inappropriate for Pradeep to have interfered in Sanju and Jay's dispute. As we were speaking, one of the boys from the ghat came over and informed Raj that Sanju was "bragging to everyone" about how Raj had come to him "to beg for his forgiveness." Raj became furious and immediately ordered the boy to go get Sanju. About ten minutes later Sanju appeared. Raj got up, stepped toward Sanju, and slapped him across the face. Then he began yelling at him (though the message seemed to be as much for our benefit): "I do not bend down to anyone! I do not beg anyone for anything! If you are going to insult me and disgrace me or my brother, I will beat you!" Sanju's face was red from the slap, as well as from embarrassment, and he began to apologize. Then, Raj took him off to the side to speak privately with him. They talked for about twenty minutes, and by the time their conversation was over, it seemed that the matter was finally resolved.

Afterward, I asked Raj what he had said to Sanju. He told me that he had "reminded" Sanju that the ghats were owned by the government and that anyone had "the right" (*haq*) to sell there and make a living there if they wanted to. He also told Sanju that he should let Jay do his business on the ghat, and if Sanju did encounter problems with his younger brother then he should come directly to him. "I told Sanju I would deal with Jay if there is a problem," Raj said. Then he turned to Jay and in an aggravated voice he warned, "And if you do not listen to me, our relationship will be finished. You should just stay away from Sanju!" Upon hearing this, Jay looked even more discouraged than he did before, as though his older brother had just sided with the enemy. "It will be impossible for me to avoid Sanju on the ghats," he protested, "I will still have to deal with him bothering me and insulting me." Trying to help, I chimed in with my own "turn the other cheek" advice, but this just seemed to make Jay feel worse. Looking at me as though I were a complete idiot, he said, "If I ignore Sanju's insults, then eventually I will end up having to fight him to keep my respect. Once you lose your respect, Jenny, you can't get it back!"

Keshwar and Jay both struggled to protect their right to earn in this informal economy, and they both struggled to protect their honor. In so doing, they experimented with different strategies. Sometimes, as Keshwar noted, diplomacy was the best policy, and "investing" in social relationships did "pay off." However, there were also times when the tyranny on the ghats had to be answered in kind, and the boys felt that violence was their only option if they were going to produce themselves as respected subjects. For Keshwar, the pressure and anxiety became too much. A few months after I interviewed him, he retired from working on the ghats and began an apprenticeship with an auto-rickshaw mechanic. One day, Keshwar stopped by my guest house on his way home from work to say hello. He was covered with grease stains and was complaining about how dirty and exhausting his new job was. But he also seemed happier and more at ease. "I got fed up selling on the ghats," he told me. "The boys there were making it too difficult for me, so I decided to do something else. At least now I don't have to fight with them all the time."

The Right to Earn versus the Fight to Earn: Envy, Greed, and Competition

Getting and giving beatings was perceived as an effective way to maintain, as well as contest the socioeconomic order on the ghats, and in some cases, secure or enhance one's reputation. However, fighting also operated as a powerful metaphor. The children often spoke of the ghats as a rough and tough "world below," where one had to learn how to abuse and swindle others in order to survive. This kind of imagery was also invoked to describe the nature of the tourist economy itself. As the children repeatedly told me, "In this line there is no unity, everyone is jealous of each other, everyone only looks after themselves" (*Is line me koi ekta nahin hota hai, sab log jalte hain, sab log bas apne ko dekhte hain*). Thus, while the children acknowledged a set of moral prescriptions that were intended to safeguard everyone's right to earn, they were also keenly aware that competition, greed, and envy played a significant role in shaping their work relations and practices. In fact, most of the disputes between the children involved accusations that these vices had gained the upper hand. For instance, one evening, I went to eat at a popular tourist restaurant in Godolia Bazaar. On my way in I encountered Arun and Mukesh Sahani standing in the corner. They were peering angrily into the dining-hall, watching Pramod and Mohan eat dinner with three French female tourists. "Why aren't you with them?" I asked, since the boys usually hung around together and frequently pursued tourists as a team. "They told those women bad things about us," Arun said. "They don't want us to earn anything from them." Pramod glanced over and with a gloating, cat-just-ate-the-canary kind of smile he began waving hello. Arun and Mukesh were incensed by the gesture and Mukesh got so angry that he began shouting across the restaurant. "Go ahead," he said, "do whatever to fill your stomach, just remember God is watching!" Then, the boys stormed out.

In this particular instance, Pramod was literally "filling his stomach." However, as Jonathan Parry has noted, in Banaras, and elsewhere in India, it is very common for people to articulate ideas about social exchanges through "a digestive idiom" (Parry 1994, 214). Indeed, the very language the children used to talk about earning almost always drew upon imagery of the stomach (*pet*). One's livelihood was described as the "earnings of the stomach" and, as Sangeeta pointed out in an earlier quotation, these earnings were not supposed to be "stolen" or denied. Yet, when it came to the reality of this informal economy, charges of stealing and allusions to the "insatiable" stomach were rampant. For instance, as Arun explained to me one day in an interview, "To fill the stomach, people fight. Some people eat one roti and they are satisfied, others eat ten rotis but they do not stick. That's how it is with the boys in this business."

Like Mukesh and Arun, many other children also complained about being double-crossed by "greedy" friends who wanted to keep them from earning their share. In fact, a few weeks after this incident, Pramod found himself on the short end of the stick when his partner at the time (Dipesh, age ten) allegedly failed to give him his percentage of a sizeable commission that they had jointly earned. When I encountered Pramod a few days later and asked him if he and Dipesh had settled matters, he said, "Not yet. He won't show his face on the ghats for a while because he knows that I will beat him for cheating me."

While accusations of "cheating" and double-crossing certainly caused animosity among the boys, the disputes they generated were usually short-lived. A foe one day was a friend the next, particularly when a common business interest could be reestablished. As Bali informed me, "With the boys at Dasashwamedh it is like this, one day we fight the next day we are friends, but we always unite against outsiders." Sometimes, the "outsiders" included shop owners in the bazaar. During my fieldwork there were several occasions when shop owners failed to pay a boy his promised commission. On each of these instances, the boys united and collectively confronted the shop owners, threatening to boycott their businesses until the commissions were granted. On another occasion, I was told that a shop owner had beaten one of the boys from Dasashwamedh for bringing customers to a competitor's shop. When the boys learned of the incident, they again collectively assembled and demanded that the proprietor publicly apologize.[7]

After this confrontation occurred, I interviewed Manoj Yadav. Manoj was in his late twenties and had worked as a guide and commission agent at Dasashwamedh when he was a young boy. With some encouragement and support from friends, he had been able to move up into "the world above" and open his own silk shop in the bazaar. In so doing he had become a celebrated success story in the neighborhood, and many of the boys sought to emulate him. When Manoj heard about the incident between the boys and the shop owner, he was not surprised:

MY: In this business there are many people who pressure these young boys and say to them, "You get this tourist for me and bring them to my shop only." They mostly say this to the young boys, like "If you don't bring customers to me then I will have your guiding stopped." "I'll have the police catch you. I will hit you" and they hit them sometimes. If a guide is twenty-three, twenty-four, then you can't threaten and intimidate boys who are this age. At this age boys are very excitable. Because you know, [in English] "young body." So because of this shop owners won't say anything to these boys. They mostly say things to the young boys. For instance, they get angry and think, "Oh, this new shop owner has come and you're bringing customers there now when it was just me who kept you for all these days and now you're not bringing customers here." So the children have some troubles. But it's like this, they are kids, you have to understand that they are kids. Sometimes they feel okay, sometimes they get angry about little things, so it's very necessary to treat them lovingly. Like me, I never force anyone, my behavior is [in English] "just like friendship." These are all my friends. These were the people who told me to do this business so that they could help me. And if they ever have a bad time, then I'm always ready to help them as much as I can. It is very important for our business to develop ties with these boys who work as guides because without them our foreign business won't be successful. If my store was on the main street then it might be possible for me to do it on my own but not completely.

In their attempts to control the flow of foreign tourists, therefore, shop owners in the bazaar often tried to invoke traditional conceptions of the patron-client relationship. They supported these young boys in their times of need and, in return, they expected their allegiance and customers in the future. However, as Manoj pointed out, the boys did not always recognize or honor such commitments, and in most cases, they actively avoided becoming beholden to one shop, for they knew it was important to have flexibility if they were going to earn from foreign tourists. Here again, therefore, there was a sense in which the boys found themselves in a conundrum, pulled between a free-market economy and a socially embedded one. As Manoj noted, some shop owners tried to impose their wills on these younger and weaker subjects by resorting to violence and intimidation, but from Manoj's perspective it was far more effective to use kindness, love, and understanding. "You have to butter these children up," he told me later in the interview. "You have to remember they are kids and be sensitive to their feelings." In fact, in some cases, this kind of sensitivity proved even more important to the boys than financial incentives. For instance, when I asked Raju how he decided where to take his customers he said: "It is not just a matter of money; some shop owners pay good commissions but their behavior is not good. It also depends on how they treat us. There was one shop owner who used to pay me commissions but he did not speak nicely with me, he never offered me tea or drinks, he did not want me to come in his shop, so I stopped taking customers there."[8]

An Economy of Desire

When shop owners like Manoj relied upon their abilities to anticipate and manipulate the children's feelings, they invoked an earning strategy that was actually very common among the children themselves. The children who pursued foreign tourists were also, to varying degrees, aware that their success was contingent upon their abilities to interpret and influence tourists' feelings. This was particularly the case when it came to guiding and commission work, which involved longer periods of sustained interaction with tourists, as well as the potential for greater earnings. In fact, the very language these boys used to talk about their dealings with tourists reflected some awareness of the affective dimensions involved in their work. When they spoke of their efforts to win over customers they usually used the verb *patana*, which literally means to impress or convince someone, but which can also have a connotation of seduction and is frequently used in the context of trying to woo or seduce a girl. This economy, therefore, was not only "submerged" in customary social relations and concerns.

It also emerged in response to tourists' desires and anxieties. Those children who were able to attune themselves to these subjective forces were often able to increase their sales and profits.

Sales Pitches and Speech Genres

One of the ways the children did this was through manipulating speech genres. As Mikhail Bakhtin proposed, speech genres consist of a "relatively stable type of utterances," which "reflect the specific conditions and goals" of each area of human activity through "their thematic content, style and compositional structure" (1986, 60). Over time, as a particular sphere of activity develops, so does the repertoire of genres accompanying it. For instance, within the sphere of selling, sales pitches may "differentiate" and become "more complex." A standard and unambiguous proposition such as, "Would you like a postcard?" may give way to a much more nuanced approach involving small talk, banter, jokes, or, eventually even a highly sophisticated advertising campaign. However, whether simple or complex, Bakhtin argued that speech genres provide organizing frames that guide our verbal interactions with others and lend a certain degree of stability and predictability to human communication.[9]

Bakhtin also recognized that people can play with speech genres and come to "master" them in ways that enhance their abilities to express their individual feelings and intentions.[10] Achieving mastery over speech genres involves being attuned to the "apperceptive background" of the listener or, in Bakhtin's language, "the addressee." It requires taking account of "the addressee's perception of my speech: the extent to which he is familiar with the situation, whether he has special knowledge of the given cultural area of communication, his views and convictions, his prejudices (from my viewpoint), his *sympathies* and *antipathies*, because all this will determine his active responsive understanding of my utterance" (96, emphasis added). In taking account of the apperceptive background of the addressee, the savvy speaker then accordingly modifies the genre and style that he or she chooses. The following examples demonstrate how the children's earning potential was influenced by their respective abilities to master and manipulate speech genres, and anticipate the "sympathies and antipathies" of their customers.

Persistence and Pestering

Priya, whom I introduced in chapter 3, was one of the most successful and yet, from the perspective of many Western tourists, one of the most "annoying" and "irritating" peddlers at Dasashwamedh. Her success selling postcards, therefore, had far less to do with her ability to endear herself to foreign tourists than it did with her ability to wear them down through a repetitive, monotone onslaught of "You buy postcard? You buy postcard?" Often Priya coupled this with tugging at tourists' clothes or hands, or trying to physically position herself in such a way that the tourists virtually had to step over or around her if they wanted to move on. For instance, one day, she was trying to sell postcards to a German couple walking along the ghats. After a few minutes of positioning herself between them and pulling on the woman's skirt, the man bent over, swiftly lifted Priya high into the air, and then placed her down on the other side of them. Priya looked shocked when her feet struck the ground and she immediately glanced over at her father, who was selling peanuts on the ghat, to see what he was going to do. He seemed nonplussed and he motioned her with his hand to move on and pursue another tourist who was walking her way.

Although tourists were typically turned off by this approach, some gave in because they sympathized with Priya's plight and recognized that she was being continually prompted by her father to pursue customers. However, most of the tourists I observed and spoke with said that they ultimately surrendered to Priya's solicitations just "to make her go away," or to put an end to her "relentless pestering." This was also the case with Rakhi Sahani, age six, who sold diyas. Rakhi, too, was regarded as a notorious "nuisance." For instance, one afternoon I was having tea on the ghats with Sara. As we were chatting, Sara pointed to Rakhi and began to tell me about their encounter from the previous evening: "I was watching the puja and I had already bought several diyas from the other kids and I just wanted to be left alone, but that one, with the curly hair, she wouldn't go away. She has one of those whiny beggar-like voices and it was really irritating me. So finally, I gave her some money and took a candle and then I stormed off." Both Laurien and Kirsten (see chapter 4) voiced similar complaints. They suggested that instead of having mastered the genre of selling, the children seemed to be completely dominated by it. As Kirsten put it, the children were utterly incapable of "jumping out of their roles."

Still other tourists insisted that the children's relentless solicitations reflected a highly intuitive and even "clever sales strategy" that was purposively intended to stir up their antipathies. As Steven, an Australian traveler, remarked: "These kids know that if they aggravate us enough, and keep asking, we will eventually break down and buy their stuff just so they will go away. It's psychological warfare out here!"[11] Although the children never suggested that aggravating tourists was part of a conscious sales strategy, by watching tourists "break down" night after night, they did, I think, come to realize that it was a potentially effective one.

Humor and Jokes

Dipesh Pandey, age ten, also worked as a peddler and guide at Dasashwamedh. His opening sales pitch was extremely successful at disarming tourists: "How many people have asked you to see their shop since you came to Banaras, 1,000?

Well I'm 1,001." Though it did not always secure him a customer or sale, it usually made tourists laugh, smile, and even praise him for his witty sense of humor and "natural talents as a little businessman." As one tourist described Dipesh, "He is not just another broken record repeating the same line, 'You come to my silk shop.' We've heard that over and over again! This kid is funny, he's different." Indeed, when I asked Dipesh about his selling strategy he told me, "I always think to myself what can I say to customers to make myself different? Or, what can I say to woo these customers so they will want to come with me?"

Like Dipesh, Anita was also inclined to use humor and jokes as a way of persuading potential customers. Often, she would forgo the standard "You want diya?" approach, and instead, she would place a diya in front of a tourist and then walk away, leaving the tourist looking bewildered. A few minutes later, she would return, and waving her finger in the air, she would reprimand the tourist for "stealing" the candle from her. On other another occasion, I saw Anita put her entire basket of diyas in a tourist's lap and say, "If you not buy from me, then you sell for me!" The tourist burst out laughing, began walking around with the basket soliciting his fellow travelers, and ended up making a number of sales on Anita's behalf.

Indeed, one of the advantages that Anita had over some of the other children was that she seemed profoundly aware that many of these tourists wanted to play. They wanted to have fun, friendly, and personable exchanges that could provide them with a break from what they often described as the stressful and "dehumanizing" experience of being a foreign tourist in India. Anita's approach was also effective because she had a talent for creating parodies that actually highlighted and inverted some of the tensions that routinely pervaded exchanges between tourists and locals. She turned the reluctant foreign buyer into the seller, the suspicious tourist who was afraid of getting ripped off into the thief. In so doing, she was able to transform these routine and potentially aggravating commercial transactions into amusing, and sometime even dramatic spectacles that could attract the attention of other tourists and locals on the ghats.

Making Friendship

Another effective strategy, particularly among the boys who engaged in guiding and commission work, involved "making friendship." For the boys, these "friendships" were first initiated through conversations on the ghats. When the boys approached a potential customer, they rarely began with a direct business proposition or an immediate offer to guide the tourist around the city. Instead, they engaged in small talk. As Pramod explained to me one day, "You never just ask a tourist to come see your shop; you have to talk to him first." However, many of the tourists I interviewed found the boys' "small talk" extremely generic. In fact, when I would ask tourists to tell me about how they were approached by children on the ghats, they often ended up mimicking and mocking the children. In a staccato voice, with their heads tilting from side to side, they would begin reciting the "standard" list of questions: "What is your name? What is your father's name? Where do you come from? What do you do? You come see my shop?" Thus, merely engaging in chit-chat was not enough for the boys to succeed at making a friendship. The boys had to be able, as Bakhtin put it, to "reaccentuate" the genre in such a way as to allow their individual charms and personalities to shine through.

For example, when Dipesh approached a potential customer, he also looked for specific conversation pieces that he could use as devices to engage tourists. One morning, we were sitting on the ghats when an Australian man with a walking stick paused in front of us to wipe some mud off his shoe. Dipesh jumped up like a firecracker and exclaimed: "Hey nice stick! What do you use it for? Can I hold it?" The man was amused and handed the stick to Dipesh so that he could examine it. Then, once Dipesh had the stick in hand, Dipesh told the man to sit down. "It doesn't look nice if you are standing up and I am talking to you." The man complied, and they took a seat on the steps below me. Then, Dipesh started in with the "standard" line of questioning but, as always, he added his own personal twist.

"What is your name?" The man replied "George." "Where are you from, George?" He replied, "Australia." "Oh," Dipesh said, "I have many friends in Australia. Sydney, Melbourne, Perth, Brisbane. I can show you the letters they send me. They all say I am a good boy." George nodded his head and again, looked very amused. "I am from Sydney," George said. "What do you do there?" Dipesh asked. "I was in the navy." Dipesh looked at him curiously, "What is the meaning of navy?" George started laughing, and quite happily, began explaining his former profession. The conversation and questions proceeded like this for about fifteen minutes before Dipesh asked George what sights he had seen in the city. "Have you seen Monkey Temple? Have you seen Golden Temple?" George shook his head no. Dipesh exclaimed, "Oh, you haven't seen anything yet! I can show you, you come with me. I show you. No money, just for friendship. Okay?" George seemed genuinely flattered, and thanked Dipesh for the "kind" offer, but he also told him that unfortunately, he was leaving the city in a couple of hours and had to go back to his guest house to pack. Upon hearing this, Dipesh again shot up like a firecracker, said good-bye, and headed off to look for other customers.

Reciprocity and Intimacy

Dipesh did not succeed in snagging the customer on that particular morning, though, having watched their interaction, I would say that he successfully wooed him. I had little doubt that George would have accompanied Dipesh on the tour if he had had the time. Nevertheless, the example is instructive, for it demonstrates how the children manipulated speech genres in their efforts to earn money from foreign tourists. It also suggests that much of their success was predicated upon their abilities to attune themselves to tourists' desires to have unique and personal encounters, rather than just generic commercial transactions. Indeed, in addition to manipulating speech genres, another way these children tried to change the terms of their relationships with tourists from "mere" commerce to friendship was by establishing and cultivating relations of reciprocity that involved the giving of material gifts and assistance, as well as emotional incentives and support.

Like Dipesh, almost all of the boys who worked as guides and commission agents offered to show tourists around the city free of charge. It was feasible for them to do so because unbeknownst to many tourists, they earned most of their money from the commissions they received in the bazaar. However, this decision to initially forgo a guiding fee went beyond the issue of feasibility and, I argue, was part of a more pervasive strategy for increasing profitability.[12] The boys often relied upon "generalized" and "balanced reciprocity" as key mechanisms for maximizing their earnings from foreign tourists (Sahlins 1972).[13] As Jaggu Mukherjee, age ten, explained, "If you ask for something you will never get it, and yet, without asking you will get pearls" (*agar aap kuch mangenge to kabhi nahin milega aur bina mangne moti milengi*). Or, as Pramod explained when I and asked him to describe his earning strategy: "I take them [tourists] around a bit and don't charge them any money, I say, 'No, I won't take any money.' Initially I won't take money because I know that later on I will be able to earn more from them. The trick is to get money out of them by making them happy" (*kush karke paisa lena*)." Kailash Sahani, an eleven-year-old guide and commission agent, provides yet another example:

KS: I make sure to remove the idea from the tourist's mind that I am following him in the quest of earning some money. I will forge a friendship with him and only after forging a friendship with him will I try to bring him into business and try to get some money out of him. And then he will give money happily.

JH: So what is necessary for making a friendship?

KS: In order to make a friendship first you have to make the tourist happy, ask him questions, find out what he likes, and after that you have to make sure that you don't talk about business at all with him. You have to tell him about whatever he asks you. You will have to get some information out of him and you too will have to give him some information in return so that you can be friends.

In repressing the material side of these transactions and downplaying expectations of an immediate return, the boys drew upon forms of reciprocity that have historically characterized a wide range of social relations within Indian society.[14]

In terms of the present discussion, however, what I find noteworthy is not just that these boys were able to appropriate traditional transactional models in their pursuit of profit. Rather, it is the emphasis they both placed on emotions. For Pramod and Kailash, the path to profit required more than just imbuing tourists with a sense of duty, or an obligation to eventually make a return and thereby uphold their end of the social contract. It required being able to produce a surplus of positive feelings within these visitors. As Pramod stated, the trick to getting money out of tourists was "to make them happy," and the happier you made them, the more they were likely to give.

This is significant because it has consequences for the way we conceptualize both the nature of this informal economy and the kind of work these children were engaged in. As Marshall Sahlins and others have proposed, in many other sociohistorical contexts, the concept of friendship, just like the concept of family, does not entail an emotional connection between the transacting subjects.[15] Indeed, anthropologists have suggested that the premium placed on emotional intimacy may itself be reflective of a particularly Western understanding of the self, which emphasizes the interiority and authenticity of human feelings. Arjun Appadurai, for instance, makes this point in his discussion of praise in Hindu India. He argues that we need to conceptualize praise as a culturally stylized emotional discourse and practice that works to create material and social bonds between transactors without presupposing communication between their "internal" states. "Praise," he writes, "is not a matter of *direct* communication between the inner emotional states of the parties involved but [a matter] of a publicly understood *code* for the negotiation of expectations and obligations" (Appadurai 1990, 101–102).

Although these anthropological reflections on friendship and praise are certainly germane, the children on the riverfront did not assume that foreign tourists shared their "publicly understood code for the negotiation of expectations and obligations." Nor did they assume that these tourists would be bound to them by the kinds of long-term exchange relations that define and sustain friendships in many parts of the world.[16] The children were keenly aware that tourists had the power to walk away from the relationship if it started to feel burdensome or, as Kailash emphasized, was not to their "liking." Thus, these children were, to varying degrees, engaged in a particular kind of emotional labor (Hochschild 1983).[17] Although the children themselves may not have been affectively invested in these transactions, their success was contingent upon their abilities to attune themselves to tourists' feelings and desires, and in many cases, create emotionally charged intimate experiences for them.

Home Is Where the Heart Is

January 31, 2000

Namaste! My dear beloved friends,

Just a quick note to say I'm thinking of you all and hope that you are doing well and staying warm. Enclosed are some sweaters and things for all the kids. I am sending a separate letter with photos. I hope you get this package. And I hope things fit. We loved being with you in Varanasi and thank you from open hearts. I think of you every day, keep you in my prayers and miss seeing your bright smiles and beautiful hearts. In *truth* we are one though, "same-same"! Much love to you Sharmila, and big hugs for all the children.

I love you,
Om Shanti Shanti Shanti!
Sophia and David

Often, the children helped create these intimate experiences for tourists by bringing them home. For instance, Sophia and David, a middle-aged couple from France, had spent a week in the city. During their stay they ended up befriending Sharmila and her daughters, whom they had initially encountered selling postcards and diyas on the ghats. Though their time together was brief, as the letter above suggests, it left a deep and lasting impression on the couple. In their subsequent letter "with photos," Sophia and David again thanked the children for inviting them to their home, and they graciously complimented Sharmila for preparing such a "delicious" dinner. When I asked Sharmila about Sophia and David's visit, she had nothing but praise for them as well. "They are very kind people. They understand my situation. My daughters have made many foreign friends who have helped us. Some of them still send money for Malika; they say it is to help pay for her marriage."

These intimate "backstage" experiences often translated into gifts or financial assistance from tourists, not just because they satisfied a desire for authenticity, as MacCannell has famously argued (MacCannell 1976), but also because they stirred up other powerful feelings such as sympathy and guilt. Like many of the other families I knew, Sharmila and her daughters shared a single-room dwelling that was considered "shockingly small" by most of the Western tourists who visited. For instance, after Sara had paid a visit to their home she remarked, "When I saw where they live I couldn't believe it, I felt so bad when I got back to my room at the guest house and realized it was twice as big! They really don't have anything!" For the children, of course, small living quarters were normal, not shocking, and inviting tourists home was more an act of strategic hospitality than a calculated attempt to make tourists feel guilty by highlighting the disparities in their standards of living. However, the visit home was often as unsettling as it was endearing, and it did frequently emerge as a decisive factor in tourists' decisions to give money to these children. Malika, I suspect, was aware of this. In recounting her earlier experiences working with foreign tourists she said: "I never asked anything from my tourist friends even though I had many. I never said to any of them, 'I want this and you must get this for me.' There were many such friends who came to my home and saw how we lived and they said to me on their own, 'Malika, I want to give you something and please don't refuse.'" Like Jaggu, therefore, Malika had also learned that the greatest gifts and rewards often came without asking.

Girls Save, Boys Spend

"So what did you do with all the money you earned from tourists?" I asked Malika during our interview.

MS: I used to give it to my mummy. I used to keep enough money to buy another set of postcards and colors and I would give the remaining amount to my mom.
JH: Always?
MS: Always.
JH: Did you ever spend money on something wasteful?
MS: No. Of course my mom used to give me five or ten rupees to spend. She would say to me, "Keep this money, when you go out sometimes you may feel like eating something all of a sudden." But then, I never let my desires get out of hand. I was never the kind to think that if I wanted something then I must have it. At that time I was very cautious not to develop a liking for something which I wouldn't be able to buy.

Within this informal economy, therefore, it was not just earning practices that were constrained by a larger set of sociocultural logics and relations, but also spending practices. Both boys and girls emphasized that they had a moral obligation to contribute their earnings to the family rather than use them as a means for pursuing individual desires and ends.[18] In practice, however, there were also significant differences between the way girls and boys spent their money and rendered their earnings meaningful.

Girls were much more apt to give the majority of their earnings to their parents than boys were. For instance, as Madhuri explained: "My daughters understand. If there is a problem and one day we don't cook food at home and no one gets to eat, or if we can't open the shop that day, then Anjali says to me, 'Don't worry, Mummy, I will earn and feed all of you.' But my son is only interested in taking money for himself. He has a lot of his own personal expenses that come from eating out, wandering around, he wants fancy clothes. But Anjali, she sells tea and then gives her money at home."

In part, the differences may be attributed to pragmatic reasons. First, it was difficult for girls to conceal the money they earned because they were more closely monitored than boys. Second, because girls were usually restricted to the space of the riverfront, they had far fewer opportunities to spend their earnings. Most of the money the girls spent was on inexpensive drinks and snacks that were sold on the riverfront, whereas the boys routinely had access to a bevy of consumer items and temptations in the bazaar.

By demonstrating their "conspicuous parsimony" (Appadurai 1986, 30), the girls were also able to prove themselves as devoted and caring daughters who deserved parental praise and blessings.[19] For instance, when I asked Mona why she sold tea on the ghats, she said: "If I listen to my parents and give them money then I will get merit (*punya*), and if I get merit then when I get big, my future will be very good." Saving rather than spending also testified to the girls' abilities to control their desires and live within their means. Moreover, it was another act of "performative deference" that contributed to the harmony of the household. Though there were certainly occasions when girls would have preferred to be able to keep the money for themselves, for the most part they all agreed that parents should be the ones to decide when and how their earnings were spent. As Malika explained, "If you do not give the money to your parents it is like stealing from them." Finally, saving rather than spending was also important because, as I noted in chapter 3, one of the ways the girls attempted to secure their reputations was by narrating their work on the ghats as an act of necessity. As such, spending on frivolous or extravagant items could undermine these efforts.[20]

All of this was markedly different from the way that boys tended to approach and talk about their earnings and spending. Although boys often contributed part of their earnings to the household economy, they also "blew" (*paisa urana*) a significant portion on themselves and their friends. Instead of adopting a strategy of conspicuous parsimony, they were very much invested in conspicuous consumption. Routine expenditures included dining out, going to films, buying new clothes, taking trips about the city, and gambling. Indeed, for the boys, there was a sense in which the money was there to be spent rather than saved, and to be used to indulge appetites and desires rather than inhibit them. The very act of spending was talked about as a quasi intoxicant that made the boys feel as though they enjoyed an unbridled freedom and a lifestyle that was frequently compared to living like "kings." "We blow our money like kings," they would often say (*hum raja ki tarah paise uraate hain*). "With the money we earn we can eat whatever want, we can take rickshaws around the city, we can go to the cinema two times a day!"

And yet, for the boys, spending also provided a vital path for establishing important friendships and business alliances on the ghats. Indeed, as Keshwar suggested, part of learning how to make money in this informal economy entailed learning how to negotiate the recurring demands that other boys made on one's income. Agreeing to pay for others' snacks, drinks, meals, or even trips to the movies was an effective way to maintain an alliance or demonstrate one's generosity. But, if a boy continually acquiesced to such demands, he risked more than just a loss of profit; he risked being perceived as a weak-willed "servant" who was unable to hold his own on the ghats.

Conclusion: Morals, Meanings, and Emotions in the Informal Tourist Economy

The tourist economy was indeed a moral economy regulated by a set of informal rules and shared expectations regarding "everyone's right to earn." Although the children did not always agree upon these rules, or adhere to them in practice, they all acknowledged that the pursuit of profit should be subordinated to other ends. The model of free-market competition and individual acquisition was not embraced as the proper way of doing business even if it did prove tempting at times.

Moreover, it was not just the pursuit of profit that was subordinated to a set of culturally shared understandings and expectations. To varying degrees, the children's spending and saving practices also fell under their sway. Girls tended to curb their individual consumption and give the majority of their earnings to their parents, thereby proving themselves as virtuous, self-sacrificing daughters. Boys, on the other hand, often spent a significant portion of the money they made. Although spending was central to the boys' attempts to establish working alliances with others on the ghats, it also reflected a more hedonistic approach to life that emphasized the importance of enjoying one's self and indulging in the pleasures of the city. Thus, earning, spending, and saving were intimately linked to the children's larger attempts to produce themselves as particular kinds of valued and respected subjects, and as we have seen, this process of self-production was gendered in very definite ways.

Finally, in order for the children to succeed in this economy it also helped if they were able to intuit tourists' feelings and desires. This was as much an affective economy as it was a moral one, and many of the children did attempt to increase their earnings by attuning themselves and their performances to the "sympathies" and "antipathies" of their customers. Yet what exactly did tourists desire? What did they want to consume in and through their interactions with these children? It is to these questions that I now turn.

7

Something Extra

Western tourists in Banaras, as we have seen, often had quite opposite experiences with the children on the riverfront. Many tourists came away feeling indebted to the children and they expressed their gratitude not only by purchasing their goods and services but also by taking the children on special outings, buying them gifts, and even sending them money and presents upon their return home. For instance, in commenting on his encounter with Mohan Mukherjee, Jorgen, a thirty-one-year-old Dutch tourist, remarked, "I know he is selling me something, but it doesn't feel like he is. There is something extra. I am very lucky that I met him!" Other tourists, however, left the city feeling assaulted and dehumanized. They complained bitterly that the children's relentless sales tactics had ruined their experience and had reduced them to the status of "walking dollar signs" or "cash cows." As Robert, a twenty-four-year-old Canadian tourist, remarked: "These kids are relentless. They make you feel like you are just a walking dollar sign. I don't want to go to the riverfront again! If I hear 'postcard,' 'postcard' one more time, I'm going to lose it!"

Though seemingly polarized, these reactions are more like two sides of the same coin, and they both speak to the topic that concerns me in this chapter: the elusive and often fraught nature of touristic consumption. In this chapter, I explore the "object" of consumption among Western tourists in Banaras. I ask: what exactly was the "something extra" that tourists sought to consume from these children? How was this "object" produced through the interactions, transactions, and performances of tourists and children on the ghats? How were tourists' desires for particular kinds of experiences both thwarted and enhanced by the misunderstandings and misrecognitions that so frequently animated these encounters? What does all of this suggest about the way that value was produced and consumed within this informal economy? And, what might these examples reveal about the changing nature of touristic consumption, both in Banaras and beyond?

Although we tend to feel awkward about putting children and sex in conversation with each other, in the discussion that follows I pursue these questions by drawing upon some of the ethnographic research that has been done on encounters between male customers and adult female entertainers and sex workers (Allison 1994; Bernstein 2007; Brennan 2004; Frank 2002). Some of this research explicitly theorizes men's visits to strip clubs and sex workers as a form of touristic consumption (Brennan 2004; Frank 2002), however there are other parallels, both conceptual and substantive, that warrant making such a comparison. These studies provide further insights into the affective dimensions of commercial exchange and the articulation of material and libidinal economies. They also provide some of the most nuanced attempts to analyze the production and consumption of particular kinds of experience. As I have been suggesting throughout this book and as I will argue here, for many tourists, the object of consumption had little to do with procuring guiding services or purchasing postcards and souvenirs. Rather, what tourists desired from their encounters with these children was a personal connection that would render both their experience of Banaras and their experience of themselves far more intimate and compelling.

Making It Personal

In her fascinating ethnography, *G-Strings and Sympathy*, Katherine Frank explores the political, economic, and psychocultural aspects of men's visits to strip clubs in the contemporary United States. Drawing upon John Urry's work on the tourist gaze, she theorizes men's visits to strip clubs as a form of "touristic practice" and "consumption" that involves the centrality of looking and "the seeking of experience through interactions" (Frank 2002, 28). "What the customers end up purchasing," Frank argues, "is an experience, an interactive fantasy through which a variety of different desires are produced and expressed" (24). In order to facilitate such experiences, Frank notes that the services offered in strip clubs "have become simultaneously more spectacular and more individualized." As she explains:

> The new individualized form of entertainment offered in the table dance and in the opportunity for one-on-one conversations with dancers means that one of the most significant services available in some of these clubs is extended personal interaction with a dancer. Now a dancer performs for her customers in a much more flexible manner, perhaps even radically changing her approach from one customer to the next. Most of her income is generated through these private performances rather than her

stage dancing. Many of these dancers are fairly steady employees of the clubs ("house dancers") rather than traveling performers ("features"), and there is thus an opportunity for the customers to return again and again to see a particular dancer: not because she is a headliner, but because of the kind of relationship that has developed between them. (Frank 2002, 27)

Influenced by David Harvey's writings on the shift from Fordism to flexible accumulation (Harvey 1990), Frank theorizes this new individualized form of entertainment, and this desire for more personal interactions, as a reflection of and response to the increasing "flexibility of the contemporary commodity form" that has come to characterize and mediate social and economic relations within the context of late capitalism. She argues, as Harvey does, that the regime of flexible accumulation has "been accompanied by accelerations in exchange and consumption" and has "led to a shift toward the consumption of 'ephemeral' services." "Strip clubs," she concludes, "provide a venue for a very particular kind of modern consumption, one that is based both on spectacle and on the commodification of an extremely ephemeral service—intimate interaction" (Frank 2002, 25).

Producing and consuming these intimate interactions involves a complex, varied, and at times, fraught process. As Frank writes, "Becoming and remaining a customer is a complicated process that is rife with ambivalence" (Frank 2002, 118). In part, this ambivalence stems from a pervasive cultural ideology that frowns upon paying for intimacy and views such practices as "desperate" or "inauthentic." In part, Frank suggests, it stems from the different desires and interests that motivate customers and dancers to participate in these encounters. This ambivalence is further engendered by the ambiguous power relations that animate these interactions. Frank argues that we must trace the "links between slippery fantasies and desire and more intractable power relationships" (154). With a keen ethnographic eye, however, she also demonstrates just how complex the issue of power can be in commodified sexualized transactions, particularly at the level of subjective experience. Within the "play space" of the strip club, it is "not simply a matter of one party or the other 'having' more power naturally, physically, financially, or emotionally" (154). Both parties may feel that they are empowered or disempowered, albeit in different ways, and this again can make the relationship between customer and performer simultaneously alluring yet difficult to sustain.

For tourists in Banaras, "becoming and remaining a customer" was also "a complex process rife with ambivalence," for many of the same reasons that Frank cites. Like strip club regulars, tourists too were hoping to establish personal relationships with the children on the riverfront that would enable them to have more intimate and individualized travel experiences. Moreover, like some of the strip club regulars Frank writes about, one of the primary ways tourists pursued this end was by giving these children gifts. Through engaging in acts of "symbolic exchange" (Baudrillard 1981), tourists tried to transcend their status as mere customers/consumers and seek personal connections with the children on the ghats. The following examples put this on display.

Gifting Chocolates and Consuming Relationships

Jacqueline was in her mid-fifties and worked as a language and literature teacher in France. As a young woman she had participated in a volunteer program to raise money for an Indian schooling project. Though she was eager to travel to India, she had a family, job, and children of her own, and Jacqueline did not make her first visit until she was in her late forties. Thereafter, she began traveling to India on an annual basis, spending three weeks of every February touring different parts of the country, sometimes alone, and sometimes escorting groups of students.

I was introduced to Jacqueline on a chilly February afternoon. She and Pramod were standing on the ghat and were involved in what looked like an uncomfortable conversation. Pramod was smiling as though he had just been caught doing something wrong, and Jacqueline's face was twisted with confusion and skepticism. As I was passing by, Pramod summoned me over to meet Jacqueline. Whether he did this as favor or as a diversion, I was not sure, but when I came up to say hello he immediately told Jacqueline that I was doing "research" on tourists and rather boldly insisted that she grant me an interview. Then, he quickly departed. Although somewhat bewildered by what had just transpired, Jacqueline was amenable, and we set up an appointment for the next day.

Jacqueline and I met the following afternoon at a rooftop restaurant. I learned that she was traveling with a female friend and that this was her second visit to the city of Banaras, which she described as "initially shocking" because of "all the pilgrims and so many people." Indeed, the initial "shock" of Banaras was something that tourists frequently emphasized when they spoke about their arrival to and experiences in the city, and for many it was also part of the allure. Instead of sequestering themselves in the upscale tourist enclave of the Cantonment Area and relying upon official tour guides to mediate their experience, they actively sought out the unpredictable and "heterogeneous" space (Edensor 1998) of the old city and riverfront, where they felt that had a better chance of being among and with "the people."[1]

About twenty minutes into our interview, I asked Jacqueline how she met Pramod. Her reply helped me understand why their interaction seemed so tense when I had encountered them on the ghat the day before. It also began to crystallize the sentiments and experiences that so many other tourists shared with me. As such, her account is worth exploring in detail:

J: We met Pramod one day on the ghat and we talked and we wanted to go by boat with him and we fixed a meeting for the next day but he was not there. And I had, because I had some chocolate from home I brought chocolates for him because it was the *only* thing I had, because he was nice, he did not ask for money. Tourists in India are usually treated like walking dollar signs, but we had a nice relationship and because he wasn't there I was very disappointed. I felt, *trumpe, trumpe* because my feeling went out to him, and I got nothing back. [In an animated and upset voice] And so he wasn't there and I ate all the chocolates because I was upset! And we met him two days after and I asked him and he told me, "I came," but I don't think he came. So I said, "I don't understand, we were here at the meeting point and we waited for a half an hour." So I was disappointed because when you speak a long time with somebody and they are nice, they explain, and I understand [pause] because I am a tourist in India, so for me to meet Indian people is very important but for him he sees so many it doesn't matter. We need a relationship with Indian people because if you don't have a relationship it's not an interesting travel. We need Indians much more than they need us. They need our money. I think that we consume relationships, we need Indian relationships, if you go to India and you have no relationships [pause]. Why do people agree to pay somebody who is nice? It is normal, they give [pause]. But also when there is money involved you are not sure if it is something true or not, that's why it is so difficult with money, because you cannot [pause]. So I don't know; it's very difficult.

JH: So you think that money makes it uncertain?

J: It depends on the way it, for example, if you, if somebody lets you feel that he wants only your money, and first money, but if first he is nice with you, at the end, you know that he needs money and he is nice and you want to give him, but immediately, it's more difficult and you don't know what he wants to give you, it's very, very difficult.

The intensely emotional nature of Jacqueline's response was rendered manifest not only in what Jacqueline said but in how she said it. Her speech was punctuated with excited flair-ups, deliberating pauses, and incomplete thoughts, and as we spoke, it seemed as though she was actually struggling to figure out why this encounter had left her so dismayed.

Jacqueline's remarks move from an account of what happened, to an explanation of why it happened, to a series of broader reflections on her status as a tourist and interactions with people in India. Beginning with the first dimension, Jacqueline reported that she and her friend met Pramod on the ghat, spoke with him for a while, and then agreed to meet him the following day for a boat ride. Jacqueline arrived bearing chocolates for Pramod; however, when he failed to show up, Jacqueline devoured the sweets in a fit of disappointment. Within the first part of her account, therefore, several questions emerge. First of all, what was Jacqueline's gift of chocolates supposed to symbolize or secure? Why did she bring them to India in the first place? And, why did she want to give them to a boy whom she had just met the day before, proclaiming that it was "the only thing" she had to offer him?

It is significant, and not at all unusual, that Jacqueline brought chocolates with her to India. Elsewhere, I have discussed the way that guidebooks continually frame India as a place for giving (Huberman 2006) and many guidebooks explicitly instruct tourists to bring small items such as candy or pens to hand out to children. In this case, however, Jacqueline's offer went beyond a mere handout and was motivated by feelings of appreciation and indebtedness. As Jacqueline remarked, Pramod "was nice, he did not ask for money." In other words, from Jacqueline's perspective, Pramod had already "gifted" her with the courtesy of not treating her like a tourist, or in her words, as "a walking dollar sign," and this surprising gesture was itself significant enough to stir Jacqueline's feelings and make her want to reciprocate. However, because Jacqueline viewed money as a potential stumbling block to a "nice relationship," and an uncomfortable reminder of her status as a tourist, she required a different medium through which to return his kindness: chocolates from home. If the gift of chocolates symbolized Jacqueline's feelings of gratitude and her desires to further her relationship with Pramod, her ultimate consumption of the sweets may be read as a self-consoling attempt to "digest" her disappointment when the reciprocity did break down and she received "nothing back" in return.

In the second part of her narrative, Jacqueline shifted from an account of what happened to an explanation of why it happened. From Jacqueline's viewpoint, the disappointing encounter was hardly the product of a personality clash or a casual misunderstanding. Rather, it reflected the way that she, as a Western tourist, and Pramod, as an Indian whose life was inundated with tourists, were differentially positioned in regards to a larger set of interests and antagonisms. According to Jacqueline, while tourists longed to develop relationships with Indians who could make their travel experiences unique and interesting, boys like Pramod, her comments imply, sought to extract the same homogenous substance from all of them.

Thus, as Frank observed, within these transactions, particularly at the level of subjective experience, it was "not simply a matter of one party or the other 'having' more power naturally, physically, financially, or emotionally" (Frank 2002, 154). Rather, the power dynamics that animated these encounters were more subtle and complex. Although Jacqueline was positioned as the "First-World, wealthy" foreign tourist, she clearly felt that she was at a disadvantage. Boys like Pramod could easily pursue another tourist if the prospects at hand did not look profitable. However, travelers like Jacqueline became emotionally invested in these relationships. They "needed" them, for they not only played upon the traveler's desire to be seen as something other than a tourist but they also provided the critical link between the tourist and his or her "passage" to India: as Jacqueline queried, if tourists went to India but had "no relationships," then what? Had they really seen or experienced the country? Jacqueline thus identified "the relationship" as the object of touristic consumption, and in so doing she suggested that the relationship itself functioned as a *sign* of an authentic experience of India.

In his writings on consumption, the theorist Jean Baudrillard famously argued that, properly understood, the object of consumption is always a sign. Indeed, Baudrillard maintained that despite what consumers might tell themselves or others, people do not purchase goods for their utility or use value, which, he argued, is merely an "alibi," but rather for their sign value: for their capacity to mark and locate the consumer within a social field of recognized differences (Baudrillard 1981). Indeed, for Baudrillard, consumption is basically a process whereby consumers use money to purchase or "appropriate" signs from an already existing system or "code" so that they may communicate their position and status to others.[2] As he wrote:

> An object specified by its trademark, charged with differential connotations of status, prestige and fashion. *This* is the "object of consumption." . . . The object does not assume meaning either in a symbolic relation with the subject (the Object) or in an operational relation to the world (object-as-implement): it finds meanings with other objects, in difference, according to a hierarchical code of significations. . . . Instead of abolishing itself in the relation that it establishes, and thus assuming symbolic value (as in the example of the gift), the object becomes autonomous, intransitive, opaque and so begins to signify the abolition of the relationship. (Baudrillard 1981, 64–65)

Baudrillard's argument deserves consideration here for two reasons. First, like Jacqueline, many tourists suggested that "relationships" with local people provided the ultimate sign of a more authentic and, thereby, more distinctive and prestigious experience of India. Indeed, in his study of backpackers in India, Tim Edensor notes that relationships with local people, rather than visits to "famous sites," provide these travelers with a "distinct form of cultural capital" that enables them to cast their experiences as more authentic, off-the-beaten-path, and unique (Edensor 1998, 178). However, Baudrillard's argument is also worth revisiting because it seems incapable of providing an adequate framework for conceptualizing and analyzing the object of consumption among tourists like Jacqueline. In their efforts to "consume relationships," these tourists were not pursuing sign objects that already existed within a code of differences and were readily available for "appropriation." Rather, like the experiences Frank writes about, they were produced in and through personal interactions.

Moreover, in order for these relationships to take on the status of sign objects, they had to first be experienced as gratifying; that is, their "use value," far from being "an alibi," was the very condition of possibility for them becoming compelling signs. This was rendered clear in the last part of Jacqueline's remarks, when she explained that on the one hand, it was "normal" and perhaps inevitable (at least when one is a tourist in India), to pay for relationships, "to pay somebody who is nice." On the other hand, however, she pointed out that as soon as money was involved it became increasingly difficult for the tourist to sustain his or her fantasy of creating a "true" relationship. At such moments, money emerged as an unsettling signifier that discouraged tourists from following their hearts and forced them to acknowledge that they were still immersed in a highly commodified system of exchange.[3]

If the act of payment threatened to obliterate the very object that tourists wanted to consume, how then, was this tension reconciled? How did tourists pay for something that, from their perspective, was not supposed to have a price tag on it (Zelizer 1985, 1994)? And, how did the children whom they encountered on the ghats facilitate this process and help them feel as though they were developing qualitatively unique relationships and were not just involved in generic business transactions?

In many cases, these tensions did prove insurmountable, and the encounter culminated with tourists feeling utterly disenchanted and the children on the ghats complaining about "stingy foreigners" who did not pay them enough. However, as Jacqueline's remarks also suggest, there were ways of reconciling these antagonisms. Through skillful performances and a keen sense of timing, the children on the ghats could make tourists feel as though they came first: the money was not a payment demanded by the children, but rather a *gift*, lovingly bestowed upon them through the tourists' own initiative and feelings of gratitude and generosity.

For instance, as I discussed in chapter 6, the children's strategy of first "making friendship" clearly played upon tourists' longings to be seen and treated as more than dollar signs. However, it also accommodated tourists' desire to feel in control of these encounters and to preserve the power of being able to decide when, where, and how much they would give. As John Hutnyk has remarked in his excellent study of low-budget travelers and volunteer tourism in Calcutta: "the Western visitor has the power to give and yet also fake the gift, and abandon the effort when the demand becomes too much" (Hutnyk 1996, 209).

Paradoxically, therefore, although many tourists longed to have "real" relationships with these children, the relationship itself required a certain amount of "misrecognition" (Bourdieu 1980) in order for it to develop. In some situations, as will be seen below, tourists derived an immense amount of pleasure and sense of empowerment by being able to reward or punish these children with money, and as Frank observed among strip club regulars, "flaunt their social status—either to themselves or to others" (Frank 2002, 194). But many tourists, Jacqueline included, did not want to acknowledge such asymmetries, or discover that they were the kind of people who would use purchasing power as a way of coercing good behavior or affection from these children. Thus, although Jacqueline may have been correct to identify the personal relationship as the object of touristic consumption, the relationship that was produced and desired in these encounters was not just one between the tourist and the Indian child. It was also one between the tourist and his or her *self*. These encounters often took on significance precisely because they enabled tourists to pursue idealized or "fantasized identities" (197).

Benevolent Benefactors

One of the most commonly recurring "fantasized identities" that tourists pursued was that of the benevolent benefactor. As John Hutnyk has pointed out, many backpackers come to India with the expressed intention to "help the poor."[4] At the time of my research, Banaras was not a major hub for volunteer tourism. Nor, to some tourists' dismay, did it have the kind of "poverty appeal" of other major cities such as Kolkata or Mumbai, which were known for their sprawling slums. However, many of the tourists I encountered did arrive in the city with a host of charitable sentiments, and their encounters with the children on the ghats often provided them with an opportunity to express and act upon these feelings. In some cases, the touristic desire to do good took a very playful form and involved treating the children to fun outings or buying them presents such as new clothes. In other cases, it involved imparting moral lessons to these children. Finally, in some situations these encounters did morph into full-blown charity cases, where tourists sought to financially help, educate, or "rescue" these children from a life of "poverty" and "disadvantage." In all of these instances the children, of course, also played a role in facilitating, or alternatively, interrupting tourists' desires and fantasies, and this, in turn, inevitably influenced the kinds of rewards and compensation they received.

Sara

Sara was a twenty-nine-year-old nurse from Canada, and she was working as a volunteer at a clinic in Nepal. In the spring of 2000 she came to Banaras for a two-week vacation, anticipating that it would be "the perfect place" to celebrate the festival of Holi. She took up residence in a low-budget guest house near the ghat and, as she put it, spent most of her time "palling around" with the children on the riverfront, treating them to "goodies" in the bazaar, and buying them "small gifts." Indeed, during her stay, there was rarely an occasion when I encountered Sara without a child on her arm. At the end of her visit, when I asked Sara how she had enjoyed her time in Banaras, she replied with a chuckle: "It's been great, I've spent two weeks here, four hundred dollars, and now I've got about twenty foster kids!"

Of these "twenty foster kids," Sara had developed a particular fondness for Sharmila's daughters, whom she had initially encountered selling postcards and diyas on the ghats. "These girls," Sara told me during our interview, "have totally made my stay here, I've gone to their house, I've met their parents, I've gotten a real insight into their lives!" The day before Holi, Sara decided to take Jaila, Ritthi, and Seenu shopping for new outfits.[5] Recounting their shopping excursion, Sara remarked: "I would have preferred to spend the money on something more useful for them, but of course every little girl wants a pretty dress! I remember how much I loved getting a new dress when I was little. When we were in the store Ritthi was petting and kissing this one dress which was ughh, very frilly and way too much like Western duds but eventually she found a different one, but I bought *salwar kurtas* for Jaila and Seenu, I just can't resist little kids in a *salwar kurta!*"

Sara's shopping trip enabled her to act out and even relive a number of fantasies. Not only was she able to vicariously experience the childhood pleasure and excitement of receiving a new dress, but she was also able to step into the role of the nurturing and even indulgent mother who spoils her children with unnecessary gifts. Moreover, by steering the girls away from the "Western duds" and ultimately outfitting them in traditional India garb, Sara was able to refashion their images in ways she found more aesthetically pleasing and, perhaps more important, in ways that enabled her to better sustain her own fantasies of an "authentic" India. Although Sara noted that spending $400 in two weeks was an "extravagance" for her, particularly given her "austere" volunteer lifestyle and budget in Nepal, one might argue that with the "twenty foster kids" she accumulated, her money did go a very long way.

Marion

Compared to Sara, Marion had a much more ambivalent experience. Marion came to Banaras in late January of 2001. I met her one morning in the e-mail shop near my guest house. She was with Pramod and Harsha, who had escorted her to the shop and were waiting with her while she checked her e-mail. Because the Internet server was so slow, Marion and I ended up having a lengthy conversation while we waited for our messages to download. Before I left the shop, I asked Marion if I could interview her. She agreed, and we set up an appointment for the following afternoon.

Marion worked as "political organizer" in California and was in her mid-fifties. She had three daughters, two grandchildren, and was entering into her thirty-fourth year of marriage with her second husband. This was her second trip to India, and she was traveling alone. At the time of our interview she had already been in Banaras for three days. Marion told me that she came to the city because everyone kept telling her "you haven't seen India until you have seen Varanasi!"

As was the case with many tourists, Marion's arrival to the city got off to a rather rough start. Equipped with a 1997 *Lonely Planet* guidebook, she knew exactly which guest house along the riverfront she wanted to go to. However, when she descended into "the swarm" of rickshaw drivers outside the train station, most of them told her that it no longer existed or that she would be happier someplace else. Finally, Marion found a driver who said he could take her to her desired destination, but when he ended up delivering her to a different guest house, Marion "exploded in a fit of anger," refused to pay the driver, and then stormed off looking for another place to stay. During her search, she stopped at a roadside restaurant for a drink. It was there that she encountered Pramod and Harsha:

> The good thing of the afternoon was I ran into two young men, I will say young men, teenagers, one twelve and one fifteen, and they were just as sharp as little tacks, and after talking to them for a while they asked me if I wanted to go for a sunset boat ride, and the price sounded right and I liked the both of them by that time and I said, "Sure, sure." And so we went out and we had a great time. I figured they were going to take me to somewhere where there was a group of other tourists going on the boat, but I guess they have an arrangement with someone who has a boat and they can take it out on their own and then they split the money with the owner of the boat. They thought I was going to be upset because they were taking some of the money and I said, "No, no, no, I would be upset if you *weren't* getting paid money to do this!" and I said, "It's fair, you worked hard" and I gave them an additional tip. I think it's very important to let people know when you appreciate them. At one point, I pulled out pictures of me and my family to show them. I showed them my grandson who is as short as them and the same age, and I had one small picture of myself and my husband and [imitating their voices] "Can I have picture, can I have picture of you?" And then they started fighting over who was going to have the picture and I don't think they would do that if they didn't really have an interest in who *I* am, you know? So I wrote on the back my name and the date and said it was up to them who was going to keep it. At the end, I told them that I would like to see some sights, and that I would like them to show me around, that I would like their company to do it. So they're going to take me out again tomorrow.

As was the case with Jacqueline, Marion's account also demonstrates just how quickly tourists came to feel indebted to the children for their simple gestures of kindness, sincerity, and goodwill. Given the rough start that Marion and so many other tourists had in the city, these seemingly unremarkable acts could take on a rather extraordinary significance for Western tourists. Indeed, several tourists narrated stories where the children seemed to "miraculously appear" to cheer them up after an aggravating experience or emerged "just at the right time" to help them find their way when they were lost.

Second, Marion's remarks suggest that money was not always construed by tourists as a sign of an inauthentic or highly commodified relationship. Indeed, in this context the "additional tip" not only enabled Marion to express her gratitude to these boys. It also enabled her to impart a moral lesson about the virtues of honesty, fairness, and hard work. Furthermore, Marion's remarks again draw attention to the ways tourists both actively sought out and attempted to produce much more personalized travel experiences and interactions. Like Marion, many of the tourists I encountered brought family photos with them as a way "to break the ice," or "have a more human exchange" with the people they met on their travels.[6] In Marion's case, this led to a profound moment of recognition. Much to her delight, the boys began "fighting over" who was going to have her picture, and in celebrity fashion, Marion even autographed the picture before she gave it to the boys to keep.

For Marion, the boys' excited reaction was proof that they were interested in her, and one of the subtexts of her comments seems to be: "I like working with somebody who appreciates *me*." Thus, for Marion, it was not just the thrill of discovery or the desire for an authentic Other that animated her interactions with these children. It was also the thrill of being discovered and being recognized by the children as an object of interest and desire.[7] In fact, after spending just one afternoon with the boys, Marion felt so good that she had already placed them on her "shopping list." As she went on to explain with a lighthearted laugh:

M: One of them, probably two of them are already on my shopping list.
JH: What do you mean by your shopping list?
M: Well there's a couple of people . . . I have one person who I'm buying binoculars for, one person a Swiss Army knife and you know a couple of watches, and when I give my word, my word is you know, something I'm going to follow through with, and I met one nice young man in Gokarna, and I had a Swiss Army knife with me and he wanted one and I said it was a gift from my husband and I can't give away presents and he agreed with me and I said, "Well, I will send you one." So that's what I mean about my shopping list. But these boys, they're a real kick, great personalities, they're funny, they're sharp, you know they're trying, they're going to make it. They have a real . . .

you know some people have a really good sense of balance and of life and in spite of whatever they have had to deal with; they're great kids!

For Marion, making good on her shopping list was clearly a way of demonstrating that she was a woman of her word. I suspect it was also a way for her to express her more charitable sentiments for, as she suggested several times throughout our interview, despite their upbeat and "great personalities," it seemed clear these boys had been forced "to deal with" a lot of misfortune in their lives. However, as was the case with Jacqueline, Sara, and so many others, Marion also used these acts of symbolic exchange—that is, the giving of gifts that were deemed inseparable from the relationships they established (Baudrillard 1981) to create more personalized and "distinct" travel experiences. Indeed, in Marion's case this culminated with a shopping list that provided a virtual map of all the people rather than places she had visited in India—thus begging the question: Was Marion shopping *for* these people, or was she shopping for *people*?

The day after our interview, an incident occurred that dramatically reconfigured Marion's experience and that forced her to reconsider her shopping list. It was the festival day of Basant Panchami, and across the city children were out flying kites in celebration of the coming spring. It was a beautiful sunny morning, and I was on my way to have tea when I encountered Marion standing in the middle of the street outside of my guest house with tears running down her face. Her voice was shaky and distraught. The woman who seemed so chipper and full of life the day before now appeared deflated and forlorn. Sensing Marion's distress, I asked her if she would like to join me. She graciously accepted my invitation and we headed off to a rooftop restaurant where we could talk without interruption and where we could still enjoy the kites that were being flown from rooftops across the city.

Once we were settled at the table Marion began to tell me why she was so upset. According to Marion, Pramod and Harsha had agreed to take her sightseeing that day and they had even fixed a price of 100 rupees. However, when Marion went to the ghats to meet the boys they informed her that they had changed their minds. According to Marion, they said, "We want to stay here and earn money to buy string for our kites; if we go with a different customer we can earn more money; there is one man who will give us 500 rupees, and if we go with you we will only get 100." With this rejection, Marion and her vacation experience quickly unraveled. Reflecting upon what had gone wrong, she remarked: "I don't know if I offended them with the money, I know that money is an issue, and then I thought, well, if they can make 500 rupees from another customer and if they can afford to give up my 100 then they must not need it so much. I just don't understand what happened. Yesterday we had such a good time together!" In her struggle to understand what went wrong, it is clear that Marion still needed to resist certain explanations. Couched in between her admissions of not being able to comprehend the situation, Marion entertained possibilities that were still too painful for her to fully embrace: her encounter with the boys really was a business transaction; money was not only an issue, but it was *the* issue; Marion was not a friend, but just another customer.[8]

Marion's experience was far from idiosyncratic. Throughout my fieldwork I came across many other tourists who walked away from such encounters in tears. Even those who did not express their distress so visibly seemed very familiar with the feelings of disappointment—and in some cases, I would even go so far as to say devastation—that these encounters could generate. Sometimes, I shared Marion's story with other travelers. For instance, in my interview with Jay, a thirty-four-year-old tourist from the United States (see chapter 4), I asked him why he thought Marion had become so upset by the boys' refusal to accompany her: "Because she is probably only here for a couple of days, or a week or whatever and she wants to experience it, she's on the deadline and she felt like if she put in her couple of rupees she could at least break the ice and after that point it wouldn't be a matter of money, you know and she got upset because she found out the reality. The reality is that if you try and play with the kids there's always going to be a price. You know they're just going to break your heart or piss you off, one or the other."

Comparatively, Jay was far more of a cynic than Marion, and he was proud of his ability to discern the "reality" of such encounters—much the same way as Frank's male strip club regulars pride themselves on "not being duped" into believing they are having authentic exchanges with strippers (Frank 2002, 182). As "a seasoned traveler" who was "not about to be made anyone's fool," Jay noted that he was "suspicious of all the people" he encountered in India. However, what I find interesting about Jay's remarks is that even though he claimed to be impervious to "these obviously contrived relationships" he, too, was able to quickly diagnose the "heartbreak" and anger that these encounters so frequently generated. The real price that tourists had to pay when they got involved with these children, he suggested, was not extracted in rupees or dollars, but rather in hurt feelings and pain.

Jorgen

Whereas Jay proposed that personal connections could help compensate for the limited time that tourists had to spend in each destination (thereby implying that when it came to travel, depth mattered more than duration), for many other travelers personal connections became the reason for extending their stay in the city. Such was the case with Jorgen, who was also introduced briefly in chapter 4 and whom I quoted at the outset of this chapter. Jorgen was a thirty-one-year-old computer network designer from the Netherlands, and he also was traveling alone. He arrived in Banaras in early May of 2000, having already spent several weeks touring in the south. Initially, Jorgen had intended to stay in Banaras for three or four days, but after meeting and befriending Mohan his plans changed, and he ended up staying over a week. Jorgen's encounter with Mohan provides a another compelling example of the way Western tourists attempted to cast themselves as benevolent benefactors and pursue more intimate and personalized travel experiences through their encounters with the children on the riverfront. Here, I want to consider this case study in detail.

Jorgen met Mohan the day he arrived in Banaras. He was sitting along the ghats sipping tea when Mohan approached him and began asking him questions. As Jorgen recounted:

J: I was sitting having tea and we started talking, and the way he was talking he sounded like a nice boy, so I talked back.

JH: What was he saying?

J: I don't really remember. It was small talk, like you get all the time, "What's your name?" "Where do you come from?" "What do you do for a profession?" "Are you married?" The standard set of questions. But the way he was talking, I mean, I had been talking to others at that moment also, I met a lot of people on the ghats, kids also, while walking around with my backpack on my shoulders, who asked the same questions but in their voice you heard their intent that they weren't interested in the answers, they were only interested in capturing my attention and taking me along to the place where they wanted to take me. And when I was sitting down talking to Mohan he gave me the impression that he wanted to talk to me only for the talking and not for taking me anywhere. And only later in the conversation he started talking about all of the nice places in Varanasi that you could visit and that he could take me there whenever I wanted and after I think an hour or maybe an hour and a half of talking there, we made an appointment for meeting the next day, maybe at nine o'clock in the morning or something and he would show me around, and that's actually what happened. And I went there and I made sure I was on time and from that moment on he showed me Varanasi city.

Jorgen's encounter with Mohan again illustrates that "how exchanges are conducted in markets are as relevant to the 'value' of something as what is being bought and sold" (Cook 2008, 7).[9] Mohan's mastery over the genre of "small talk," and his ability to "re-accentuate" (Bakhtin 1986, 79) "the standard set of questions" and convey a sense of intimate interest not only made Jorgen feel special but it also set Mohan apart from the homogenous echo of veiled business propositions that Jorgen had grown so tired of. Jorgen detected a special quality in Mohan's voice and behavior, and instead of immediately presenting Jorgen with offers to guide him around the city, Mohan had the insight to wait until they had established a good rapport. From the outset, Jorgen was aware that Mohan was not the most knowledgeable guide whom he could have selected. Indeed, most of the time Jorgen had to inform Mohan about the places they visited by reading to him from his guidebook. However, as I noted earlier, Jorgen actually "preferred" having a child guide him because he feared that an adult would be "much more difficult to control."

During Jorgen's eight-day stay, Mohan was by his side from morning until night. As he explained, "The only thing I have had to do by myself since I arrived in Banaras was find a guest house. Since then he's helped me with everything." Mohan mediated all of Jorgen's transactions, from getting his laundry done, to arranging boating and sightseeing excursions, to accompanying him for meals, to managing the other children on the ghats who wanted to sell Jorgen their goods or ask him for money. Despite complaining that so many of the children on the ghats "were simply after [his] money," Jorgen seemed to delight in flaunting his wealth in front of them. Every evening he would come to the puja with Mohan and break out a thick wad of rupees to disperse to the children, asking Mohan to tell him which children were "worthy" and "really in need." In fact, after a few days of this, Mohan confided in me: "Jenny *Didi*, Jorgen has spent so much money in Banaras, every time someone comes up to him he gives him 50, 100 rupees!"[10]

Like Marion, Jorgen also used monetary rewards to teach the children moral lessons. For instance, recalling an incident from the day before he remarked:

J: Yesterday I was on the ghat with Mohan and Pramod. I don't like this other boy Pramod much. I don't think he's a very nice kid. I was sitting on the ghats and a little beggar boy was trying to sell me a flower and that boy Pramod was being so mean to him and giving him such a hard time that I ended up giving the little beggar boy fifty rupees just for one flower. Then later on we were going to eat dinner and Pramod asked if he could come and I said "No, I did not like the way you treated that little beggar boy."

Here again, Jorgen's remarks reveal the kinds of assumptions that animated tourists' interpretations of the children on the riverfront. Though this child was selling diyas, Jorgen assumed that he was a "beggar," and he was deeply disturbed by Pramod's apparent lack of compassion for this apparently destitute child. To teach Pramod a lesson, therefore, Jorgen overcompensated the boy who was selling the "flower" and denied Pramod "the privilege" of coming along for dinner.

When it came to his dealings with Mohan, Jorgen's rewards were also disbursed on a conditional basis. Indeed, the primary condition seemed to be Mohan's capacity to accommodate and satisfy Jorgen's desires. For instance, from the very first day of "their arrangement," as Jorgen put it, Jorgen claimed that he was keenly aware that he would be paying Mohan for more than just his guiding services. As Jorgen remarked:

J: The first day I asked him, "You are going to guide me, what is it going to cost me?" And he told me, "I'm not guiding you for money, I'm guiding you because I would like to be your friend and I want to build up a friendship." At that moment I realized that it would cost me more, eventually, than it would cost me if he had just named his price. But he seemed like a nice kid and I thought, "If you're doing this out of friendship then either this friendship is going to develop and I'm going to like you and I won't mind paying you more than I would pay for a guide, or I'm not going to like you and then there will be no friendship and there will be no reason for you to ask me for money." And indeed it has developed as a friendship and I think it's going to cost me more than it would have cost me otherwise. And I'm comfortable with that, it doesn't matter. Because now there is also the aspect that I know a little bit about his life, and I think I know why he wants the money, why he needs it, and I know it's much easier for me to earn that money and give it to him than it would ever be for him. I'm giving him a little, whereas it's a lot for him.

In certain respects, Jorgen's remarks recall Elizabeth Bernstein's discussion of "bounded authenticity." In *Temporarily Yours: Intimacy, Authenticity and the Commerce of Sex*, Bernstein argues that we have entered "a brave new world of commercially available intimate encounters that are subjectively normalized for sex workers and clients alike" (Bernstein 2007, 7). Instead of just selling sexual services, female sex workers increasingly market themselves as "girlfriends" for hire, who provide customers with intimate experiences that satisfy their desires for authentic, yet circumscribed relationships.

Mohan, for instance, was clearly prepared to offer his friendship for hire, and Jorgen was clearly prepared to pay for it. Although Mohan made a conscious effort to demonstrate that he was not interested in money, Jorgen immediately recognized the financial implications of this "friendly" gesture. Mohan's opening maneuver was successful, therefore, not because it was convincing but rather because, like Bernstein's informants, Jorgen did not view paying for friendship and intimacy as an untenable contradiction. Indeed, his response also recalls Viviana Zelizer's discussion of "the sacrilization effect." Arguing against theories of commercialization that posit an inherent contradiction between a monetary economy and personal values, Zelizer examines "the processes by which values shape price" and invest them with social, religious, or sentimental meaning (Zelizer 1985). For Jorgen, "the conversion" of feelings into quantifiable amounts of cash became a testimony to the successful development and value of their friendship rather than a detriment. Moreover, within this encounter, and so many others that I observed, the sacrilization effect was itself augmented by favorable exchange rates for tourists. The disparity between the value of tourists' currencies and the Indian rupee provided a powerful incentive for Jorgen and other travelers to translate their feelings of generosity and kindness into monetary rewards. As Jorgen remarked, "I'm giving him a little, whereas it's a lot for him." In fact, many travelers, Jorgen included, exhibited an almost obsessive interest in calculating "how rich" they were in India, and this could prompt them to engage in acts of charity that would have been unthinkable for them at home.[11]

Although Mohan initially refused to speak about money with Jorgen, after a few days he did broach the subject. Instead of requesting to be paid for his guiding services, however, Mohan asked Jorgen to give him 4,000 rupees for his "schooling fees." To Mohan's dismay and concern, Jorgen did become suspicious and the following morning Jorgen arrived at my guest house to "verify" why Mohan required the money.[12] He instructed Mohan to wait outside while we talked. "I know you are familiar with his situation and you know his family," he began. "Do you think this is a reasonable request?" It was not the first time that a tourist had come to me to "verify" a child's request and as had been the case before, I tried to stay out of the matter. I told Jorgen that I was not in a position to assess whether or not Mohan needed the money for school, and that the decision was one he would have to make on his own. Looking dissatisfied with my answer, Jorgen thanked me and left.

About two hours later, Jorgen and Mohan returned. Jorgen informed me that he was going to give Mohan the money but certain conditions needed to be met first. "I am only going to give him half of the amount now," he said, "and then I will send him the rest when I return home. Also, I already told Mohan that I want to hand the money over directly to his parents so we are going to his house for lunch." Jorgen and Mohan asked if I would come along in case they need me "to translate" and I agreed.

I showed Jorgen the way to the house while Mohan ran ahead to pick up a few supplies and prepare his mother for our visit. By the time we climbed the narrow steps leading up to the small, cramped room where Mohan, his brother, sister, and parents lived, Mohan was already there unpacking some fruits, sweets, and yogurt that he had purchased in honor of Jorgen's visit. Mohan's mother, Devika, was leaning over the pressure cooker, which sat atop a single gas cylinder on the floor. When we entered Devika greeted Jorgen with a *namaste* and pleasant smile, eyeing him from head to toe, and motioned for Jorgen, who was a very tall man, to be seated on the double bed that occupied almost all of the space in the tiny room. Mohan sat next to him, and Jorgen put his arm around Mohan, incredulously marveling at the size of the living space that was shared by a family of five.

Jorgen spoke graciously to Devika. He told her how pleased he was to come to their home and praised her for having raised such a "wonderful son." Devika was not the kind of woman who was easily swayed by flattery and, with her sardonic sense of humor, she quickly replied, "Good, you take this useless boy back with you!" When I translated this to Jorgen he laughed but then, with a more serious expression, he reached into his pocket and pulled out a thick wad of fifty-rupee bills, which he began counting out in front of us. When he reached 2,000 he separated the notes from the rest of the fold, put the remainder back in his pocket, and then, in a voice beaming with pride, almost as though he were expecting a drum roll, he remarked, "This is for Mohan's future!"

He extended the money to Devika who was sitting next to me on the floor, and waited for her to take it. For Jorgen, it was clearly a grand and meaningful moment and I sensed he was a bit let down when Devika countered with a sincere, yet not overwhelmingly emotional thank you. Jorgen quickly began to explain that he was going to send Mohan more money when he got home, and he was making plans to open a bank account for Mohan so that he would be able to wire the money from Holland. In addition to the original 4,000 rupees that Mohan had requested, Jorgen had decided that he would try to send Mohan some money every couple of months to help him. Devika insisted that a money order would be much better, but Jorgen maintained that it would be more expensive and more difficult for him to transfer funds that way. For a while, the technicalities of the arrangement were discussed and debated, and when the topic was finally exhausted, Devika served us lunch.

Jorgen and Mohan ate together on the bed (something unthinkable in their everyday family life), and afterward, they stretched out and watched an old movie on the black-and-white television set that was propped up in the corner. Mohan presented Jorgen with a carved wooden frog "to remember" him and Jorgen was delighted with the gift. While Mohan and Jorgen rested on the bed, I spoke with Devika. She was still very concerned about how the money would actually arrive from Holland and she was not pleased about having to go through the procedure of opening a new bank account for her son.

Although Jorgen had already extended his stay and was supposed to depart the next day, he postponed his plans once again. In the wake of his visit to Mohan's home, or what Dean MacCannell would describe as his glimpse "backstage" (MacCannell 1976), Jorgen's determination to help Mohan financially had taken on a new urgency. Not only had he "upped the ante" by offering to send Mohan money every couple of months, but he seemed almost obsessed with making sure that "all the arrangements" were, as he put it, "properly in place" before his departure. On his final evening in Banaras, Jorgen, Mohan, and I had dinner together. "I've spent the whole day running around to make sure everything is just right," Jorgen informed me. "I have even set up an e-mail account for Mohan so we will be able to keep in touch." When I asked Jorgen how he felt about his visit and his decision to give Mohan the money, he began shaking his head from side to side and with a smile spread wide across his face he replied, "I feel *really* good about this, *really* good!" The next day, he was gone.

Why was this encounter so gratifying for Jorgen? What was he looking for and what did he find? It is obvious that Mohan was at the center of Jorgen's experience in Banaras, or rather that he *was* Jorgen's experience of Banaras. Although other tourists suggested that personal relationships could help compensate for the limited amount of time that a tourist spends in a particular destination, in Jorgen's case, the relationship itself became the reason for extending his stay from three or four days to over a week.

During our many conversations, Jorgen noted that he had little contact with children at home. Despite this lack of experience, however, from the very beginning of their relationship Jorgen responded to Mohan in a very paternalistic manner. Having spent a considerable amount of time observing their interactions, I was struck, and honestly rather disturbed, by the way Jorgen so quickly insinuated himself as a fatherlike figure. This was something that was common with other tourists as well, but in Jorgen's case it was even more extreme. His demeanor toward Mohan was protective, affectionate, and yet also authoritative. He was constantly advising Mohan on what he should and should not do. For instance, after his encounter with Pramod and "the beggar boy" on the ghats, Jorgen instructed Mohan that he should not spend time with Pramod because Pramod was a "bad boy." In other instances, he would reprimand Mohan for behavior he felt was risky or inappropriate, as when Mohan was leaning "dangerously" out of the auto rickshaw on one of our tours around the city. Moreover, in assuming this right to monitor and control Mohan's behavior, Jorgen not only established himself as a fatherlike figure, but he also asserted his rights as a consumer who was going to make sure that he got what he paid for, even if it meant transgressing boundaries and demanding access to private spaces and relationships, such as Mohan's parents and home. As he noted in one of our conversations: "If he asks me for more money for school, I'm going to ask him for proof that he's going to spend it on school." Unlike the customers that Bernstein writes about, therefore, Jorgen did demand full disclosure, and the boundaries of their relationship had to be pushed beyond a brief circumscribed encounter in order for Jorgen to authenticate it.

Jorgen's encounter with Mohan was clearly overdetermined by a much broader set of relationships and representations. While Jorgen noted that he was initially drawn to Mohan because he seemed to stand out from the rest of the children who had approached him with guiding offers, by the end of his stay, Mohan had emerged as the "classic" charity case and Jorgen the paradigmatic Western benefactor who delivers aid, technology, and education to the "less advanced" peoples of the world. It was a common "script" that tourists pursued and enacted in their interactions with these children. However, in Jorgen's case the attraction to this role also seemed to be motivated by more personal reasons, as well. In many of our conversations, Jorgen talked at length about the extremely fraught relationship he had with his own father, who had passed away several years before. As he remarked rather sheepishly one afternoon, "I know it sounds terrible but I am glad that my father died."

Perhaps it might be pushing the analysis too far, or rather too deep, to argue that Jorgen unconsciously sought to resolve his conflicts with his father by establishing a paternalistic relationship with Mohan—but I certainly would not want to discount such possibilities, either. For many tourists these children did become "objects of psychic investment" (Baudrillard 1981), and this investment stemmed not only from the shared fantasies and fears that tourists experienced in India but also from the personal baggage they brought with them.[13]

Conclusion: The Touristic Turn Inward, from Places, to People, to Selves

Certainly, not all of the tourists I met during my fieldwork were seeking personal connections with the children on the riverfront. Some tourists really did just want postcards and souvenirs, while others bought these items with the hopes of putting an end to the children's "relentless pestering." However, for many tourists the personal connection was an integral if not central part of their experience. As Carla, a twenty-six-year-old traveler from Canada, remarked: "These days so many people are traveling in these countries and I think everyone is looking for a unique experience. If you meet a child and spend time with them, it glorifies your experience because you're seeing what every other traveler is but you know, you're making a personal connection and that feels really good, especially when you think the connection is genuine. It makes it just a hundred percent more of the experience really."

In the remainder of this chapter, I argue that this desire for personal connections points to more profound shifts in the nature of touristic consumption. I develop the concept of the "touristic turn inward" to discuss what these shifts have entailed and what they may suggest about contemporary tourist experiences and motivations. At the most general level, I use this concept to refer to a shift in both the modality and object of touristic consumption in which gazing is displaced by more interactive forms of appropriation, and in which the consumption of places is not only enhanced by the production and consumption of personal connections but, in some cases, displaced by them as well.[14] The touristic turn inward is a response to the ongoing commodification of places and peoples that has accompanied the expansion of the global tourism industry.[15] But it may also be viewed as another manifestation of the more "flexible" nature of commodity consumption and production within the era of late capitalism.

As we have seen, unlike their colonial predecessors, most of the tourists in this study were not satisfied with just gazing at the city from relatively safe and secure distances. Rather, they sought to establish personal connections that would render their experiences more authentic and, as Carla emphasized, more "unique." The tourism scholar John Urry notes that the desire for unique travel experiences provides yet another instance of how consumption patterns are changing within the context of post-Fordist or "disorganized" capitalism. Travelers, he argues, have increasingly come to reject forms of mass tourism in favor of an increase in "diversity of preferences . . . the proliferation of alternative sights and attractions . . . and forms of refreshment which are individually tailored to the consumer" (Urry 1995, 151). Although Urry argues that tourists are still fundamentally motivated by the desire to escape the "ordinary" contexts and routines of their everyday lives and encounter something "extraordinary," he proposes that the spread of global tourism has drastically affected how this plays out. As he observes, "every potential object of the tourist gaze has to compete internationally and this has led to substantial changes in what is extraordinary and what is internationally ordinary" (Urry 1990, 39). The examples in this chapter suggest that one of the ways travelers render international tourist destinations more extraordinary is precisely by going beyond gazing and by interacting with local people.[16] For instance, both Jacqueline and Carla maintained that personal connections were crucial to their abilities to access and experience a destination. Indeed, for Jacqueline, there was no "passage to India" without them, and for Carla they enhanced the experience "a hundred percent."

For other tourists such as Marion and Jorgen, however, these connections were not necessarily valued because they augmented their "cultural capital" by signifying an authentic encounter with an exotic Other or place. Rather, they were valued because they satisfied tourists' desires for intimacy, recognition, and even aggrandized experiences of the self. Recently a number of anthropologists and sociologists have begun to explore how "shifts in late modern economies and the forces of globalization influence intimate experiences" and affect the ways that "desires, pleasures and emotions circulate as commodities in the global marketplace" (Padilla et al. 2007, x).[17] Earlier attempts to link desires for intimacy with the changing nature of modern capitalism can be found in Richard Sennett's work. In both *The Fall of Public Man* and *The Corrosion of Character*, Sennett elaborates the notion of "the turn inward" to describe a profound reorientation in the psychic and social lives of modern subjects. According to Sennett, this reorientation can in large part be attributed to a modern capitalist system, which increasingly demands flexibility and makes long-term commitments to others much more difficult to sustain. As he argues, "Western societies are moving from something like an other-directed condition to an inner-directed condition" (Sennett 1976, 5).[18] We now live in an "intimate society" where:

> the reigning belief today is that closeness between persons is a moral good. The reigning aspiration today is to develop individual personality

through experiences of closeness and warmth with others. The reigning myth today is that the evils of society can all be understood as evils of impersonality, alienation, and coldness. The sum of these three is an ideology of intimacy: social relationships of all kinds are real, believable, and authentic the closer they approach the inner psychological concerns of each person. (Sennett 1976, 259)

Some have proposed that Sennett's thesis provides an overly pessimistic view, for as he sees it, not only does the ideology of intimacy have incredibly corrosive political implications but our very desires for intimacy, Sennett argues, are continually frustrated by our narcissistic personality disorders that entail an inability to separate the self from the Other.[19] Although this thesis may be bleak, Sennett's diagnosis of the turn inward again raises interesting questions. It suggests that in addition to pursuing desires for authenticity and distinction, both of which have been widely discussed and debated in the literature on tourist motivations and typologies, and both of which have been noted above, increasingly tourists may be motivated by more narcissistic needs, which lead them to look for or "toward" something else in their vacation experiences.[20] Paradoxical as it may seem, perhaps some people do travel halfway around the world to have Others see and recognize them. Perhaps, increasingly it is the tourist's self that is pursued and cathected as the object of desire in these "intimate" encounters.[21]

The question still remains, however: if tourists in Banaras were striving to achieve a sense of recognition or enhanced experiences of the self through their personal connections with local people, then why were these connections so frequently forged with children? Why would tourists choose, and in many cases prefer, to have intimate interactions with kids? Certainly, in some cases, children seemed a "safer bet." As Jorgen and many others emphasized, they were more "innocent" and "easier to control," and in an environment where tourists frequently felt exposed and at risk, the children, like good teddy bears, could provide tourists with an enhanced sense of comfort and security. There is also the fact that in the midst of their travel experiences, many tourists experienced, even if not consciously, a regression to a more childlike state that may have made it easier for them to identify with these "playful" and "excited" children (as was the case with Sara), or alternatively, to project their fears and fantasies onto them (as was the case with Jay in chapter 4). Another possibility, however, and the one that intrigues me the most, may be gleaned from the historian Carolyn Steedman's fascinating study of childhood and the idea of human interiority. Steedman argues that such "uses" of the child, "especially those attitudes of projection on to and identification and empathy with children," are not inevitable products of psychological regression, but rather represent "a fairly recent historical development in Western societies," in which "children have come to be closely identified with adult selfhood" (Steedman 1995, x). If this is indeed the case, and if, as Steedman puts it, children continue to be "understood as a component part of selfhood—perhaps as interiority itself" (7), then it seems even less arbitrary that the touristic turn inward and the desire for more compelling experiences of the self would so frequently involve establishing relationships with kids. And yet, as will be seen in the following chapter, although the children on the riverfront may have provided tourists with access to a lost, hidden, or fantasized self, for people in Dasashwamedh they typically provided opportunities to articulate anxieties about an external world that was viewed as rapidly transforming. That is, for locals, the concerns and interests these children evoked were not with interiority but rather with the changing and uncertain nature of contemporary social life.

8

Money, Gender, and the (Im)morality of Exchange

People in Dasashwamedh also had opposite reactions to the children on the riverfront. The boys' behavior evoked fears of dark futures, barren money, and loafer lifestyles. For instance, Anand Sahani, a local silk merchant, explained: "These boys loaf around and have fun, but their futures will be dark. No one can digest the money earned in the tourist line. When these boys die they will not even have money for a shroud; they will be cremated without one. This is the meaning of the guiding line." By contrast, the girls were frequently commended for their work with foreign tourists. As Sharmila recounted, "When Malika began working with foreign tourists, we received so many things, and tourists gave her so much money that it was like the Goddess Laxmi had entered my house. She saved our family by doing this work!" How are we to interpret these differences? Why were the boys' earnings typically cast as indigestible, whereas the girls' earnings were viewed as fecund?

In this chapter I pursue this question by drawing upon some of the anthropological literature on "money and the morality of exchange" (Parry and Bloch 1989). As Jonathan Parry and Maurice Bloch propose, the symbolism of money "relates to culturally constructed notions of production, consumption, circulation and exchange." "In order to understand the way in which money is viewed it is vitally important to understand the cultural matrix into which it is incorporated" (1). In what follows, therefore, I explore how people in Dasashwamedh evaluated the earning, spending, and saving practices of the girls and boys on the riverfront. As will be seen, through their earnings and savings, girls were praised for contributing to the reproduction of their families, as well to the reproduction of a social and moral order that was highly valued. When it came to the boys, however, people in Dasashwamedh often felt that their earning and particularly spending practices were at odds with traditional conceptions of the good life and emblematic of some of the larger ills of Indian modernity. Thus, despite their varying efforts to regulate this economy through an informal division of labor, and moral expectations regarding "everyone's right to earn," most of the time the boys were depicted as perpetuating an *immoral* economy that placed individual pursuits and pleasures over and above a concern for others.

Little Laxmis

During her four-year tenure working on the ghats, Malika had managed to establish a number of ongoing relationships with tourists who had become fairly regular benefactors for her and her family. As Sharmila explained:

> Westerners were really impressed with how sensible Malika was at such a young age. They became so fond of her, just as though she was their daughter. Some of them actually called her their own daughter. They would ask me to give them Malika and I would say, "No, she is my life, if I give her away what will I do?" Many people said to me, "Give her to me, I will get her educated and keep her properly and when she grows up your daughter will come back to you." And it was Westerners who used to buy her all the things that she needed for school. All of them said the same thing: "Educate her so that her brain may become sharper than it already is!" I began receiving letters from abroad every month. Not a month passed when we did not get a letter from abroad for Malika. We began receiving so many gifts from abroad, people began sending her photographs, books, toys, all these things, money. One man even bought her a boat so that we would be able to continue to earn money.

Certainly, not all of the girls on the riverfront achieved the kind of financial success that Malika enjoyed as a young girl. Nor were they all likened to Laxmi, the goddess of wealth. However, like Sharmila, people in Dasashwamedh were far more apt to cast the girls as productive contributors to the household economy than they did the boys. They repeatedly emphasized that whereas boys might give a little of their earnings to their parents, girls typically passed on most, if not all the money they made. As Sharmila went on to explain: "As for boys, when they start doing this work, they do what they want. When they get money from tourists they go off and get into some addiction or the other, they smoke cigarettes, or they will go see movies. They will only hand over 100 rupees to their parents, thinking this is enough to make their parents happy. But my daughters are not like that. Now that Jaila and Ritthi are doing this work, they give me whatever they earn. Only after handing me all the money do they take whatever they need." Or, as Madhuri noted when contrasting her daughters Anjali, Mona, and Gulab, with her son Maneesh, "My girls always think of me first, they understand my troubles, they bring their money home. They do not always make very much but they think of me first and give me whatever they make. My son thinks only of himself. He goes and blows most of his money in the bazaar" (*bazaar me paisa uraata hai*).

In addition to augmenting the family income, the girls' earnings were rendered fecund because they helped to reproduce important social relationships and values.[1] By relinquishing their earnings, the girls helped to sustain the normative hierarchies that structured relationships between parents and children. They also demonstrated their feminine capacity for self-restraint and reinforced the ideology that "belonging to a group is more important than individual goals and aspirations" (Wadley 2002, 11). Moreover, these examples suggest that the "productivity" of the girls' money was not necessarily linked to the amount earned, but rather to whether or not it was properly circulated.[2] In fact, many people claimed that one of the advantages that the girls had over the boys was precisely the fact they did not earn *too much*. I was often told that the girls made an appropriate (*ucit*) amount of money. As Diraj Sahani observed: "This work is okay for girls. Their earnings are appropriate. They sell diyas, some sell postcards. They make some money to give at home, but they don't make too much. Too much money is not good for kids. They will start to develop desires for all these goods in the bazaar. They will want to buy fancy clothes, they will want to eat in hotels. They will blow their money on useless things. I have seen this happen with the boys who do guiding. All they want is a luxurious life."

Thus, by working in this male-dominated public space, the girls on the riverfront indexed the impact of foreign tourism and the way it was generating new kinds of socioeconomic relations and concerns for people in the city. However, through the restrictions imposed upon them, and through their own efforts to portray themselves in a positive light, the girls also testified to the capacity of people in Dasashwamedh to reproduce cultural meanings and values that provided their lives with some sense of familiarity and order. As will be seen in the rest of this chapter, this stood in marked contrast to the boys.

The Dangers of *Dalali*

Like Anand, most people in Dasashwamedh emphasized the multiple dangers associated with guiding and commission work (*dalali*) and the "bad" and "barren" money that it yielded.[3] As I was repeatedly told: "The money these boys make from foreign tourists is bad money" (*galat paisa*). "It never sticks" (*nahin tikta hai*). "It cannot be digested by anyone" (*kisi se nahin pachta hai*). "It will not reap any fruit" (*nahin phalta hai*). "It is 'cheating' money" (*cheating ka paisa*). "It is wicked money" (*haram ka paisa*). "One way or another it must be spent!" (*kisi na kisi rasta usko karch me kiya jaaega!*).[4] Anthropologists have observed that conceptions of bad, barren, and even magic money tend to develop in situations where the pursuit of commercial profit is perceived as undermining traditional values and ways of life.[5] What interests me here, however, are not the just the cross-cultural comparisons that these responses invite but also the culturally and historically specific significance that such claims took on for people in Dasashwamedh.

Sin, Pollution, and Contagion

The *dalal*, or commission/brokerage agent, has surfaced as a rather suspect and even despised figure in other anthropological and historical accounts of South Asia. Both van der Veer (1985) and Parry (1994) have noted some of the general criticisms that surround agents operating in the pilgrimage industries in Ayodhya and Banaras, respectively. Likewise, Chakrabarty has pointed out that during the 1930s, in the jute mill industry of Bengal, the *dalal* evoked such hostility that the word itself became a "working-class term of abuse" to be applied to those who represented the interests of the employer (Chakrabarty 1989, 122–123).[6] Although far from exhaustive, therefore, there is some evidence to suggest that within other Indian contexts, as well, engaging in commission work has been viewed as a potentially degrading if not unscrupulous occupation. However, for people in Dasashwamedh, this work and money went beyond degrading. It was regarded as morally problematic.

One explanation for this, which can be quickly discounted, was the illegal status of the boys' work. Unlicensed guiding in Banaras was and still is illegal, and all of the boys had stories and complaints about being harassed by the police. Although this certainly exacerbated the perception that unlicensed guiding was not a particularly prestigious way to earn a living, for both the boys and onlookers in the neighborhood it by no means provided the foundation for raising moral objections. For instance, even in cases where boys did earn commissions off of the sale of illegal drugs (which most of them claimed not to do), the criticisms focused on other aspects that were believed to make this kind of activity morally wrong and dangerous. As Mohan explained in our interview: "I never think that I should eat [use] bad money. It is absolute poison (*bilkul zahr hai*). If I sell poison then the parents of these foreigners will be sad that their son is bad, his soul will attach to me (*uski atma, matlab hamare par lagega*). This is why I won't do any bad work for money. I can do everything, I know all about everything, but I will never think about it." Or as Bali remarked when also explaining why he refused to sell drugs to foreign tourists: "We do the work of guiding but even we have some sense of humanity inside of us. That's bad money. Because if you sell drugs then some else's life will become bad. It will cause problems for his family, the tourist's family. And his family will lament the situation and their grief will strike me (*to unka aah ham ko lagega*) and since their grief will come to me, then if I use that money at home then it will also affect my family members and both me and my family members will have to suffer."

When it came to eliciting moral outrage, therefore, condemnations typically stemmed from, or at least, were articulated in terms of, the way guiding/commission work was perceived as exposing the boys and their families to various forms of sin, pollution, and contagious substances. Mohan and Bali's comments draw us back into some very familiar ethnographic findings regarding Hindu notions of karmic retribution (Babb 1983; S. Daniel 1983; V. Daniel 1983, 1984; Wadley and Der 1990), the idea that persons and their acts are not entirely separable (Daniel 1984; Marriott 1976), the reliance upon biological models of digestive malfunction to express forms of irregular exchange (Parry 1994, 214), and the belief that sin and inauspiciousness are transmittable among people in the family line, or among "one's own" (*apna*) (Raheja 1988).

One of the most common objections stemmed from the perception that guiding was a highly polluting form of work. It required these boys to closely interact with foreigners, who were perceived as both morally lax and physically dirty. Throughout my fieldwork I heard people in Dasashwamedh speak with visceral disgust about the way foreign tourists wiped their behinds with toilet paper or kept dirty tissues in their pockets. To recall Gappa's comments: "Foreigners live in a very dirty way. They don't keep their bodies clean. They wipe their noses with paper and keep it in their pockets; they don't wash their hands. People think Angreze are dirty." Or, as Mr. Joshi noted, "When backpackers started coming to Banaras and I opened my guest house people were very concerned about having these 'dirty foreigners' so close to their sacred sites!"

If the physical dirtiness of foreigners evoked such strong reactions and concerns, this is also because Hindu conceptions of the person do not posit sharp distinctions between physical impurities and moral ones; in many cases, they are viewed as indexical of each other.[7] Furthermore, because the person is conceptualized as a more "fluid" "dividual" who is continually made and remade through their interactions with others, these impurities are regarded as potentially contagious (Daniel 1984; Lamb 2000; Marriott 1990; Wadley and Der 1990). Indeed, one of the practices that most disturbed people in Dasashwamedh was the way tourists seemed to flagrantly disregard any concern with contaminating and contagious substances by sharing drinks with each other or eating each other's *jhutha* (contaminated) food. In fact, there were several occasions when I was on hand to hear Devika sternly warn Mohan against adopting such practices: "I know some of those boys on the ghats drink *jhutha wali* cokes from tourists. I better not find out that you are!"

Not Real Work

Another recurring charge was that guiding was merely a form of "loafing" and as such, the money it engendered was inferior to "the money of hard work." For instance, echoing sentiments I heard many times over, Anand remarked:

"Consider this work absolutely useless because this is not money that is earned by working hard (*mehnat ka paisa*). They do not work hard and get this money. It is only money that is earned by roaming around and wandering like loafers." Or as Rahul, himself a former guide, remarked: "These children are earning money but they also spend it on wasteful things, because if one earns money in a useless way, then one will spend it in a useless way (*jaisa phaltu kamae to phaltu karch karenge*). If they earned money by hard work, (*mehnat se*), say 100 rupees, then they would be afraid to spend even 10 rupees."

Similar distinctions have been documented by both Parry and Gloria Raheja. They have pointed out that the money procured from the unreciprocated gift of *dan* is frequently contrasted with the superior money of hard work, and is viewed as unlikely to yield any productive returns (Parry 1994; Raheja 1988). This comparative data might lead us to conclude that the moral opprobrium surrounding the proceeds of guiding/*dalali* derived from more general concerns about "negative reciprocity" (Sahlins 1972). However, the idea that these boys were basically getting something for nothing was not, I argue, the sole or even primary source of moral rebuke. For many people, an equally troubling issue, even if it was not necessarily a conscious one, was that these boys seemed to be challenging the very category of work, and more specifically, of what constituted appropriate work for people of their class and caste background. Sporting "fancy" clothes and chaperoning tourists through the bazaar, often sharing meals and movies with them, seemed a far cry from the work world of the ghats, where Mallah livelihoods were still secured through calloused hands and physical labor.

Ill-gotten Money

Moral condemnations also stemmed from the perception that guiding/commission work was fundamentally a form of cheating. For instance, in my interview with Vinod and Rohit, two of the retired guides in Dasashwamedh, I encountered responses that I heard many times over in the course of my research:

VY: What will one do with that money? He will drink, smoke, go to the cinema, go to prostitutes, what else will he do?
JH: It's possible that he will save his money and build a house. . . .
VY: He won't save it. That money won't be saved because it is cheating money. He won't be able to (*nahin rakh payega*).
JH: Why?
VY: Because it's wicked money (*haram ka paisa*).
RS: One way or another that money will find a way to leave this guy, it will disappear (*kisi na kisi rasta voh chala jaaega*).
VY: Or someone will fall sick at home, or there will be an accident, or the police will catch him. That money simply has to leave him.

In this dialogue, it is not so much the concept of cheating that is elaborated as the consequences. Illegitimate money bears no fruit. It cannot, as Parry has noted in regard to the proceeds of mortuary *dan*, which are given to the Mahabrahman funeral priests, be "productively re-invested" (Parry 1989, 69). As I was told on many occasions: "If one earns money in the wrong way, then he will spend it in the wrong way" (*galat se kamaen to galat karch karega*). Once again, therefore, these remarks highlight some culturally pervasive ideas regarding understandings of sin, its circulation, and the way that the money itself can transmit negative qualities and emerge as much more than just a homogenous exchange value. However, people in Dasashwamedh also elaborated understandings of cheating that invoked other cultural concerns and idioms.

Some people explained that guiding was a form of cheating because it was predicated upon lies and deceit. In the first instance, tourists were usually led to believe that these boys were interested in establishing friendships with them, when in reality they were concerned with doing business. It was also pointed out that tourists were coaxed into paying high prices for relatively worthless goods. As Gopal Sahani, age sixteen, explained to me in a tone that mixed both pride and defensiveness: "Even if something is useless we will say to the customer that it is good, that is why it is called cheating. For example, we will sell something worthless for 500 rupees and tourists will bring it back to their countries and show it to people and say 'Look at this nice stuff' and someone else will say 'This isn't good stuff, it's worthless,' that's why we are called cheaters. But even the guys working in this line have to earn, they have to feed themselves" (*unko bhi kamana, unko bhi pet dekhna hai*).

Although cheating and lying were both condemned, they did not reflect a categorical moral imperative around which people lived and evaluated their actions. Indeed, many of the boys pointed out that the "right to earn a livelihood," to "fill the stomach," trumped the means by which this was accomplished. For example, as Pramod commented: "If I am cheating you in the name of business then it's not bad work (*agar mai dhandha ke marfat me apko cheating kar raha hoon to galat kam nahin hai*). If I even tell you a hundred lies for business then God will never be angry with me because it's my business, my livelihood. Because if I don't tell lies then I won't earn anything, how will I eat? It's very necessary for me to tell lies. It's not just me, it's like this for any businessman."

Within Hindu India, what is considered right or wrong, appropriate or inappropriate, is often contextually determined and predicated upon one's position and station in life rather than decreed by a set of moral universals (Vatuk 1990). There are clearly defined stages and spaces where the self-interested pursuit of business is both culturally sanctioned and expected. While Western societies (and scholars) still tend to draw romanticizing distinctions between the virtues of gift exchange and immorality of commerce, this is not necessarily the case elsewhere. Parry himself arrives at a similar conclusion in his study of the mortuary industry: "Neither in the Banaras of my informants, nor in the tradition at large, is the *normal* run of commercial profit seen as a particular ethical problem.... It is not business in general, but the business of death, which is morally loaded" (Parry 1994, 130).[8] To substantiate this claim, Parry provides an example of a young man who worked as a guide/commission agent with foreign tourists:

> The point was brought home to me by the case of a young man I knew well, whose family owns one of the shops which specializes in the sale of "goods of the skull-breaking." Most of the time he himself works as one of Banaras's numerous commission agents (*dalals*) or "guides," showing foreign tourists around the city and taking a cut on any purchase they can be persuaded to make. These sometimes include narcotics, and one day I met Bhola in a jubilant mood after he had made a very considerable sum on a sale of morphine. Despite the fact that he had many times told of the terrible misfortunes his family have suffered as a result of selling the goods required for cremation, he denies any qualms about transactions such as these. (Parry 1994, 131)

Parry's example does not mark an isolated case, for I also knew boys who had few qualms about selling drugs, and I knew many like Pramod who defended guiding and commission work as a valid, although not necessarily honorable, way to earn money. However, as the examples above make clear, and as the ones below will further demonstrate, there were many people in Dasashwamedh who did find this work and money morally problematic, and again, the question is why?

More than Necessary

The reason, I suggest, is because the boys' participation in this informal tourist economy was not perceived as "the *normal* run of commercial profit." Rather, for many people in the neighborhood the boys' work with foreign tourists represented a way of earning and spending that seemed incompatible with more pervasive cultural understandings of social life, roles, and relations. As Soni Yadav remarked:

SY: It is not wrong to take a commission, what is wrong is to take more than necessary (*zarurat se zyada lena*) like the kids of today do.
JH: So how can you decide what "more than necessary" means?
SY: "More than necessary" means this. Suppose I helped you buy this scarf for 50 rupees and I will get 5 rupees as my commission from this and I should be happy with that. But suppose I persuaded you to buy this scarf for 250 rupees, then I'll end up making 60 rupees from that and if you happen to

go to some other shop or market and you find out that you could buy the same scarf for 60 rupees there then you will come back to me and say to me, "Soni, you aren't a good man. You have cheated me." So all of the love and talk it's all finished. So I took commission and I still do but in an honest manner (*imandar ka khata hoon*).

Like Soni, many people in the neighborhood, criticized the boys for their short-sightedness and seemingly unbridled self-interest. Rather than trying to build and sustain productive relationships with customers in the future, the boys (like the Mahabrahman funeral priests) were often castigated for being excessively rapacious and for trying "to suck every rupee out of the tourist" before he or she left. Considering the fact that most tourists do not return to Banaras for second visits, from a pragmatic standpoint such concerns might seem misplaced. However, when I would point this out to people in the neighborhood, they usually replied: "Look, Jenny! One bad fish dirties the whole pond!" "People will hear about how these boys treat tourists, they will hear that we are cheaters and in the future all the tourists will stop coming to Banaras. Then we will all suffer." Thus, the boys' "cheating" also elicited concern because they were perceived as jeopardizing "everyone's right to earn."

The most common concern, however, stemmed from the perception that these boys were actually earning *too much* money. Throughout my research I was repeatedly told, "There is no limit in this work (*is kam mein koi seema nahin hoti hai*). When one dollar is equal to forty-five rupees of course the children will be able to charge so much, and the tourists also will be willing to pay so much because they know that for them it is little but for the children it is a lot." This was particularly problematic because people in Dasashwamedh placed tremendous emphasis on spending and living in accordance with one's capacity or means (*auqaat ke hisab se karch karna chayiye*).[9] They frequently suggested that the transient prosperity the boys experienced by working with foreign tourists had caused them to lose sight of their real economic position. As Diraj noted, "These boys earn money from tourists and they forget what their capacity is" (*yeh larke tourists se paisa kamate hain aur apna auqaat bhool jaate hain*). Or as Bali remarked: "When these boys begin to earn money from foreigners they start to spend beyond their means (*jab yeh larke pasie kamane lagte hain videshiyon se to apne auqaat se zyada karch karne lagte hain*). They start buying fancy clothes. They start eating in restaurants. They want very expensive things." Thus, when it came to assessing the boys' participation in this informal economy, discourses about illicit and inappropriate earnings quickly gave way to discourses about inappropriate forms of spending, leisure, and consumption. Indeed, in certain respects, people in Dasashwamedh were far more concerned with how the boys actually spent their money (and leisure time), than with how they earned it.

The Joy of Life

In her wonderful ethnography, *The Artisans of Banaras: Popular Culture and Identity, 1880–1986*, Nita Kumar describes the central role that leisure practices play in organizing the cultural system of Banarsipan among lower-class males. As she writes:

> Banarsipan is a way of life that can best be understood by describing the activities it encompasses. . . . It can also be summed up in its essential features of simplicity, carefreeness, contentment, and a love of certain "Banarasi" things such as natural beauty, darshan, pan, *bhang* (an intoxicant), and *malai* (cream). . . . Most of all, Banaras is special and superior to other places because its people are not enslaved by work, do not care about money or hoarding it, and certainly do not like to be dominated by getting involved with *naukri* (service) and *tankhwah* (salaries). They are devoted to leisure: music, melas, processions, celebrations, wrestling, bathing, bhang, and going to *bahri alang*. (Kumar 1988, 82)

The central tenets of this "Banarasi" way of life were actively embraced by the boys who worked on the riverfront. As I discussed earlier, many of the boys said that they preferred to work as guides precisely because it enabled them to be their own masters, enjoy the manifold pleasures of the city, and "spend like kings." However, according to many people in the neighborhood, the boys' leisure activities did not represent a culturally lauded expression of Banarsipan, which was premised upon a carefree attitude toward money and wealth. Instead, their spending and consumption in the bazaar seemed to suggest that their pursuits, as well as conceptions of the good life, were significantly changing. For instance, as Harsha's father Ashish remarked when I asked him to compare his own childhood with his son's:

> Today these boys just want money, because their expenses have increased tremendously. For instance, earlier we did not know the meaning of a [in English] "hotel" or what this word meant. Today there are hotels on every street. People go to eat in hotels, and there it costs at least 150 or 200 rupees for four people to eat in a hotel, and in our time we friends used to get together and go to the ghats, and we used to go to the river and cook food ourselves. So we used to make a program to eat outside, we used to go somewhere far from our home, to cook there and eat there and just to have fun. Today these kids do the same thing just in hotels. But you won't get the same pure atmosphere in the hotels as you get on the ghats. Outside, you take a bath in the Ganga and after bathing you eat and then relax. This is the intoxication/joy of living in Banaras (*yeh to Banaras mein rahene ki masti hai*).

Ashish's account of the "program" provides a vivid example of bahri alang. Literally translated, *bahri*, which derives from *baahar*, meaning "outside," and *alang*, which translates as "portion or side," *bahri alang jaana* is the activity of going out. However, as Kumar explains, bahri alang is also a "matter of mood, time, and a ritualized pattern of activities" that are geared toward revitalizing the body and mind.[10] To "go out" is to escape the crowds, congestion, and "busy life of men" in the city and it is to indulge in the "fresh," "free," and purifying elements of nature and open space (Kumar 1988, 90). As a matter of mood, bahri alang represents "the way of feeling that . . . is taken by Banarasis to be characteristic of them in general: *mauj*, or *masti*" (Kumar 1988, 99). According to Kumar, intellectuals talk about masti as a "philosophy of pleasure" or "science of life" that informs people's actions and orientation to the world. However, among "ordinary folk," she observes that masti is described as the *product* of certain pleasurable practices and spaces. "Mauj masti is the sense of freedom and contentment that comes from the *maalish* (oil massage) and *snaan* (bath), the exercise, the *safa-pani*, the bhang, and the outdoors . . . it means to feel on top of the world, and also to feel intoxicated" (Kumar 1988, 99).[11]

Although Kumar proposes that these two ways of conceptualizing masti reflect a difference between "intellectuals" and "ordinary folk," in Ashish's account both are invoked. Ashish construed masti as an orientation to the world and as the emotional and physical product of a particular kind of praxis, and the tensions between these two understandings generated uncertainties for him: Were these boys who worked in the foreign tourism line simply transposing a traditional cultural logic or "philosophy of pleasure" onto a different set of spaces and consumptive practices, that is, did hotel parties represent a new manifestation of the traditional "outside program"? Or, did this reorientation from the riverfront to the bazaar entail significant differences?

An Unwholesome Life of Luxury

Ashish and others were ambivalent about the answers to these questions. However, many people in Dasashwamedh asserted that it was not the joy of life that was driving these boys from the riverfront into the bazaar, but rather, it was *aiyaashi*, the love of luxury and comfort. The goods and fantasies produced in the market had seduced these boys away from the more "wholesome," simple, and nourishing pleasures of the riverfront and the home.[12] For instance, Kailash liked to spend his earnings dining in restaurants where he could order his favorite dish, *shahi paneer* (which literally translates as royal or kingly cheese). However, as Kailash himself noted, the excessive oil and spice that was used to make this food so "tasty" was detrimental to his health: "It is bad for us to eat in hotels. It is bad for our bodies. They put too much spice and too much oil in the food to make it more tasty." Or as Arun Yadav (age twelve), who also sold postcards at Dasashwamedh, remarked in our interview:

AY: Many kinds of goods have come into Banaras so that boys will eat them and get sick.
JH: For example, what will you get sick from eating?
AY: For instance, if a man opens a shop near a drain and it is a sweet shop and he has any kind of sweets and it's near the drain then those worms that are in the drain go and sit in the shop. So a man just sees the shop and thinks it's a good shop but he doesn't know what happens, he doesn't know what really happens in the sweet shop.

In both of these remarks, the tempting yet dangerous food from the bazaar may be read as a metaphor for the bazaar itself. As Dipesh Chakarabarty has suggested, in India, the bazaar represents an inherently ambiguous space: viewed as a site of both pleasure and peril, it is ultimately "a place against which one needs protection" (Chakarabarty 1991, 25). Not only was bazaar food regarded as harmful to the boys' physical health, as Kailash and Arun proposed, but it also was perceived as loaded with potential social and moral dangers. In Hindu culture, food provides one of the central conduits through which the qualities and affections of a person may pass.[13] Consequently, to consume food that has been prepared by a stranger exposes one to receiving potentially inferior or incompatible substances, while to consume food made by one's own (*apna*) is to share in their substance and increase the bonds of solidarity between giver and receiver.

Moreover, as Chakarabarty has also noted, within India, the home and sphere of domesticity, which is so often signified by women at the hearth, is still frequently valued as the true center of vitality and nourishment. Therefore, when people in Dasashwamedh criticized these boys for eating in the bazaar, or expressed concerns about harmful bazaar food that "did not stick" or satisfy, they also reinscribed a pervasive cultural ideology that posited the primacy of the domestic over the commercial or public sphere.[14] For example, as Bali remarked: "The food from outside does not stick to the body. If you eat four rotis outside they will not stick, if they are made by hand they will." Or, as Aashaa (age thirteen), one of the girls who occasionally sold tea on the ghats, commented: "Look, if you eat outside every day, then of course the food will not be taken into your body (*nahin lagega sharir mein*). Of course, once in a while if you don't have time to make food at home then you can eat outside and that's perfectly okay, and that food will be taken into your body. But if you think, 'I'm not going to eat at home even though food is being made there, I'm going to eat outside,' then of course, that grain won't stick to your body."

Thus, boys who regularly ate in the bazaar became signs that social roles and relations within the home were fundamentally askew: they spoke of parents who were unable or unwilling to provide for their offspring, and they also conjured up images of defiant children who refused to be contained by the rules and expectations of their elders. Indeed, the boys themselves were extremely cognizant of this. In most cases, even on days when they had eaten out in restaurants with friends or tourists, they made sure to save enough room to be able to eat some food at home. As Harsha remarked, "Even if I eat out with my friends I make sure to go and eat some food at home. If I don't eat, my mother gets very upset, she thinks the love between us is finished."

The idea that the bazaar tempted these boys with a "rich" lifestyle that was actually far from enriching was reiterated in many ways. Rani Goswami, who ran the bead kiosk on the main road above Dasashwamedh Ghat, observed:

> Children before used to pay a lot of attention to physical exercise, they were always playing on the ghats, swimming, they were strong. But the children who work with tourists today are not like this, they earn money, they wander around in the bazaar, they go see movies and after seeing them they simply believe that they are movie stars. They want to live in that style. They are always wearing [in English] "first-class jeans and t-shirts." They want to be comfortable, they want to eat everything in the bazaar and not work too hard. This is what they like.

Similarly, Tulu, whose eleven-year-old son worked as a guide, remarked:

> These boys are definitely much farther ahead when it comes to fashion. Back in my days there was no fashion, or fashion consciousness. The fashion consciousness and the imitation (*naqal*) that you see today through movies was not there. For example, if a hero or heroine dress a certain way in a movie, then the next day that very same model of dress will arrive in the marketplace and all these children will want it. A big difference has come into the lifestyle now. Today, if you take these boys to the village area or the rural society they will not enjoy being there. And as for us, even today if you take us to a village we will enjoy being there.

In both of these accounts the boys' consumptive practices were cast as a form of mimicry, and the market was identified as the primary site in which their desires were produced and pursued. The fantasy world of Bollywood, not the riverfront of Banaras, was seen as providing the model of the "good life," and the boys' bodies were disparaged as mere sign vehicles that expressed the fluctuations of fashion rather than the enriching effects of exercise and healthy living.[15] In Tulu's assessment, these cosmetic transformations and imaginative reorientations bespoke significant internal differences as well; the boys had lost their capacities to enjoy the quintessential pleasures of India. In such commentaries, therefore, the movement from the riverfront to the bazaar, and from masti to aiyaashi, reinstated a commonly espoused meta-narrative of Indian modernity that lamented the loss of traditional values and ways of life.[16]

In other instances, however, people questioned what the boys' newfound love of luxury would lead to in the future. For instance, Rana was the father of Mohan and Jaggu, and he worked as a low-paid and low-ranking attendant in a government sari shop near Lanka. Usually he was at work when I made my regular Saturday visits to eat kitchery with his wife Devika and daughter Bharati. However, on the few occasions when he did stay home, we had lengthy conversations, and before I left Banaras he agreed to set some time aside for me to interview him. On the designated afternoon, I arrived with my tape recorder. Rana, Mohan, and I sat together on the bed while Devika and Bharati sat by the gas cylinder on the floor making tea. After hearing Rana narrate his own life story, I asked him what he thought about the work that his sons did with foreign tourists. In an impassioned outburst, which subsequently made Mohan blush with embarrassment and tears, Rana replied:

> If they had jobs where they had to sit in a shop all day, or be supervised, then they would not be able to go around and eat all these things in the bazaar, spend their money on "fancy pant-shirts" and go to the movies. These boys just want a life of luxury and comfort (*aish araam ki zindagi chaahte hain*). They do not know about work or study. Since the day my son bought these pant-shirts he has become crazy. The boy whose mind is focused on studies or work does not care for pant-shirts! [Giving Mohan a slap to the head] You should see this boy powdering his face before he goes out now, cleaning his shoes and clothes, always looking at himself. Combing his hair all the time, wandering around in the bazaar and acting like a "hero"!" Where is this going to get him?

Rana's volatile reaction was, I suspect, in part linked to his own frustrations and failed aspirations. Rana hated working in the sari shop and despised the tedium of his days. As he told me on more than one occasion, had his life been different, he would have chosen to be a "scholar." Moreover, his inability to financially provide for his family did grate on his self-esteem, especially when Devika belittled him. On many occasions when I spoke with Devika, she explained, or rather complained: "If my husband wasn't so weak, if he could do more than work as a servant in a government shop and earn more than a thousand rupees a month, then these boys would not have to work. It is because he is weak that they are on the ghats. If they didn't do this work then what would we eat?" However, although Rana's response was certainly animated by a set of personal frustrations, it echoed widely shared concerns among people in the neighborhood. When Rana surveyed his son's spendthrift practices in the bazaar, he did not see evidence of masti or a "carefree attitude" toward money and wealth, but rather he saw troubling signs of fixation.

Dangerous Addictions and Dark Futures

Indeed, some of the most vehement critiques of the boys' spending and consumption practices explicitly drew upon idioms of addiction. In many local accounts, the figure of the *aishebaaz,* or pleasure seeker, quickly gave way to the figure of the addict, *nashebaaz.* As Avi Sahani remarked: "Look, children get ruined (*bigar jaate hain*) from doing this tourist work. They earn too much money in this line and then they begin spending it in the bazaar. They eat bad foods in restaurants. They buy fancy clothes. They see too many movies. They become addicted to money and drugs. They develop a greed for these things. But when they become bigger and the tourists don't love them anymore, and they don't get so much money, then what will they do? They will still be longing for all these things. Then what will they do?" Or, as Rahul remarked when reflecting upon his own experiences as a child guide:

> In my childhood I saw so much money, tourists gave me so much money. I earned so much, that the greed that was inside of me, it came to the surface (*hamare jo andar se lobh tha, voh upar ho gaya*). After doing this work, these children's hunger increases (*bukh barh jaati hai*). They get greedy for things. They start using bad things, wasting their money, they gamble, use drugs. It is all very bad. And then, suppose tomorrow they have no money for these things, then they will really feel a lot of anguish. Maybe they will do some kind of bad work to get money for these things.[17]

The problem, therefore, was not only that these boys were challenging traditional conceptions of the good life. People in Dasashwamedh also worried that their newfound lifestyles and seemingly insatiable consumption would render them, and potentially their families, unfit for any kind of productive future. As Devika remarked one afternoon when we were discussing her son's involvement with guiding and commission work, "Sons are our walking sticks in old age. If they break, so will we."

Conclusion: Transactional (Dis)orders

If the boys' participation in this informal economy elicited so much more concern from people in Dasashwamedh than that of the girls, and if their earnings were far more apt to be symbolically elaborated as bad or barren money, this is because, as Parry and Bloch astutely note: "The symbolism of money is only one aspect of a more general symbolic world of transactions which must always come to terms with some fundamental human problems. One of these is the relationship between the individual human life and a symbolically constructed image of the enduring social and cosmic order within which that life is lived" (Parry and Bloch 1989, 28). In exploring the way that money "is symbolically represented in a range of different societies," Parry and Bloch argue that underneath this incredible diversity there is also "a unity" to be found which stems from "the totality of transactions" that "form a general pattern which is part of the reproduction of social and ideological systems concerned with a time-scale far longer than the individual human life" (1). As they argue, all societies must symbolically resolve the tension between "a short-term transactional order," which typically provides a sanctioned space for "individual appropriation, competition, sensuous enjoyment, luxury and youthful vitality" (24), and "a long-term transactional order," which is oriented around reproducing the social and moral values of the collective.

Although these two orders share a necessary relationship with each other, Parry and Bloch observe that usually the short-term transactional order is morally underdetermined, while the long-term cycle is "positively associated with the central precepts of morality" (Parry and Bloch 1989).[18] Therefore, when individual or short-term transactions are seen as reinforcing the tenets of the long-term cycle (or rather, when money accrued in the short-term transactional order is transformed through "symbolic operations" into the long-term order), they often become morally valorized. When "the opposite possibility" prevails, however, "this evokes the strongest censure." As they argue, it conjures up "the possibility that individual involvement in the short-term cycle will become an end in itself which is no longer subordinated to the reproduction of the larger cycle; or more horrifying still, that grasping individuals will divert the resources of the long-term cycle for their own short-term transactions" (26–27).

When people in Dasashwamedh reflected upon the children who participated in this informal tourist economy, and when they symbolically elaborated the money that they earned, spent, and saved, they suggested that both of these possibilities were playing out, albeit along gendered lines. By relinquishing their earnings to their parents and curbing their personal expenditures and consumption, the girls established themselves as virtuous subjects who were seen as adhering to and perpetuating the moral order of society. That is, the girls were praised for putting others' interests and traditionally valued ways of life before their individual aspirations or desires.

The boys, however, did evoke "the strongest censure" and, as we have seen, the criticism and concerns that they and their earnings generated were culturally elaborated in multiple ways. In some cases, the moral condemnation stemmed from the perception that the boys were violating traditional logics of production or engaging in dishonorable, illicit, or impure work. In other cases, the concerns centered more on their lives as consumers. However, whether articulated in terms of production or consumption, when it came to the boys, people suggested that the short-term cycle had "become an end itself." The boys' behavior and actions were perceived as challenging a "general set of ideas regarding the place of the individual" in the larger social and cosmic order (Parry and Bloch 1989) and, instead of working to symbolically resolve the tensions between these two orders, as the girls did, the boys were seen as undermining any kind of harmonious relationship between the two. Anand's warning, issued at the outset of this chapter, captures this fear vividly: "These boys loaf around and have fun, but their futures will be dark. No one can digest the money earned in the tourist line. When these boys die they will not even have money for a shroud, they will be cremated without one. This is the meaning of the guiding line."

9

Conclusion

This book developed from a yearning to understand why the children on the riverfront of Banaras elicited such powerful reactions from Western tourists and locals in their community. It also stemmed from a determination to explore how these young peddlers and guides rendered their work meaningful. In the preceding chapters, I have argued that the children emerged as polyvalent symbols that enabled tourists and locals to express a range of desires and concerns. I have also made it clear, however, that the children played upon adult fantasies and fears, thereby actively shaping the outcomes of these encounters.

By organizing my analysis around these three sets of actors, one of my aims has been to show how people moving through the same space come to perceive and experience it in very different ways. I have sought to illuminate "the structure of the conjuncture" (Sahlins 1981) that brought these children, tourists, and locals into ambivalent relationships with one another.[1] I have explored how these encounters were influenced by the conscious strategies and performances of the participants involved, as well as by forms of miscommunication, misrecognition, and contingent circumstances. Although these encounters were certainly open to contingency, they were also overdetermined. They were informed by varying cultural expectations; by conflicting discourses on childhood; by the respective positions that these different actors occupied vis-à-vis the global tourist economy; and by their specific locations and emotional experiences within the city of Banaras. In this concluding chapter, I want to return to some of the broader questions that animate this book and briefly discuss the implications raised by this ethnography.

HOW ARE CHILDREN DEFINED AND VALUED WITHIN THE GLOBAL SPHERE?
Within the global sphere, children are defined and valued in multiple and often

conflicting ways. As we have seen, for many of the tourists in this study, the category of the child was still intimately linked to modernist and romantic ideas about the innocence and playfulness of youth. Other tourists, however, were far more likely to invoke premodern and postmodern conceptions of the child as a "miniature adult," variously praising the children for their savvy business sense or mourning their apparent "corruption." Still other tourists viewed the children on the riverfront as exploited street kids who were perceived as the "victims" of abusive parents, "despotic masters," or a negligent Indian state. Scholars have proposed that such varied yet patterned responses require us to explore how conceptions of children are forged through a complicated interplay of political-economic structures, ideological agendas, discourses that constitute children as particular kinds of subjects, and by the everyday practices that inform interactions within and between local cultures.

Although I have tried to attend to this interplay, one of the conclusions of this study is that the classification and valuation of children should not be reduced to an exclusively social phenomenon. For if "practice has its own dynamics," as Marshall Sahlins has proposed, then surely these include psychodynamics as well. In many cases, tourists' reactions to the children were as much determined by their desires to defend against feelings of guilt and anxiety as they were by sociocultural factors. Through processes of splitting, idealization, and denial, tourists, albeit unconsciously, found ways of coping with the extreme anxiety that these children and the surrounding environment provoked in them.

Such powerful feelings may be particularly pronounced in contexts where adults encounter children outside of their routine and taken-for-granted worlds. Yet, even if this is the case, there are likely to be many other situations where adults' reactions to children are animated by similar kinds of processes. As such, one of my intentions in this book has been to suggest that psychoanalytic theory can provide useful conceptual tools for deepening our understanding of the ways children are affirmed and denied in different contexts.

WHY DO CHILDREN SO FREQUENTLY EMERGE AS SOURCES OF ANXIETY? When it comes to theorizing the way that people in Dasashwamedh responded to the children, however, I have refrained from utilizing psychoanalytic theory. This decision does not stem from a conviction that to do so would risk inappropriately imposing Western models of the mind and self cross-culturally; for while there are certainly good reasons for considering such critiques, my hunch is that some of the of unconscious processes discussed in this book are probably universal.[2] Rather, it is because I suggest that locals' reactions to the children were more culturally and socially motivated than those of Western tourists. As I proposed in chapter 5, locals were far less likely than tourists to relate to these children as "personal symbols" (Obeyesekere 1981). Although the children also elicited powerful and conflicting feelings from people in Dasashwamedh, these feelings stemmed more from concerns about the changing nature of social life than from concerns with interiority, personal fantasies, feelings of persecution, or desires to recover or discover more compelling experiences of the self.[3] Nor, is this unique to people in Banaras. If children frequently emerge as objects of anxiety it is, in part, because childhood is an enduring structural category (Qvortrup 1994, 6). In all societies, children provide the very conditions of possibility for social reproduction. As the once-famous Whitney Houston song goes, "children are the future." Or as Mohan's mother Devika so poignantly expressed it, "sons are our walking sticks in old age, if they break so will we."

WHAT ROLE DO CHILDREN PLAY IN CONFIGURING PEOPLE'S EXPERIENCE OF SOCIOECONOMIC CHANGE? Thus, it is also not surprising that children frequently emerge at the center of anxieties regarding social change. Many anthropologists have written about the ways that larger-order transformations are read off of the behaviors and bodies of children. Although this study provides yet another example of this, it also highlights the central role that gender plays in such processes. As both Caitrin Lynch and Sandya Hewamanne have shown in their insightful ethnographies of female garment workers in Sri Lanka, gender emerges as a "key element" in responses to globalization (Hewamanne 2008; Lynch 2007). "Cultural norms and expectations concerning gender" play a central role in determining how women both participate in and signify the impacts of economic processes around the world (Lynch 2007, 237). Similarly, throughout this book, I have shown how girls and boys participated in this informal economy in very different ways, and I have argued that they emerged as very different kinds of symbols for locals in the city. By subordinating their participation in this informal economy to dominant gender norms and expectations, the girls on the riverfront testified to the capacity of people in Dasashwamedh to reproduce cultural values and relations that rendered their lives meaningful and familiar. In so doing, the girls nurtured the hope that although foreign tourism might be changing life in the city, it wasn't changing it too much. By contrast, the boys' participation in this economy generated fears of "dark" and uncertain futures and it made many locals suspect that both their laboring and leisure practices were antithetical to traditional Banarasi conceptions of the good life. In this respect, therefore, it might be argued that local reactions to the children on the riverfront also evidenced processes of splitting, idealization, and denial, but in contrast to the Western tourists whom I observed and interviewed, they explicitly played out along gendered lines.

Finally, narratives about good girls and bad boys clearly provided locals with a way to articulate their ambivalence about the impact of foreign tourism. Throughout this analysis, however, I have also suggested that part of the reason the children at Dasashwamedh became such evocative symbols was because through their work with foreign tourists they put a very local face on some of the more pervasive changes and problems typically associated with Indian modernity. Although foreign tourism was typically portrayed as the cause of these social changes and disruptions, in many instances, it functioned more as an alibi.

HOW AND WHY HAVE CHILDREN INCREASINGLY BECOME OBJECTS OF 'THE TOURIST GAZE'? John Urry points out that tourism often provides a "scapegoat" for "undesirable social and economic developments" (Urry 1990, 59). Yet in many parts of the world, tourism has had a drastic impact on local ways of life. One result is that an increasing number of children have been drawn into the global tourism industry. This phenomenon has been noted by scholars and activists working to publicize and criminalize the spread of child sex tourism. However, the kinds of encounters described here have received hardly any attention. I find this surprising because in the course of writing this book, I was struck by how many people shared similar tales of encounters with children on their vacations. Thus, although further research has yet to confirm it, I suspect that elsewhere as well children do often emerge as objects of touristic desire and disdain.

There are complex economic, historical, cultural, and psychological reasons for this, which, in terms of future research, would need to be carefully distilled in each context. In the case that I have been dealing with, we have seen that these encounters emerged as the product of both social and subjective transformations. As I discussed in chapter 2, children's participation in this informal economy coincided with a significant increase in the number of foreign tourist arrivals during the late 1980s and 1990s, and with development of a low-budget tourist hub near Dasashwamedh Ghat.

The prevalence of these encounters has also stemmed from a subjective transformation among Western tourists. Unlike their colonial predecessors, the tourists in this study wanted much more than just to gaze at local places and people. They wanted affectively charged, interactive experiences. Many of the tourists in this study could be aptly described by MacCannell's depiction of the alienated, modern-day "pilgrim" who seeks authenticity in other times, places, and people. I have also suggested, however, that some tourists were driven by more narcissistic needs and longings. Coining the concept of the touristic turn inward, I have tried capture this subjective reorientation by highlighting a form of touristic consumption in which gazing is increasingly displaced by more interactive forms of appropriation, and in which the consumption of places is not only enhanced by the production and consumption of personal connections but in some cases displaced by them, as well. For instance, although some tourists sought out personal relationships with children on the riverfront in the hopes of achieving a more authentic or unique experience of India, many others were far more concerned with having the children discover *them*.

And yet the question still remains, why did children in particular so frequently figure into these divergent, yet not completely incommensurable quests? The answer, again, seems to lie in a combination of psychosocial factors. At the cultural level, we can conclude that children were symbolically predisposed to facilitate such desires, as they were routinely associated with greater innocence, sincerity, authenticity, and even interiority. These symbolic determinations, in turn, were often reinforced by the psychodynamics of these encounters. Tourists in Banaras often experienced a profound sense of de-routinization, which led them to regress to a more childlike state. Their own feelings of insecurity and wonder, and in some cases, their desires to play and have fun, often prompted tourists to identify with children on the riverfront, or alternatively, turn to them for reassurance. Moreover, in many cases, the children facilitated forms of projection and identification that enabled tourists to more effectively manage their desires and anxieties. While in some cases, this played out as a celebration of the child as a culturally distant yet romanticized "noble savage," in other cases it led tourists to discover themselves and their own childhood aspirations in these "budding young entrepreneurs."

HOW DO CHILDREN ACTIVELY NAVIGATE THEIR LIVES AND WHAT MIGHT IT TAKE TO INSCRIBE THEIR EFFORTS WITHIN THE ANTHROPOLOGICAL RECORD MORE EFFECTIVELY? Much of this book, therefore, has been concerned with showing how and why these children became susceptible to "symbolic amplifications" (Sahlins 2004, 190). One of the merits of anthropology, or at least good ethnography, however, is the commitment to trying to understand people as creative, willful human beings who approach the world from unique perspectives. By making the children's voices central to this book, I have tried to provide a more balanced, and yet also complex, picture of these encounters. As we have seen, the children often understood their participation in this informal economy in ways that were quite different from the way foreign and local adults understood it. For instance, whereas local adults criticized the boys for their corrupt and wayward practices, the boys often maintained that both their laboring and leisure activities were very much in concert with traditional Banarasi conceptions of the good life. Similarly, although girls were praised by adults for the contributions they made to the household economy, the girls themselves often expressed feelings of inadequacy and "regret" that they could not earn as much as the boys who guided tourists around the city.

Such examples are interesting, in part, because they have broader implications for the ways anthropologists attempt to understand and study children's lives. They suggest that even when children and adults do arrive at very different interpretations of their actions, this is not because, as some scholars have argued, children occupy an "autonomous" culture. Indeed, when it came to participating and succeeding in this informal economy, and even when it came to their play, both girls and boys were very much aware of adults' desires, and they drew heavily upon cultural norms and expectations that informed relations among their elders. From an analytical standpoint, therefore, it seems more prudent to explore how children creatively appropriate cultural resources in different contexts rather than fall back upon a reified notion of "children's culture."

This is also preferable because, although children are indeed "willful, purposeful creatures who possess selves" (Bluebond-Langner 1978, 12) and who, as we have seen in this book, work hard to protect and promote certain images of themselves to others, there is also a sense in which children's conceptions of themselves are more fluid and open to ongoing negotiation than those of adults. As Myra Bluebond-Langner has noted, "any meaning that children attach to themselves, others and objects varies with respect to the physical, social and temporal settings in which they find themselves" (12).[4] For instance, in chapter 3, we saw how encounters on the ghats provided girls like Jalia and Priya with opportunities to revise, or at least question, their conceptions of themselves, their work, and their families.

If we take the contextually shifting nature of children's interpretations seriously, there are methodological implications, as well. When it comes to doing research with children, there really is no substitute for being there and being in the moment.[5] Although I was able to procure some extremely rich interviews with the children, by far the most interesting and revealing data came from hanging around, watching, listening, and accompanying the children as they went about their daily lives and interactions with others.

WHAT CAN THESE ENCOUNTERS TEACH US MORE GENERALLY ABOUT THE HIGHLY MEDIATED AND OFTEN AMBIVALENT NATURE OF HUMAN INTERACTION? HOW ARE WE TO TRACE AND THEORIZE THE COMPLICATED INTERPLAY OF INTIMATE AND SOCIAL REALITIES? "What is your book about?" For a long time, I actually dreaded having to answer this question. Aside from the difficulties I had translating my theoretical interests into something that made sense to the person sitting next to me on the airplane, I also found that the various answers I provided never quite seemed to hit it on the head. "It's a book about kids and tourists in India," I would answer. "It's about consumption and exchange." "It's about children and Indian modernity." "It is about the relationship between affect and economy." "It's a book about the articulation of different forms of value."

There is no doubt that these varying responses reflected a lack of analytical clarity on my part. But I also suspect that they stemmed from a felt need to try and adequately, or perhaps more advantageously, position my research within a scholarly market that has become increasingly specialized. As such, when I finally did make my way to an answer that I was satisfied with, and that turned out to be very general in its scope, I must confess, I felt a bit nervous.

At the broadest level, this book has been about the highly mediated, often fraught, and frequently ambivalent nature of human interaction. According to Freud, of course, all human relations are fraught with ambivalence. Our capacity to experience conflicting feelings, and repress or redirect them in the service of society and others is a pan-human phenomenon. It is also part of what renders human psychic and social life so interesting and complex. By foregrounding ambivalence in this analysis (and in this book's title), I have hoped to do more than just highlight a central feature of the human psyche. I have also sought to understand the way that ambivalence is produced in and through the mediations of particular sociohistorical contexts.

Reaching beyond the riverfront of Banaras, I have tried to use these examples as a means to explore, and I hope, more productively theorize, the way that human encounters are shaped by myriad forces and relations. C. Wright Mills saw this as one of the central "tasks" and "promises" of "the sociological imagination." In a passage that occasionally still brings tears to my eyes, he described the sociological imagination as "the most fruitful form of self-consciousness"; as the "capacity to shift from one perspective to another . . . to range from the most impersonal and remote transformations to the most intimate features of the human self—and to see the relations between the two" (Mills 1959, 7). It does not matter if the "point of interest" is a "great state power or a minor literary mood, a family, a prison, a creed," or even, as has been the case here, a tourist's heartfelt letter. So long as it provides us with an opportunity to "grasp the interplay of man and society, of biography and history, of self and world" it fulfills its promise (4). I hope this book has provided such an opportunity and will inspire readers to keep grasping their ways toward fuller understandings of their own ambivalent encounters with other human beings.

NOTES

1. CHILDREN, TOURISTS, AND LOCALS

1. Many studies have explored how the classification and treatment of children is shaped by sociocultural, economic, and political determinations. For instance, see: Ariès 1962; Chin 2001; Cunningham 2005; De Mause 1974; Gottlieb 2004; Higonnet 1998; Kett 1977; Kusserow 2004; Lareau 2003; Morton 1996; Postman 1994; Reynolds 1989; Scheper-Hughes 1992; Scheper-Hughes and Hoffman 1998; Whiting 1963.
2. As other anthropologists have noted, children's access to resources, both economic and emotional, frequently hinge upon their abilities to conform to adults' expectations (Rosen 2005; Scheper-Hughes and Sargent 1998; Stephens 1995).
3. Some of the first attempts to displace adult-centered perspectives on the child grew out of the Opies' research on children's play. They argued that children possess their own world of meanings, rituals, and social rules for interaction that are inherently foreign to adult life (Opie and Opie 1969, 1977). These observations prompted some scholars to propose that children have their own "culture" (Davies 1982; Hardman 1973; Reynolds 1974). This position has since been critiqued. Mayall argues that the concept of children's culture obscures the fact that children's lives and experiences are intimately wed to their relations with adults. It also risks reducing the concept of culture to a mere aggregation of playground games, lore, and rituals (Mayall 1994). Others argue that the category of children's culture is itself too broad, and fails to account for the way that race, class, and gender shape children's experiences (Corsaro 1979; Grugeon 1988; Lever 1976).
4. Some scholars have talked about the ways tourists themselves become more childlike on vacation and "psychologically regress" (Cocker 1992; Dichter 1981). Others have focused on how the tourism industry seeks to control and entice travelers by treating them as children and by framing vacation destinations through tropes of a romantic return to the world of childhood innocence and bliss (Dann 1989, 1996; Turner and Ash 1975). Finally, one exception to the striking absence of children in the tourism literature can be found in Jan Gamradt's article on Jamaican children's representations of tourism (Gamradt 1995).
5. The work on tourist typologies has made it eminently clear that not all tourists are driven by the desire to encounter culturally exotic or authentic others. See, for instance: E. Cohen 1979; Feifer 1985; Hamilton-Smith 1987; Urry 1990; Wickens 2002.
6. For other contributions to the authenticity debate, see: Adams 1996; Boorstin 1964; Bruner 2005; Cameron 1987; Culler 1981; Desmond 1999; Duggan 1997; Frank 2002; Greenwood 1989; Hughes 1995; Lacy and Douglass 2002; MacCannell 1992; Olsen 2002; Urry 1990.

7. The idea that the tourist's journey through space often entails, or at least is motivated by, a desire for an inner psychological journey and a quest for self-discovery has also been widely remarked upon (Bruner 1991; E. Cohen 1979; Galani-Moutafi 1999; Graburn 1989; Noy 2004). However, the self-discovery involved in these encounters was not necessarily procured through trying ordeals, "sacred journeys" (Graburn 1983), or transformative growing experiences. Rather, it was primarily produced through the affirmation and recognition of the Other.
8. Some have cautioned against using the tourist as a kind of paradigmatic modern or postmodern figure that enables us to speculate upon the nature of subjectivity in contemporary capitalist society (Edensor 1998). However, I find that it is useful to consider how tourist experiences and practices may be viewed as reflective of larger societal dynamics and shifts.
9. Within the recent literature on tourism there has also been an emphasis on exploring the articulations "between place and performance." For instance, see Bærenholdt, Haldrup, Larsen and Urry 2004; Coleman and Crang 2002; Edensor 1998.
10. For discussions of such representations, see Hutnyk 1996; Inden 1990; Said 1979.
11. Both Nita Kumar and Assa Doron have written insightful ethnographies that explore the riverfront from other vantage points. See Doron 2008; Kumar 1988.
12. Banaras also attracts many Japanese backpackers and independent travelers. However, most of the Japanese tourists I met had very rudimentary English and it was difficult for me to communicate with them. As such, they do not figure prominently in this book. Moreover, the Japanese tourists whom I did observe often tended to be more interested in establishing relationships (in some cases, of a romantic nature), with the older guides and boatmen who worked along the riverfront.
13. See, for instance, E. Cohen 1972, 1973, 2004; Desforges 1998; Edensor 1998; Hutnyk 1996; Loker-Murphy 1996; Loker-Murphy and Pearce 1995; Maoz 2004, 2005; Muzanini 2006; Riley 1988; Sörensen 2003; Uriely, Yonai, and Simchai 2002; Westerhausen 2002.
14. For studies that attend to the role of national and cultural characteristics in shaping tourist behaviors and motivations, see: Graburn 1995; Pizam and Sussmann 1995; Richardson and Crompton 1988; Ritter 1987.
15. See Baker 1982; Briggs 1986; Clifford and Marcus 1986; Denzin 1970; Maseide 1990.

2. A TOURIST TOWN

1. As Eck notes, however, there was also an interesting trend in which writers harked back to the classical world and wrote about Banaras as the "Athens" of the East (Eck 1983, 16).
2. In 1943, Dr. A. S Altekar, who was the head of the Department of Ancient Indian History and Culture at Banaras Hindu University, prepared a small publication prior to the convening of the Twelfth All India Oriental Conference, which was intended to serve "as a guide for the cultured visitor of Benaras" (Altekar 1947, 1). In the appendix entitled "Useful Information for Visitors," Altekar listed the hotels in the Cantonment Area where Europeans could stay, but he advised Indian visitors that they would find it more "convenient" to take rooms in Dharamshalas. Ironically, today the Cantonment Area's five-star hotels throw their gates open to affluent Indian travelers and businessmen, while the smaller, low-budget guest houses near the riverfront, which cater to Western backpackers, actively discourage, if they do not outright reject Indian visitors who seek accommodations there. During the course of my fieldwork, a formal complaint was filed by an Indian traveler who was denied lodging by one of these

guest houses, and the tourism department issued a statement saying that this kind of discrimination was illegal and would be investigated.
3. For more on the grand tour, see Towner 1985.
4. Article entitled "The Hippy Trail."
5. Indeed, as both Tushar Hathi and Subas Kumar note in their studies, tourism was not granted official "industry status" in India until 1986. See Hathi 1998 and S. Kumar 1998.
6. W. S. Caine's 1890 *Handbook for European Travelers* mentions that guides sought to earn commissions off of their European customers in the colonial era. However, while travelers in the colonial period were also marked as sources of potential profit, the development of the tourism industry in Banaras over the last hundred years has significantly augmented possibilities for official and unlicensed guides to earn money from foreign visitors.
7. These figures were taken from the 1997 Tourist Statistical Book issued by the Directorate of Tourism, in Lucknow, U.P.
8. In his article, "Behavioral Perspective of Pilgrims and Tourists in Banaras (Kashi) India," Pravin Rana notes that according to the U.P. Tourism Department, the number of international tourists declined from 108,546 in 2001 to 86, 267 in 2002.

3. GIRLS AND BOYS ON THE GHATS

1. Exceptions to this included allowing the girls to go to the market to buy flowers for their diyas or to replenish their postcard supply. The children procured postcards and souvenirs from shopkeepers in the bazaar, and they usually were given the materials to make diyas by their parents.
2. Other anthropologists of South Asia have argued that sexual purity should not be posited as the sole or dominant value against which girls and women are assessed. For instance, McKim Marriott has pointed out that within Hindu India, girls and women are judged in relation to the particular contexts and roles they occupy and that sexual purity is but one of several qualities used to assess them (Marriott 1998, 292).
3. Threats to sexual purity may take several forms: men who try to molest girls in public or tempt them into inappropriate relationships; girls who begin to develop the "wrong kinds of feelings" and lose their capacity for self-restraint; and rumors and gossip that can malign a girl's reputation if she is perceived as "wandering" around too much.
4. Being perceived as asexual was not the only criteria that defined the category of childhood. Many people in Banaras maintained that so long as one was not married, he or she was still a child. This idea is also noted by Anthony Carter in his essay, "Hierarchy and the Concept of the Person." His Hindu informants suggest that "a human being does not really become a person . . . until after he or she is married" (Carter 1992, 129).
5. Much has been written on female gender norms and expectations in South Asia. For some further discussions, see Grima 1994; Inden and Nicholas 1977; C. Lynch 2007; Majumdar 2002; Seizer 2000; and Wadley 2002. For perspectives on how women in South Asia challenge or subvert these norms, see the collection of essays entitled *Women as Subjects*, edited by Nita Kumar in 1994; Raheja and Gold 1994; and Ramanujan 1991.
6. Before I began my official fieldwork, I visited Banaras for several months in 1999, and during this time I lived in a guest house that was directly opposite Malika's home. This is part of the reason why we ended up spending so much time together.

7. For a critique of the "anthropological story of India and its essentially familial self," see L. Cohen 1998, 105.
8. Clearly, when it comes to gender there is variation across caste, class, religious, regional, and generational lines. However, as numerous anthropologists have noted, within Indian society, and South Asia more generally, there still remains a set of highly pervasive norms and expectations that configure the lives and outlooks of girls and women. The idea that females should affect a modest, deferent demeanor, be chaste, compliant, self-sacrificing, virtuous, and make domestic and family life their number-one priority is still taken as axiomatic in many parts of the subcontinent. For discussions of these expectations and notions of ideal femininity, see Das 1988; Dube 2001; Grima 1994; Kakar 1981; Kumar 2007; Lamb 2000; C. Lynch 2007; Raheja and Gold 1994; Seizer 2000; Vatuk 1990; and Wadley 2002.
9. In a certain sense, albeit in an inverse form, this recalls Anne McClintock's discussion of the "labor of leisure" that middle-class European housewives had to perform by the end of the nineteenth century. McClintock argues that as the image of the "useless" and leisured woman triumphed, middle-class housewives had to work harder than ever to prove that they were living a life of leisure (McClintock 1995, 162).
10. The concern with comportment and presentation of self extended to other areas, as well. There were many discussion about the proper way for a girl to sit on the ghats, what constituted appropriate clothes to wear, which girls spoke in a nice and polite manner, and which ones did not.
11. This was also possible, in part, because as others have pointed out in Banaras, the public/private distinction is not as rigidly instantiated. See for instance, Chakrabarty 1991 and Kumar 1988, 2007.
12. These kinds of attacks were reserved for female-only company.
13. This is not to say that there weren't difficulties involved, as well. While Anjali enjoyed being able to come to the ghats, she was also under considerable pressure from her parents, particularly her father, who according to Anjali and her sisters would occasionally hit the girls if they did not return from the ghats with enough money.
14. Most of the other girls who lived in the immediate neighborhood of Manmandir and came from the Mallah caste did have actual kin relations on the ghats. Anjali did not. She lived about ten minutes away, near the Chowk market.
15. Also drawing upon the work of Mead and subsequent symbolic interactionists, Myra Bluebond-Langner (1978) has noted a similar dynamic in her study of children with terminal cancer. In many cases, these children came to arrive at new understandings of themselves and their illness not by direct questioning, or statements, but rather by reading the cues and reactions of their adult interlocutors.
16. Working as a domestic helper also came with a set of stigmas attached, but it had the advantage of being less "visible." It was not something that most girls and women liked to advertise.
17. Because I had been in Banaras for nine months between September of 1997 and May of 1998, and then returned for another visit in 1999 before officially beginning my fieldwork in February of 2000, I had the chance to see some of these boys transition from arrestingly cute-looking little kids to more mature-looking adolescents.
18. For a further discussion of the way anthropologists and historians have attempted to deal with the relationship between "emotional needs" and "material interests" in the family, see Medick and Sabean 1984.
19. In Pramod's situation, the idea of conditional love was even more pronounced. He often described his relationship with his aunt as being very similar to the widely

remarked-upon relationship that exists between a child and the often vilified stepmother, *sautali ma*. This is a figure whose affection and intentions are commonly regarded with great suspicion.

20. For an excellent discussion of intergenerational reciprocity in Hindu family life, see Lamb 2000, 2002, 58. As she notes, the care of parents is often perceived as integrating both material and spiritual dimensions. Not only are sons expected to provide economic support to parents but they are also asked to provide *seva*, or respectful loving service, and attend to essential rituals at the time of death. In his discussion of parent-child relationships in Hindu India, Sudhir Kakar also comments on the pervasive belief that children are considered to be "gifts from God" (Kakar 1981, 12). Moreover, he notes that mothers, too, experience a sense of debt to their sons and often respond to them as "saviors" who augment their respect and position in the family home (88).

21. In his fascinating study of blood donation and religious experience in North India, Jacob Copeman uses the concept of "interoperability" to describe the ways that different pursuits, such as making money (or in his case, soliciting blood donations) and proving one's devotion can work in conjunction with each other. As he demonstrates, although concerned with different ends, each activity may "contribute usefully to each other's priorities and aims" (2009).

22. In part, this sense of centrality derived from the sacred geography of Banaras. As Jonathan Parry notes: "Those with the eyes to see know that Kashi is both the origin-point and a microcosm of the universe; that it stands outside space and time and yet all space is contained within it; and that it provides for the attainment of all the four conventionally enumerated goals of human existence (the *purusharthas*): in life for the fulfillment of moral and religious duty (*dharma*), material and political advantage (*artha*), and of the sensual appetites (*kama*)." Parry 1994, 11–13

23. During my research, there were many articles published that outlined plans for this development; for example, in April of 2000, the newspapers *Denik Jagran* and *Aaj* featured several articles about the development of a tourist police force in Banaras that would help put an end to unlicensed guiding. In the years following my fieldwork, it seems that the harassment of unlicensed guides grew even more considerable. As Assa Doron has noted, in early October of 2005, in response to the demands made by the Government Approved Tourist Guide Association, eighteen boatmen were arrested by the Dasashwamedh ghat police for operating as "fake tour guides." This resulted in a formal protest by the boatmen community at Dasashwamedh (Doron 2008, 167).

24. Here it is interesting to note, as Assa Doron points out in his study of the boatmen of Banaras, that itinerant work was also stigmatized by the colonial administration in Banaras (Doron 2008).

4. INNOCENT CHILDREN OR LITTLE ADULTS?

1. As they note, it is being undermined by the growing need for child labor; as well as by human rights discourses that prioritize the universal rights of the individual over specific needs or protectionist policies for children, and by the emergence of increasingly hostile policies and attitudes that express "the ambivalent and declining, social value of children" in advanced industrial societies.

2. As Lionel Trilling has pointed out, in contexts where people are not assured of others' identities and intentions sincerity can emerge as a privileged virtue (Trilling 1972).

3. Although the girls sometimes playfully teased their Western customers, I rarely observed this kind of behavior when they were interacting with Indian customers.
4. This sentiment was also echoed by a middle-aged American traveler, Laurien. As she put it, "What I observe here is that affluence makes kids stupider, there's a stupidness that goes with affluence as well . . . the rich kids here act more childlike longer."
5. "Colonial mimicry," Homi Bhabha writes, is "the desire for a reformed, recognizable Other, as a *subject of a difference that is almost the same, but not quite*" (Bhabha 1997, 153). Etty did not want a reformed Other, but rather she longed to encounter an "authentic" Other who could help her live out her own fantasies of being in traditional India. However, at the same time, Bhabha's observation that mimicry is "at once resemblance and menace" (154), that it has the potential to disrupt the authority of the colonial discourse (or fantasy) and that the residue of difference can produce an unsettling reminder of what the colonizer and colonized do and do not share, also seems apropos to this example.
6. A number of scholars have explored when and why the figure of the playful child emerged as a dominant cultural ideal within Western capitalist societies. See, for instance, Field 1995; Higonnet 1998; James, Jenks, and Prout 1998.
7. Elsewhere, I have drawn upon Donald Winnicott's work, and I have considered how these children came to function as "transitional objects" that provided tourists on the riverfront with "a defence against anxiety" (Winnicott 1989, 4). See Huberman 2006.
8. For a more detailed discussion of Locke's formulation of the child as tabula rasa, and how Locke's conception of the child differed from Rousseau's, see James, Jenks, and Prout 1998, 15–16.
9. Here, it is interesting to note that when I met with the information officer at the Department of Tourism office in Banaras, he could not see any reason why a tourist would want to employ the services of one of these "uneducated children" as a guide. In fact, he emphasized how they end up giving the city a bad name.
10. Much of the anthropological, sociological, and even psychoanalytic research on childhood over the last thirty years has been devoted to demonstrating that through play, children come to develop crucial cognitive and social skills. For a review of this literature. see James, Jenks, and Prout 1998.
11. In the collection of essays entitled *Small Wars: The Cultural Politics of Childhood*, edited by Nancy Scheper-Hughes and Carolyn Sargent (1998), both of these social trends are discussed. See, for another example, Norma Field's 1995 essay, "The Child as Laborer and Consumer: The Disappearance of Childhood in Contemporary Japan."
12. In making this argument, I also draw upon Melanie Klein's 1946 paper, "Notes on Some Schizoid Mechanisms" and her 1948 paper, "On the Theory of Anxiety and Guilt". In both of these papers, Klein elaborated her thesis on the "paranoid-schizoid position" of early infancy and the subsequent development of the "depressive position," which, she argued, under normal circumstances occurs after the first six months of a child's life. While Klein initially derived these two positions, and their respective anxieties and defense mechanisms, from the study of infancy and childhood development, she ultimately concluded that human beings move in and out of these positions throughout the course of their lives. As such, she proposed that these two positions could be viewed as ideal types that would provide analysts with a useful way of "understanding and unraveling emotional situations" (Klein 1975, 37).
13. Numerous scholars have argued that tourists frequently undergo a psychological regression to a more childlike state during their travels (Cocker 1992; Dichter 1981; Selwyn 1993). This regression is induced by the experience of being taken out of a

familiar environment and by the discursive apparatus of the tourism industry itself, which, as Graham Dann argues, often seeks to control and entice travelers by treating them as children (Dann 1996, 104).
14. Given the fleeting nature of their encounters, this is not very surprising.
15. Usha's use of the word "rubbish, rubbish" may have been reflective of her difficulties with the English language rather than suggesting an unconscious Freudian slip; however, I would not want to discount the latter as a possibility either.
16. Like many "travelers" I encountered, Usha resisted being labeled as a tourist, and aside from our informal visits in the guest house, she actively avoided spending time with other Westerners.

5. THE MINDS AND HEARTS OF CHILDREN

1. In this regard, my discussion is influenced by Steven Parish's writings on Nepali Hindu Newar culture and the concept of *nuga*, or "heart," which, as Parish writes, "embodies a person's feelings and sense of self in ways that integrate self and moral order. Newars place much that Western culture conceives of as "mind" in this "heart-self," and also much that Western culture conceives of as belonging to the separate domain of religion (Parish 1994, 190). In a footnote Parish also notes that it is very similar to the Nepali concept of *man*, which is also understood as located in the chest and is a seat of cognition, intention, memory, and emotion. This also resonates precisely with the definition provided in the McGregor Hindi-English Dictionary, which is as follows: *Man*: masc. noun. 1. the mind (as seat of perception and feeling). 2. the heart. 3. the soul. 4. wish, inclination; will purpose. 5. character, temperament (McGregor 1993, 788).
2. This observation has been noted by other anthropologists working in India. For example, see Lynch 1990; Markus and Kitayama 1991; Shweder and Bourne 1984; and Shweder and Miller 1991.
3. Both these neighborhoods are about a fifteen- to twenty-minute rickshaw ride from Dasashwamedh.
4. As Cohen astutely observes, the quality of the old voice and the way it is interpreted are always contingent upon a "community of listeners and their interrelationships" (L. Cohen 1998, 178). For outsiders, the disgruntled old voice may be heard as a sign of the elder's neglect, and therefore an indicator of the family's state of moral decay. For children and caretakers within the family, on the other hand, unhappy old voices may be heard as making insatiable demands, exposing age-inappropriate desires, or may signify elders' unwillingness to relinquish their former roles and adjust to the new balance of power in the home.
5. I emphasize "in certain respects," because as the concept of karma implies, people in Banaras also suggested that children come into the world configured by the acts, deeds, and sins of their past lives. As Urvashi Misri notes, within Hindu India, "the child is not perceived as a blank slate." In addition to inheriting certain properties or qualities from the collective, the newborn child is also construed as a unique individual whose disposition has already been configured by other forces such as karma, the time of conception, and the unique combination of parental substances the child inherits (Misri 1985).
6. This is also noted by Anthony Carter in his essay "Hierarchy and the Concept of the Person." As he writes, "neither the uninitiated boy, the unmarried girl, nor the *sanyasin* is thought to have *dharma* (religion, duty, or code)" (Carter 1992, 138).

7. A. K. Ramanujan has also noted that "unmerited suffering" plays a pivotal role in women's stories in India (Ramanujan 1991, 1994, 53).
8. The idea that daughters are actually wiser, more mature, and more discerning than sons is one I repeatedly encountered throughout the course of my fieldwork, and it stands in sharp contrast to what Susan Wadley has observed among joint families in rural north India, where women are often talked about as being more childlike and having less judgment (*vivek*) than men. See Wadley 2002, 12.
9. Thus, as Cohen noted in his analysis of aging narratives among Chamars, here, too, social weakness (*kamzori*) was "quantified" and embodied (L. Cohen 1998, 230). However, unlike some of the weakness narratives that Cohen encountered among Chamars in Nagwa, in this commentary, weakness did not function as an ideology that "challenges the moral order" of caste and class "by substituting for it" a different one (232).
10. Here, it is also interesting to note that one of the ways older guides attempted to maintain and express their seniority and dominance on the ghats was precisely by refusing any gifts or offerings from the younger children. As Ganesh Sahani explained to me one day, "I will never let these boys pay for my tea or food. If we are having tea on the ghats, I pay for them, this is the way it is, elders always pay." This resonates with the Vatuks' findings that "In general, the direction of gift-giving . . . is from elder to younger, from senior to junior" (Vatuk and Vatuk 1971, 217).
11. For further discussions of the role of purity and pollution in Indian social life, see: Bean 1981; Carman and Marglin 1985; Dumont 1970; Glucklich 1984; Madan 1991; Marglin 1977; Marriott 1968, 1976; Marriott and Inden 1977; Parry 1994.
12. For further discussion of the way social hierarchies are both reproduced and challenged through the monitoring and modulating of emotions, see Lutz 1988.
13. The Hindi word *tez* has multiple connotations. It can be used to describe someone who is bold and strong, or it can be used to describe someone who is mentally sharp and quick-witted.
14. However, as Mattison Mines has persuasively argued, within Indian society there is certainly room for individual autonomy and rebellion. He argues that while much of the scholarship has emphasized the ways individualism in India is subordinated to the demands of a sociocentric, hierarchical society, ethnographic data reveals that the qualities of autonomy and rebellion may be highly valued within the context of people's own understandings of their lives and life histories (Mines 1988, 1994).
15. Valentine Daniel alludes to a similar idea when he discusses the preoccupation that Hindus have with compatibility. In describing what he calls the "person-centric orientation of Hindu culture," he notes that "because each person has a uniquely proportioned composite substance, in his search for equilibrium he must observe unique codes for determining what substance is compatible with his bodily substance" (Daniel 1984, 70). Although I did encounter this idea in my fieldwork, I also encountered the idea that one's caste identity plays a considerable role in configuring what may or may not be compatible. Daniel notes this as well, when he says, for instance, that "minimally" transacting castes find "cooling" foods more compatible, whereas "maximally" transacting castes favor "heating foods" (70–71).
16. As Jonathan Parry has noted, this caste of ritual specialists, who are charged with cremating the dead, are not only infamous for their "chicanery" (Parry 1994) but they are also believed to reside in a permanent state of ritual pollution, and are "likened to a sewer through which the moral filth" of their patrons is passed (Parry 1989, 68).

17. Indeed, although some scholars have argued that class is displacing caste as the most salient category configuring social hierarchy in India (Liddle and Joshi 1989), the examples presented here suggest the need to more carefully consider how these categories get constructed and mobilized in particular contexts and communities (Natrajan 2005).
18. This is reminiscent of what Bernadette Barton discovered in her study of female strippers. See Barton 2007.
19. When I first met Vinod in 1997, he primarily worked near Assi Ghat; however, during the course of my fieldwork he befriended several of the older guides from Dasashwamedh and had become a regular presence in the area.
20. As Jonathan Urry points out, local populations often blame "undesirable social and economic developments on tourists" (Urry 1990, 59). Moreover, as Cohen observes, within Banaras, and within the larger context of urban Indian modernity, such narratives of "the Fall" which cast "the West" as a central villain, require more than "a hermeneutic of suspicion" (L. Cohen 1998, 104). Their telling, he argues, is itself, a performative act that enables speakers to both mourn the loss of a previous way of life and nostalgically "recover" a more gratifying, unspoiled identity. To hear only tragedy in such narratives, would therefore, be a mistake.
21. As she writes: "According to the well-known theory of the four *yugas* or ages, things get progressively worse rather than better as time passes. When this world first came into being many thousands of years ago, people lived in the Satya Yuga, the age of truth and goodness in which *dharma* or moral-religious order flourished. But ever since then, the social and material world has gradually deteriorated, until, according to my informants, about five thousand years ago we entered the fourth and most degenerate of ages, the Kali Yuga" (Lamb 2000, 94). For other discussions of how the Kali Yuga provides people with an interpretive frame for making sense of their current experiences, see Pinney 1999.
22. In such accounts, the modern world was cast as site and source of social and moral incoherence, or to borrow a term from the anthropologist McKim Marriott, "unmatching" (Marriott 1990, 20).
23. This notion is formally expressed through *asramadharma* or the four-stage theory of the life course (see L. Cohen 1998; Kakar 1981), but it is also articulated through more common distinctions that people draw between childhood (*bacpan*), young adulthood (*javaani*), and old age (*burhaapa*) (Vatuk 1990, 60).
24. In his classic study *Learning to Labor*, Paul Willis notes a similar dynamic among working-class lads in Great Britain. They too rejected the ideology that educational qualifications provide "equivalents" for entering "into other successive exchanges that are to the advantage of the individual" (Willis 1977, 64).
25. As Obeyesekere proposes, as anthropologists, we must "articulate the symbol to the cultural, social and psychological dimensions" of our informants, and explore "the interdigitation of deep motivation and public culture" (Obeyesekere 1981, 1).

6. EARNING, SPENDING, SAVING

1. The concept of the moral economy has been influential among anthropologists, historians, classicists, and more recently, political scientists. At its core, it seeks to highlight the way that economic relations are embedded within, or regulated by, larger sets of social-cultural logics and imperatives. For further discussion of this concept and its legacy within the social sciences, see Booth 1994; Polanyi 1957; Sahlins 1972; Scott 1976; Thompson 1971.

2. See, for instance, Appadurai 1986; Carsten 1989; Gell 1986; Munn 1992; Parry and Bloch 1989; Polanyi 1957; Stirrat 1989.
3. For a discussion of the boli system, also see Parry 1994.
4. The children who sold other items or who approached tourists as guides were also concerned with territorial boundaries. They did not want children from outside Dasashwamedh infringing on their turf, and when such an infraction was perceived, they were, like the boatmen, quick to unite against these outsiders. However, at this very local level, the children who sold postcards, colors, or tea were able to traverse the four adjacent ghats more freely than the children who sold diyas. One of the reasons for this seems to be that selling diyas was primarily construed as a part of the pilgrimage industry and part of the boatmen's long-standing "ritual economy," which Doron has also described in fine detail (2008). As such, the children who sold diyas were more "religious" about observing traditional territorial boundaries on the ghats than children who sold other goods and, notably, only girls from the Mallah caste participated in this business.
5. Though official records were impossible to come by, most of the people I knew and interviewed told me that the first children to enter into this informal tourist economy at Dasashwamedh were primarily from lower-caste families who were already established in the immediate area and working on the riverfront, such as the Mallahs, Domes, and Yadavs. At the time of my research, the majority of children working at Dasashwamedh still came from such families. But children from different castes and neighborhoods had also begun selling on the Main Ghat, and this was a source of irritation and concern to the children from the immediate neighborhood.
6. For further discussion of these valued attributes, see Alter 1992; Kumar 1988.
7. According to everyone I spoke with, he did.
8. Raju may have been extra sensitive to such slights because his family belonged to the Dome caste and he was closely affiliated with the "polluted" ritual specialists who oversaw cremations at Manikarnika Ghat.
9. The implication of this is that even in our most intimate encounters or in our most strident efforts to express our individuality, we often end up sounding "generic."
10. "The better our command of genres the more freely we employ them, the more fully and clearly we reveal our own individuality in them" (Bakhtin 1986, 80).
11. Indeed, I was struck by how frequently the reference to "psychological warfare" came up when tourists described their interactions with the children on the riverfront.
12. Doron also describes how the boatmen of Banaras rely upon such strategies in their attempts to increase trust between themselves and their customers. Moreover, he notes that this refusal to accept a payment or return animates one of the central myths that the boatmen invoke to enhance their status. As one of his informants pointed out, the boatman who ferried Ram, Sita, and Lakshman across the river was "very clever" because he "refused to take the ring from Sitaji as payment for his services" and in so doing "won his heart" (Doron 2008, 148).
13. Unlike the highly calibrated and symmetrical give-and-take of balanced reciprocity, which variously animates relations in trade, friendship, and even good dinner conversation, generalized reciprocity refers to a realm of "more personal transactions" where "assistance is freely given" (Sahlins 1972, 191), "goods move in one way . . . for a long period of time," and "the expectation of a direct material return is unseemly" (193–194). As Sahlins points out, therefore, generalized reciprocity can provide a key mechanism for creating and maintaining social relations and obligations.

14. For instance, such forms of reciprocity commonly underscore relations between patrons and clients, parents and children, and politicians or "big men" and their followers.
15. Also see Hénaff 2010.
16. There were some children who had successfully established long-term friendships with tourists by continuing to send letters and gifts; however, for the most part, their relationships were short-lived.
17. I emphasize particular kind, because what I am trying to describe here both resonates with and diverges from the concept of emotional labor as it was initially laid out by Arlie Hochschild in her ethnographic study of flight attendants. In her now-classic text, *The Managed Heart: The Commercialization of Human Feeling*, Hochschild defines emotional labor as a form of labor that "requires one to induce or suppress feeling in order to sustain the outward countenance that produces the proper state of mind in others." She proposes that this kind of labor "calls for a coordination of mind and feelings, and it sometimes draws on a source of self that we honor as deep and integral to our individuality" (1983, 7) Finally, she emphasizes that in contrast to "emotion work" or "emotion management," which have "use value" and may be done in private, emotional labor is a public activity that is "sold for a wage and therefore has an exchange value" (7).

    Like Hochschild's airline attendants, the children on the ghats were also concerned with managing the experiences and emotions of their customers and sustaining a "countenance" that would help them produce the "proper" state of mind in others. Moreover, although they were not wage workers (and this in itself is an important difference), they clearly realized that their abilities to maintain such a countenance often translated into financial returns. However, in contrast to Hochschild's informants, these children did not seem overly concerned or bothered by having to manage their feelings. I would not argue that they came to feel "alienated" from their emotional lives, or viewed managing their emotions as a violation against some "integral" part of the self, and in this respect, Appadurai's insights do seem particularly poignant.
18. In many societies, particularly precapitalist ones, the primary consumptive unit has not been the individual, but rather the family or the larger community. Moreover, as Colin Campbell notes, in such cases, "the efforts of any one individual to 'better' his condition by striving after new wants are not only seen as threatening to the whole community but as fundamentally immoral" (Campbell 1989, 39).
19. Elizabeth Chin has noted a similar dynamic among young African American girls. In her excellent ethnography, *Purchasing Power: Black Kids and American Consumer Culture*, she discusses the way that girls' consumption practices were frequently oriented not toward their individual needs and wants, but rather toward the needs of the household. See Chin 2001.
20. In her study of sex tourism in the Dominican Republic, Denise Brennan also notes a similar tendency. As she reports, female sex workers were extremely careful not to "dwell on the material rewards of sex work. To do so would be tantamount to an admission that they spend their earnings on nonessential items for themselves rather than remit them to their children back home" (Brennan 2004, 177).

7. SOMETHING EXTRA

1. Edensor draws a useful distinction between enclavic and heterogeneous tourist spaces. In enclavic spaces, tourists are "characteristically cut off from social contact with the local populace and are shielded from potentially offensive sights, sounds

and smells" (Edensor 1998, 45). In "heterogeneous spaces," tourists and locals "must mingle with each other," indeed, "the opportunities for meeting locals are part of the tourist experience" (55).
2. Baudrillard, of course, also argued that capitalism systematically produces subjects who are in constant need, whose "consummativity" becomes just as important to the recuperation of surplus value as their productivity (Baudrillard 1981, 83). As such, he was also interested in the unconscious forces that shape modern consumption.
3. Katherine Frank notes a similar difficulty among strip club regulars. She writes: "The payment of money thus has the potential to unsettle an interaction because its symbolic value is one that is ideologically incommensurable with romantic love or true friendship" (Frank 2002, 191).
4. From Hutnyk's perspective, charity and volunteer tourism in the "Third World" "deserves no alibi," as it represents "the soft edge of an otherwise brutal system of exploitation" (Hutnyk 1996, ix). Instead of treating poverty as a complex social problem that needs to be eradicated through structural realignments in the global political economy, he argues that volunteer tourism renders poverty a spectacle to consume.
5. It is customary for children to receive new clothes on Holi, though usually such gifts are given by parents or related elders.
6. This was also recommended by many guidebooks.
7. Both Frank (2002) and Allison (1994) note similar desires in their writings on interactions between male customers and female entertainers.
8. As a caveat, I should note that after my discussion with Marion, I went to Pramod's house, where I found him up on the roof flying his kite. I asked him why he hadn't taken Marion sightseeing, and he said he just wanted to fly his kite at home. As far as I could tell, there never was another higher-paying customer whom he was holding out for.
9. The emphasis on performance has also animated the work of an increasing number of tourism scholars who have sought to understand how tourist places and experiences are continually produced and reconstituted through embodied performances. See, for instance, Bærenholdt, Haldrup, Larsen, and Urry 2004; Coleman and Crang 2002; and Edensor 1998.
10. As was the case with many tourists, for Jorgen, the poverty of India was a recurring source of fascination, and he was one of several tourists whom I encountered who actually expressed disappointment that Banaras did not have gigantic sprawling slums for him to visit. For instance, at one point during his stay he hired Jay Yadav's older brother Raj to take him on a rickshaw tour of the city's slums and came back complaining that there was not enough "squalor" to see.
11. However, this also made tourists feel that that their gifts were far more generous than they really were. For instance, tourists would speak proudly about the "thousands of rupees" they gave to these children, and almost lose sight of the fact that they were only giving $50 or $100 in U.S. currency. For example, Jorgen acted as though the 4,000 rupees he was giving Mohan was a significant investment in "his future."
12. Several months before, in similar fashion, Mohan had brought me home to meet his family, and after my first visit his mother began inviting me every Saturday for a *kitchery* lunch. She knew it was one of my favorite meals, but she also knew about my research project and my interest in her sons, and she suspected that I might be in a position to help them financially. Occasionally, I was called upon to assist with "schooling fees" for her sons and daughter. However, to Mohan's relief, this was not information that I shared with Jorgen.

13. As Baudrillard writes, "the objects of psychic investment" is one of "passion and projection—qualified by its exclusive relation with the subject who cathects it" (Baudrillard 1981, 64–65).
14. Recently, within studies of tourism there has been an increasing interest in moving beyond the "gaze" and exploring the multisensory modes of touristic practice and appropriation that shape tourist experiences. For one such example, see Coleman and Crang 2002.
15. In this regard, it may be appropriate to view the touristic turn inward as the latest manifestation of what MacCannell described many years ago as "the dialectic of authenticity" (MacCannell 1976). However, in this manifestation, people as opposed to places, and increasingly the tourist's self as opposed to the other's, become the site around which the compelling travel experience is pursued and produced.
16. This is also to suggest that perhaps "the internationalization" and democratization of the tourist gaze are, in a sense, sowing the seeds of its destruction and thus, paradoxically, displacing the gaze as the primary mode through which tourists want to consume places and experiences.
17. For other attempts to explore the articulations between intimacy and larger socioeconomic transformations, see Berlant 2000; Hochschild 2003; Illouz 2007; Povinelli 2006; Zelizer 2005.
18. As Sennett himself notes, his notion of the turn inward or inner-directed subject is quite different from the concept that David Riesman developed in his seminal text *The Lonely Crowd*. See Sennett 1976, 5.
19. For instance, although Anthony Giddens also argues that modern subjects have developed a preoccupation with intimacy and what he calls "pure relationships," he challenges the idea that this can be simply cast as a form of pathological narcissism. See Giddens 1991, 1992.
20. Yet does the desire for intimacy and recognition differ from the other kinds of motivations and experiences that have been so widely discussed and debated within the tourism literature? For this research has made it immanently clear that not all tourists seek to encounter culturally exotic or authentic others (Cohen 1979; Feifer 1985; Hamilton-Smith 1987; Urry 1990; Wickens 2002). Feifer, for instance, argues that the post-tourists' travel experiences are much more oriented around a set of playful dispositions and an acceptance of, if not delight in, the staged and fabricated nature of tourist attractions. Moreover, the idea that the tourist's journey through space often entails an inner psychological journey as well, and a quest for self-discovery, has also been widely remarked upon (E. Cohen 1979; Galani-Moutafi 1999, Graburn 1989; Noy 2004). Finally, as John Urry has pointed out, the quest for intensely emotional experiences and connections has a long history within the romantic tradition of travel, and thus cannot be portrayed as a unique development of late capitalism (Urry 1990).

    It might seem, therefore, that the tourists discussed in this chapter could be adequately described and understood by referencing this existing literature. However, to do so would leave two important differences unattended to. First, although the tourists I have discussed were frequently driven by a quest for self-discovery, the discovery they longed for was not just the product of an inner psychological transformation that was facilitated by their physical journey through space or their ability to gaze into the lives of the other, as some scholars have noted. But rather, again, it was predicated upon receiving recognition from these others and through their more intimate connections with them, being made to feel that they were human beings and not just opportunities for profit.

Second, while Urry has argued that romanticism gave rise to an unprecedented yearning for highly individual and emotionally engaging travel experiences, and while he proposes that "the romantic gaze" has been one of the main "mechanisms" which has helped "spread tourism on a global scale" as it "seeks ever-new objects of the gaze" (Urry 1990, 46), in his description of romantic or scenic tourism, the landscape is still the central object of the tourist gaze, and the gaze is still the primary mode of appropriation.

21. The examples that I have given in this chapter resonate with Vincanne Adam's illuminating study of encounters between Western tourists and Nepali Sherpa. By employing the concepts of mimesis and seduction, Adams explores the way that Western tourists and Sherpa become mutually implicated in the production of each other's identities and subjectivities. In addition to seeking an authentic Sherpa Other, Adams argues that Western tourists also yearn for "self realization by way of intimacy with the other" (Adams 1996, 176).

8. MONEY, GENDER, AND THE (IM)MORALITY OF EXCHANGE

1. Janet Carsten documents a similar phenomenon in a Malay fishing community. She shows how women are regarded as "purifying" or "cooking" money by transforming men's earnings "from a means of exchange to a consumption good so that it ceases to threaten and actually sustains the household" (Carsten 1989, 118).
2. This stands in marked contrast to what the Vatuks reported in their writings on the "The Social Context of Gift Exchange" in India. As they observed, "it is considered a 'sin' (*pap*) to accept any gift or material assistance from a daughter, unless it is immediately returned and augmented in quantity" (Vatuk and Vatuk 1971, 216). Although I did encounter this idea among many people in Banaras, it is interesting how mothers like Sharmila and Madhuri tried to ameliorate this stigma by emphasizing their desperation.
3. The boys far preferred the term "guide" over *dalal*, which translates as "commission man" or "broker," but guiding and commission work (*dalali*) were recognized as one and the same activities. *Dalali* is the term used for the actual commission received but also refers to the activity of doing commission work (*dalali ka kam karna* or *dalali karna*).
4. In fact, as I have discussed elsewhere (see Huberman 2010), the moral perils associated with the earnings of dalali bore a striking resemblance to the moral perils typically associated with the proceeds of dan. Moreover, although numerous anthropologists have debated and tried to account for the morally perilous nature of this typically unreciprocated gift (Östör, Fruzzetti, and Barnett 1992; Gregory 1997; Laidlaw 1996; Parry 1980, 1985, 1986, 1989, 1994; Raheja 1988; Snodgrass 2001), within anthropological studies of India, far less attention has been paid to the way that "commercial exchanges become the focus of a very similar symbolic elaboration" (Parry 1989, 66).
5. For examples of such analyses and other writings on the symbolism of money, see Bloch 1989; Carsten 1989; Comaroff and Comaroff 1999; Ndjio 2008; Parry and Bloch 1989; Stirrat 1989; Taussig 1980; Toren 1989.
6. More recently, in his research on laborers at the Bhilali steel plant in Chhattisgarhi, Parry also reports that the term *dalal* is used as a term of abuse. See Parry 2008, 240.
7. Within anthropological studies of India, a tremendous amount of discussion and debate has been devoted to the concepts of purity and pollution. Indeed, as Susan Bean notes, "there are probably no ethnographies that do not discuss the role of

purity and pollution in Indian social life" (Bean 1981, 575). Although this is certainly not the place to enter into a detailed discussion of these concepts, interested readers might consult Bean 1981; Dumont 1970; Glucklich 1984; Madan 1991; and Marglin 1977.
8. Italics added.
9. While *auqaat* can be used to talk about one's current financial capacities, people in Dasashwamedh commonly used it to reference to one's enduring economic standing or position.
10. As Kumar notes: "The rites of bahri alang and their constituent elements—the peace of the outside, the freshness of the early morning, and the ritual of cleansing—are all centered in the body. It is the body that is given a treat, that is allowed to indulge in sensation. In Banaras, as perhaps in popular Hindu thought in general, tremendous importance is attached to the maintenance, beautification, and satisfaction of the body, made possible by complex and systemic notions of diet, rest, health, balance, and pleasure" (ibid., 111).
11. For other accounts that have cited the pursuit of masti as a central feature in the Banarasi worldview, see Parry 1994 and Sukul 1974. For further accounts of the mastram as an idealized cultural figure, see Lynch 1990.
12. As Kumar points out, the riverfront is by no means the only traditionally recognized site of pleasure and leisure among lower-class males in Banaras. *Ghumna phirna*, or wandering through the city's crowded bazaars and narrow galis, is also recognized as one of the primary delights of living in Banaras (Kumar 1995, 89). However, as will be seen, these children were not perceived as simply wandering through the bazaars, but rather they were viewed as consuming their way through the bazaar, of being fixated with it.
13. See, for example, Alter 2002; Appadurai 1981; Babb 1970; L. Cohen 1998; Conlon 1995; Daniel 1984; Lamb 2000; Lynch 1990; Marriott 1968, 1976; Parry 1985, 1994.
14. In this regard, Frank Conlon's (1995) article "Dining Out in Bombay" provides an interesting site of contrast. Drawing upon the work of Appadurai and Breckenridge, who, as Conlon notes, also suggest that there may exist a "more subtle cultural desire to insulate commercial dealings and food transactions from each other . . . [because of] the Hindu view of food as a central to the links between men and gods" (Conlon 1995, 92), Conlon examines the way that the public dining and the restaurant scene in Bombay has developed in tandem with an emerging middle- and upper-class "cosmopolitan public culture." As opposed to evoking fears of an untamed outside, Conlon discusses the way that restaurants provide consumers with new and "modern" forms of identity, excitement, and pleasure.
15. Kumar also notes that the cinema has become one of the primary sources of entertainment for the youth in Banaras, and she ascribes it a central role in processes of cultural change (Kumar 1988, 109).
16. Here it should be noted that *aish karna* also frequently connotes indulging in sexual pleasures, and the term for "a place of pleasure; inner women's quarters" is *aishgaah*. One of the common concerns that people articulated about the boys who worked in the foreign tourism line was that they got "caught in the Western woman's trap" (*maim ke chakar mein phas jaate hain*).
17. Although all of these speakers maintained that the influx of foreign tourist wealth was making these children greedier, and even proposed that the solution might lie in keeping tourists out of Banaras, Rahul's reference to the "greed that was *inside* of him," implies, as Parry observed, that "material acquisition and self-interest" were recognized as "mainsprings of human action" regardless of whether or not the foreign tourism industry was there to exacerbate this quality.

18. Parry and Bloch further note that "the articulation between the two spheres is, however, by no means unproblematic. If the long-term cycle is not to be reduced to the transient world of the individual, they must be kept separate. . . . But if the long term is to be sustained by the creativity and vitality of the short-term cycle, they must also be related—hence the concern with the kinds of transformative processes of which the 'cooking' of money . . . is just one example" (Parry and Bloch 1989, 26).

9. CONCLUSION

1. As Marshall Sahlins writes, "nothing guarantees that situations encountered in practice will stereotypically follow from the cultural categories by which circumstances are interpreted and acted upon. Practice, rather, has its own dynamics—a 'structure of the conjuncture'—which meaningfully defines the persons and the objects that are parties to it" (Sahlins 1981, 35).
2. Psychoanalytic approaches have generated significant skepticism within anthropology. Some have argued they have no place within analyses of social life, while others have noted the problems involved with trying to apply such models cross-culturally. For an excellent review of both the critical reception and more recent development of psychoanalytic theory in anthropology, see Lindholm 2001.
3. In other words, I am suggesting that both tourists and locals had to contend with feelings of ontological insecurity. For tourists, this insecurity came from the sudden and acute experience of de-routinization that came with being a foreign visitor in India. For locals, this insecurity was a product of some of the more pervasive, and not yet fully metabolized changes that have accompanied Indian modernity.
4. From the standpoint of symbolic interactionism, such may be the case with all human beings. However, I suggest that this tendency is more pronounced among children who, in certain respects, have yet to fully establish a firm sense of their identity.
5. The anthropologist Elizabeth Chin also notes that anthropological methods that are heavy on talk, such as rambling oral histories or informational interviews, are often "entirely inappropriate" for children. In her ethnography, *Purchasing Power: Black Kids and American Consumer Culture*, she writes, "I found there was no surer way to render chatty kids suddenly monosyllabic than to directly engage them in conversation" (Chin 2001, 189).

REFERENCES

Adams, Vincanne. 1996. *Tigers of the Snow and Other Virtual Sherpas: An Ethnography of Himalayan Encounters*. Princeton: Princeton University Press.
Allison, Anne. 1994. *Nightwork: Sexuality, Pleasure, and Corporate Masculinity in a Tokyo Hostess Club*. Chicago: University of Chicago Press.
Altekar, A. S. 1947. *Benares and Sarnath: Past and Present*. 2nd ed. Varanasi: Banaras Hindu University.
Alter, Joseph. 1992. *The Wrestler's Body: Identity and Ideology in North India*. New Delhi: Munshiram Manoharlal.
———. 2002. "Nervous Masculinity: Consumption and the Production of Embodied Gender in Indian Wrestling." In *Everyday Life in South Asia*, edited by Diana Mines and Sarah Lamb, 132–145. Bloomington: Indiana University Press.
Appadurai, Arjun. 1981. "Gastro-Politics in Hindu South Asia." *American Ethnologist* 8(3): 494–511.
———. 1986. "Introduction: Commodities and the Politics of Value." In *The Social Life of Things: Commodities in Cultural Perspective*, edited by Arjun Appadurai, 3–63. Cambridge: Cambridge University Press.
———. 1986. "Is Homo Hierarchicus?" *American Ethnologist* 13(4): 745–761.
———. 1988. "Putting Hierarchy in Its Place." *Cultural Anthropology* 3(1): 36–49.
———. 1990. "Topographies of the Self: Praise and Emotion in Hindu India." In *Language and the Politics of Emotion*, edited by Catherine Lutz and Lila Abu-Lughod, 92–112. Cambridge: Cambridge University Press.
———. 1996. *Modernity at Large: Cultural Dimensions of Globalization*. Delhi: Oxford University Press.
Appadurai, Arjun, Frank Korom, and Margaret Mills, eds. 1994. *Gender, Genre, and Power in South Asian Expressive Traditions*. Delhi: Motilal Banarsidass.
Argyle, Michael. 1996. *The Social Psychology of Leisure*. London: Penguin.
Ariès, Phillip. 1962. *Centuries of Childhood: A Social History of Family Life*. New York: Vintage.
Babb, Lawrence. 1970. "The Food of the Gods in Chhatisgarh: Some Structural Features of Hindu Ritual." *Southwestern Journal of Anthropology* 25: 287–304.
———. 1983. "Destiny and Responsibility: Karma in Popular Hinduism." In *Karma: An Anthropological Inquiry*, edited by Charles Keyes and E. Valentine Daniel, 163–184. Berkeley: University of California Press.
Bærenholdt, Jørgen, Michael Haldrup, Jonas Larsen, and John Urry, eds. 2004. *Performing Tourist Places*. Aldershot: Ashgate.
Baker, C. D. 1982. "Adolescent-Adult Talk as a Practical Interpretive Problem." In *Doing Teaching: The Practical Management of Classrooms*, edited by G. Payne and E. Cuff, 104–125. London: Batsford.

Bakhtin, Mikhail. 1986. *Speech Genres & Other Late Essays*. Austin: University of Texas Press.
Barton, Bernadette. 2007. "Managing the Toll of Stripping: Boundary Setting Among Exotic Dancers." *Journal of Contemporary Ethnography* 36(5):571–596.
Baudrillard, Jean. 1981. *For a Critique of the Political Economy of the Sign*. Translated by Charles Levin. St. Louis, Mo.: Telos.
Bean, Susan. 1981. "Toward a Semiotics of 'Purity' and 'Pollution' in India." *American Ethnologist* 8(3): 575–595.
Bernstein, Elizabeth. 2007. *Temporarily Yours: Intimacy, Authenticity, and the Commerce of Sex*. Chicago: University of Chicago Press.
Berlant, Lauren, ed. 2000. *Intimacy*. Chicago: University of Chicago Press.
Bhabha, Homi. 1997. "Of Mimicry and Man: The Ambivalence of Colonial Discourse". In *Tensions of Empire*, edited by Frederick Cooper and Ann Laura Stoler, 152-162. Berkeley: University of California Press.
Bhattacharyya, Deborah. 1997. "Mediating India: An Analysis of a Guidebook." *Annals of Tourism Research* 21(2): 371–389.
Bloch, Maurice. 1989. "The Symbolism of Money in Imerina." In *Money and the Morality of Exchange*, edited by Jonathan Parry and Maurice Bloch, 165–190. Cambridge: Cambridge University Press.
Bluebond-Langner, Myra. 1978. *The Private Worlds of Dying Children*. Princeton: Princeton University Press.
Blumer, Herbert. 1969. *Symbolic Interactionism: Perspective and Method*. Englewood Cliffs, N.J.: Prentice-Hall.
Boorstin, Daniel. 1964. *The Image: A Guide to Pseudo-Events in America*. New York: Harper.
Booth, William. 1994. "On the Idea of the Moral Economy." *American Political Science Review* 88(3): 653–667.
Borocz, Josef. 1996. *Leisure Migration: A Sociological Study of Tourism*. Oxford: Pergamon.
Bourdieu, Pierre. 1980. *The Logic of Practice*. Stanford: Stanford University Press.
———. 1984. *Distinction: A Social Critique of the Judgment of Taste*. Translated by Richard Nice. Cambridge: Harvard University Press.
———. 1993. *The Field of Cultural Production*. New York: Columbia University Press.
Bourgois, Philippe. 1996. *In Search of Respect: Selling Crack in El Barrio*. Cambridge: Cambridge University Press.
Breckenridge, Carol, ed. 1995. *Consuming Modernity: Public Culture in a South Asian World*. Minneapolis: University of Minnesota Press.
Brennan, Denise. 2004. *What's Love Got to Do with It?: Transnational Desires and Sex Tourism in the Dominican Republic*. Durham: Duke University Press.
Briggs, Charles. 1986. *Learning How to Ask: A Sociolinguistic Appraisal of the Role of the Interview in Social Science Research*. Cambridge: Cambridge University Press.
Britton, Robert. 1980. "Shortcomings of Third World Tourism." In *Dialectics of Third World Development*, edited by Ingolf Vogeler and Anthony de Sousza, 241–248. Montclair, N.J.: Allanheld, Osmun.
Bruner, Edward. 1991. "Transformation of Self in Tourism." *Annals of Tourism Research* 18: 238–250.
———. 2005. *Culture on Tour: Ethnographies of Travel*. Chicago: University of Chicago Press.
Caine, W. S. 1890. *Pictureseque India: A Handbook for European Travelers*. London: George Routledge and Sons.
Cameron, Catherine. 1987. "The Marketing of Tradition." *City and Society* 1: 162–174.
———. 1989. "Cultural Tourism and Urban Revitalization." *Tourism Recreation Research* 14: 23–32.

Campbell, Colin. 1989. *The Romantic Ethic and the Spirit of Modern Consumerism*. Oxford: Blackwell.
Carman, John B. and Frédérique Apffel Marglin, eds. 1985. *Purity and Auspiciousness in Indian Society*. Leiden: E.J. Brill.
Carneiro da Cunha, Manuela. 1995. "Children, Politics and Culture: The Case of Brazilian Indians." In *Children and the Politics of Culture*, edited by Sharon Stephens, 282–291. Princeton: Princeton University Press.
Carsten, Janet. 1989. "Cooking Money: Gender and the Symbolic Transformation of Means of Exchange in a Malay Fishing Community." In *Money and the Morality of Exchange*, edited by Jonathan Parry and Maurice Bloch, 117–141. Cambridge: Cambridge University Press.
Carter, Anthony. 1992. "Hierarchy and the Concept of the Person." In *Concepts of the Person: Kinship, Caste, and Marriage in India*, edited by Ákos Östör, Lina Fruzz Etti, and Steve Barnett, 118–142. Delhi: Oxford University Press.
Castañeda, Claudia. 2002. *Figurations: Child, Bodies, Worlds*. Durham: Duke University Press.
Chakrabarty, Dipesh. 1989. *Rethinking Working-Class History*. Princeton: Princeton University Press.
———. 1991. "Open Space/Public Place: Garbage, Modernity and India." *South Asia* 14(1): 15–32.
———. 2000. *Provincializing Europe: Postcolonial Thought and Historical Difference*. Princeton: Princeton University Press.
Chambers, Erve. 2000. *Native Tours: The Anthropology of Travel and Tourism*. Long Grove, Ill.: Waveland.
Chatterjee, Partha. 1986. *Nationalist Thought and the Colonial World*. Minneapolis: University of Minnesota Press.
Chevrilllon, André. 1896. *In India*. Translated by William Marchant. New York: Holt.
Chin, Elizabeth. 2001. *Purchasing Power: Black Kids and American Consumer Culture*. Minneapolis: University of Minnesota Press.
Clifford, James, and George Marcus. 1986. *Writing Culture: The Poetics and Politics of Ethnography*. Berkeley: University of California Press.
Cocker, M. 1992. *Loneliness and Time: British Travel Writing in the Twentieth Century*. London: Secker and Warburg.
Cohen, Erik. 1972. "Toward a Sociology of International Tourism." *Social Research* 39(1): 164–182.
———. 1973. "Nomads from Affluence: Notes on the Phenomenon of Drifter-Tourism." *International Journal of Comparative Sociology* 14(1–2): 89–103.
———. 1974. "Who Is a Tourist? A Conceptual Clarification." *Sociological Review* 22(4): 527–555.
———. 1979. "A Phenomenology of Tourist Experiences." *Sociology* 13: 179–201.
———. 2004. "Backpacking: Diversity and Change." *Tourism and Cultural Change* 1(2): 95–110.
Cohen, Lawrence. 1998. *No Aging in India: Alzheimer's, the Bad Family, and Other Modern Things*. Berkeley: University of California Press.
Cohn, Bernard. 1996. *Colonialism and Its Forms of Knowledge*. Princeton: Princeton University Press.
Coleman, Simon, and Mike Crang, eds. 2002. *Tourism: Between Place and Performance*. New York: Berghahn.
Coles, Robert. 1986. *The Political Life of Children*. Boston: Houghton Mifflin.
Comaroff, Jean, and John Comaroff. 1999. "Occult Economies and the Violence of Abstraction: Notes from the South African Postcolony." *American Ethnologist* 26(3): 279–301.

Conlon, Frank. 1995. "Dining Out in Bombay." In *Consuming Modernity: Public Culture in a South Asian World*, edited by Carol Breckenridge, 90–130. Minneapolis: University of Minnesota Press.

Cook, Daniel. 2002. "Introduction: Interrogating Symbolic Childhood." In *Symbolic Childhood*, edited by Daniel Cook, 1–16. New York: Peter Lang.

———. 2004. *The Commodification of Childhood: The Children's Clothing Industry and the Rise of the Child-Consumer.* Durham: Duke University Press.

———. 2008. "Introduction: Dramaturgies of Value in Market Places." In *Lived Experiences of Public Consumption: Encounters with Value in Marketplaces on Five Continents*, edited by Daniel Cook, 1–10. New York: Palgrave Macmillan.

Copeman, Jacob. 2009. *Veins of Devotion: Blood Donation and Religious Experience in North India.* New Brunswick: Rutgers University Press.

Corsaro, W. A. 1979. "'We're Friends, Right?': Children's Use of Access Rituals in a Nursery School." *Language and Society* 8: 315–336.

Culler, Jonathan. 1981. "Semiotics of Tourism." *American Journal of Semiotics* 1: 127–140.

Cunningham, Hugh. 2005. *Children and Childhood in Western Society since 1500.* 2nd ed. London: Pearson.

D'Andrea, Anthony. 2007. *Global Nomads: Techno and New Age as Transnational Countercultures in Ibiza and Goa.* London: Routledge.

Daniel, E. Valentine. 1983. "Karma Divined in a Ritual Capsule." In *Karma: An Anthropological Inquiry*, edited by Charles F. Keyes and E. Valentine Daniel, 83–118. Berkeley: University of California Press.

———. 1984. *Fluid Signs: Being a Person the Tamil Way.* Berkeley: University of California Press.

Daniel, Sheryl. 1983. "The Tool Box Approach of the Tamil to the Issues of Moral Responsibility and Human Destiny." In *Karma: An Anthropological Inquiry*, edited by Charles Keyes and E. Valentine Daniel, 27–62. Berkeley: University of California Press.

Dann, Graham. 1989. "The Tourist as Child: Some Reflections." *Cahiers du Tourisme, Serie C.* No. 135. Paris: Centre des Hautes Études Touristiques.

———. 1996. *The Language of Tourism: A Sociolinguistic Perspective.* Wallingford, UK: CAB International.

Das, Veena. 1977. *Structure and Cognition: Aspects of Hindu Caste and Ritual.* Delhi: Oxford University Press.

——— 1988. "Femininity and the Orientation to the Body." In *Women: Explorations in Gender Identity*, edited by K. Chanana, 193–207. New Delhi: Orient Longman.

Davies, B. 1982. *Life in the Classroom Playground.* London: Routledge and Kegan Paul.

De Mause, Lloyd, ed. 1974. *The History of Childhood.* New York: Psychohistory Press.

Denzin, N. 1970. *The Research Act in Sociology.* London: Butterworth.

Derné, Steve. 1995. *Culture in Action: Family Life, Emotion, and Male Dominance in Banaras, India.* Albany: State University of New York Press.

Desforges, L. 1998. "'Checking Out the Planet': Global Representations/Local Identities and Youth Travel." In *Cool Places: Geographies of Youth Cultures*, edited by Tracey Skelton and Gill Valentine, 175–192. London: Routledge.

Desmond, Jane. 1999. *Staging Tourism: Bodies on Display from Waikiki to Sea World.* Chicago: University of Chicago Press.

Dichter, E. 1981. "Foreword" to *The Psychology of Leisure Travel*, edited by E. Mayo and L. Jarvis, ix–xi. Boston: CBI.

Doron, Assa. 2008. *Caste, Occupation, and Politics on the Ganges: Passages of Resistance.* Farnham: Ashgate.

Dube, Leela. 2001. *Anthropological Explorations in Gender*. New Delhi: Sage.
Duggan, Betty. 1997. "Tourism, Cultural Authenticity, and the Native Crafts Cooperative: The Eastern Cherokee Experience." In *Tourism and Culture: An Applied Perspective*, edited by Erve Chambers, 31–57. Albany: State University of New York Press.
Dumont, Louis. 1970. *Homo Hierarchicus*. Chicago: University of Chicago Press.
Eck, Diana. 1983. *Banaras: City of Light*. London: Routledge and Kegan Paul.
Edensor, Tim. 1998. *Tourists at the Taj: Performance and Meaning at a Symbolic Site*. New York: Routledge.
———. 2001. "Performing Tourism, Staging Tourism: (Re)Producing Tourist Space and Practice." *Tourist Studies* 1: 59–82.
———. 2007. "Foreword" to *Raj Rhapsodies: Tourism, Heritage and the Seduction of History*, edited by Carol Henderson and Maxine Weisgrau, xv–xxvi. Aldershot: Ashgate.
Elliott, Anthony. 2002. *Psychoanalytic Theory: An Introduction*. Durham: Duke University Press.
———. 2004. *Social Theory since Freud: Traversing Social Imaginaries*. London: Routledge.
Feifer, Maxine. 1985. *Going Places*. London: Macmillan.
Field, Norma. 1995. "The Child as Laborer and Consumer: The Disappearance of Childhood in Contemporary Japan." In *Children and the Politics of Culture*, edited by Sharon Stephens, 51–78. Princeton: Princeton University Press.
Frank, Katherine. 2002. *G-Strings and Sympathy: Strip Club Regulars and Male Desire*. Durham: Duke University Press.
Galani-Moutafi, Vasiliki. 1999. "The Self and the Other: Traveler, Ethnographer, Tourist." *Annals of Tourism Research* 27: 203–224.
Gamradt, Jan. 1995. "Jamaican Children's Representations of Tourism." *Annals of Tourism Research* 22(4): 753–762.
Gell, Alfred. 1986. "Newcomers to the World of Goods: The Muria Gonds." In *The Social Life of Things: Commodities in Cultural Perspective*, edited by Arjun Appadurai, 110–138. Cambridge: Cambridge University Press.
Giddens, Anthony. 1991. *Modernity and Self-Identity: Self and Society in the Late Modern Age*. Stanford: Stanford University Press.
———. 1992. *The Transformation of Intimacy: Sexuality, Love & Eroticism in Modern Societies*. Stanford: Stanford University Press.
Glauser, B. 1990. "Street Children: Deconstructing a Construct." In *Constructing and Reconstructing Childhood: Contemporary Issues in the Sociological Study of Childhood*, edited by A. James and A. Prout, 145–161. London: Falmer.
Glucklich, Ariel. 1984. "Karma and Pollution in Hindu Dharma: Distinguishing Law from Nature." *Contributions to Indian Sociology* 18(1): 25–44.
Goffman, Erving. 1959. *The Presentation of Self in Everyday Life*. New York. Anchor Books.
———. 1963. *Stigma: Notes on the Management of Spoiled Identity*. New York: Simon & Schuster.
———. 1963. *Behavior in Public Places: Notes on the Social Organization of Gatherings*. New York: Free Press.
———. 1967. *Interaction Ritual*. Chicago: Aldine.
Gold, Ann Grodzins. 1994. "Gender, Violence and Power: Rajasthani Stories of Shakti." In *Women as Subjects: South Asian Histories*, edited by Nita Kumar, 26–48. Charlottesville: University of Virginia Press.
Goldstein, Donna. 1998. "Nothing Bad Intended: Child Discipline, Punishment, and Survival in a Shantytown in Rio de Janeiro, Brazil." In *Small Wars: The Cultural Politics of Childhood*, edited by Nancy Scheper-Hughes and Carolyn Sargent, 389–415. Berkeley: University of California Press.

Gottlieb, Alma. 2004. *The Afterlife Is Where We Come From*. Chicago: University of Chicago Press.

Graburn, Nelson. 1983. "The Anthropology of Tourism." *Annals of Tourism Research* 10(1): 9–33.

———. 1989. "Tourism: The Sacred Journey." In *Hosts and Guests: The Anthropology of Tourism*, edited by Valene Smith, 21–36. Philadelphia: University of Pennsylvania Press.

———. 1995. "The Past and Present in Japan: Nostalgia and Neo-Traditionalism in Contemporary Japanese Domestic Tourism." In *Change in Tourism: People, Places, Processes*, edited by R. Butler and D. Pearce, 47–70. London: Routledge.

Graeber, David. 2001. *Toward an Anthropological Theory of Value: The False Coin of Our Own Dreams*. New York: Palgrave.

Greenwood, Davydd. 1989. "Culture by the Pound: An Anthropological Perspective on Tourism as Cultural Commoditization." In *Hosts and Guests: The Anthropology of Tourism*, edited by Valene Smith, 171–186. Philadelphia: University of Pennsylvania Press.

Gregory, Chris. 1997. *Savage Money: The Anthropology and Politics of Commodity Exchange*. London: Routledge.

Grima, Benedicte. 1994. "The Role of Suffering in Women's Performance in *Paxto*." In *Gender, Genre, and Power in South Asian Expressive Traditions*, edited by Arjun Appadurai, Frank Korom, and Margaret Mills, 81–101. Delhi: Motilaal Banarsidass.

Grugeon, Elizabeth. 1988. "Children's Oral Culture: A Transitional Experience." In *Oracy Matters: The Development of Talking and Listening in Education,* edited by Terry Phillips and Andrew Wilkinson, 159–173. Philadelphia: Open University Press.

Guttman, Matthew. 1998. "*Mamitis* and the Traumas of Development in a *Colonial Popular* of Mexico City." In *Small Wars: The Cultural Politics of Childhood*, edited by Nancy Scheper-Hughes and Carolyn Sargent, 389–415. Berkeley: University of California Press.

Hall, Kathleen. 1995. "'There's a Time to Act English and a Time to Act Indian': The Politics of Identity among British-Sikh Teenagers." In *Children and the Politics of Culture*, edited by Sharon Stephens, 243–264. Princeton: Princeton University Press.

Hamilton-Smith, Elery. 1987. "Four Kinds of Tourism?" *Annals of Tourism Research* 14: 332–344.

Hardman, C. 1973. "Can There Be an Anthropology of Children?" *Journal of the Anthropology Society of Oxford* 4(1): 85–99.

Harvey, David. 1990. *The Condition of Postmodernity*. Cambridge: Blackwell.

Hathi, Tushar. 1998. "Tourism and Indian Development: In Search of a New Perspective." In *Tourism in India and India's Economic Development*, edited by Kartik Roy and Clement Tisdell, 11–20. New York: Nova Science.

Havell, E. B. 1905. *Benares the Sacred City*. London: Blackie and Son.

Heber, Reginald. 1829. *Narrative of a Journey through the Upper Provinces of India from Calcutta to Bombay, 1824–1825*. London: John Murray.

Hénaff, Marcel. 2010. *The Price of Truth: Gift, Money, and Philosophy*. Translated by Jean-Lous Morhange. Stanford: Stanford University Press.

Henderson, Carol, and Maxine Weisgrau, eds. 2007. *Raj Rhapsodies, Tourism, and Heritage in India*. Aldershot: Ashgate.

Hewamanne, Sandya. 2008. *Stitching Identities in a Free Trade Zone: Gender and Politics in Sri Lanka*. Philadelphia: University of Pennsylvania Press.

Higonnet, Anne. 1998. *Pictures of Innocence: The History and Crisis of Ideal Childhood*. London: Thames and Hudson.

Hochschild, Arlie. 1983. *The Managed Heart: Commercialization of Human Feeling*. Berkeley: University of California Press.

Huberman, Jenny. 2005. "Consuming Children: Reading the Impacts of Tourism in the City of Banaras." *Childhood: Special Edition, Children and Global Consumer Culture* 12(2): 161–176.
———. 2006. "Working and Playing Banaras: A Study of Tourist Encounters, Sentimental Journeys and the Business of Visitation." Ph.D. dissertation, University of Chicago.
———. 2008. "Shopping *for* People, or Shopping for *People?* Deciphering the Object of Consumption among Tourists in Banaras." In *The Lived Experiences of Public Consumption: Encounters with Value in Marketplaces on Five Continents*, edited by Daniel Cook, 50–68. New York: Palgrave Macmillan.
———. 2010. "The Dangers of *Dalāli*, the Dangers of *Dān*." *South Asia: The Journal of South Asian Studies* 33(3): 399–420.
———. 2011. "Tourism in India: The Moral Economy of Gender in Banaras." In *A Companion to the Anthropology of India*, edited by Isabella Clark Decès, 169–185. Malden, Mass.: Wiley-Blackwell.
———. 2012. "Of Sales Pitches and Speech Genres: Peddling Personality on the Riverfront of Banaras." In *Global Tourism; Cultural Heritage and Economic Encounters*, edited by Sarah Lyon and Christian Wells, 304–335. Lanham, Md.: Alta Mira.
Hughes, George. 1995. "Authenticity in Tourism." *Annals of Tourism Research* 22(4): 781–803.
Hutnyk, John. 1996. *The Rumour of Calcutta: Tourism, Charity, and the Poverty of Representation*. London: Zed Books.
Illouz, Eva. 2007. *Cold Intimacies: The Making of Emotional Capitalism*. Cambridge: Polity.
Inden, Ronald. 1990. *Imagining India*. Oxford: Blackwell.
Inden, Ronald, and Ralph Nicholas. 1977. *Kinship in Bengali Culture*. Chicago: University of Chicago Press.
Ivy, Marilyn. 1998. "Have You Seen Me? Recovering the Inner Child in Late Twentieth-Century America." In *Children and the Politics of Culture*, edited by Sharon Stephens, 79–104. Princeton: Princeton University Press.
James, Allison, Chris Jenks, and Alan Prout. 1998. *Theorizing Childhood*. New York: Teacher's College Press.
James, Allison, and Alan Prout, eds. 1997. *Constructing and Reconstructing Childhood: Contemporary Issues in the Sociological Study of Childhood*. London: RoutledgeFalmer.
Jenks, C. 1996. *Childhood*. London: Routledge.
John, Mary. 1998. "Children's Rights in a Free-Market Culture." In *Children and the Politics of Culture*, edited by Sharon Stephens, 105–137. Princeton: Princeton University Press.
Kaiser, Susan, and Kathleen Hunn. 2002. "Fashioning Innocence and Anxiety: Clothing, Gender and Symbolic Childhood." In *Symbolic Childhood*, edited by Daniel Cook, 183–208. New York: Peter Lang.
Kakar, Sudhir. 1981. *The Inner World: A Psycho-analytic Study of Childhood and Society in India*. Delhi: Oxford University Press.
Kaplan, Caren. 1996. *Questions of Travel: Postmodern Discourses of Displacement*. Durham: Duke University Press.
Kett, Joseph. 1977. *Rites of Passage: Adolescence in America 1790 to the Present*. New York: Basic Books.
Keyes, Charles. 1983. "Introduction: The Study of Popular Ideas of Karma." In *Karma: An Anthropological Inquiry*, edited by Charles Keyes and Valentine Daniel, 1–26. Berkeley: University of California Press.
Klein, Melanie. [1946] 1987. "Notes on Some Schizoid Mechanisms." In *The Selected Melanie Klein*, edited by Juliet Mitchell, 175–200. New York: Free Press.
———. [1948] 1975. "On the Theory of Anxiety and Guilt." In Klein, *Envy and Gratitude and Other Works 1946–1963*, 25–40. New York: Delacorte.

———. [1955] 1987. "The Psychoanalytic Play Technique." In *The Selected Melanie Klein*, edited by Juliet Mitchell, 35–54. New York: Free Press.

———. 1975. *Envy and Gratitude and Other Works 1946–1963*. New York: Delacorte.

Kovarik, J. 1994. "The Space and Time of Children at the Interface of Psychology and Sociology." In *Childhood Matters: Social Theory, Practice and Politics*, edited by J. Qvortrup et al., 101–122. Aldershot: Avebury.

Kumar, Nita. 1988. *The Artisans of Banaras: Popular Culture and Identity, 1880–1986*. Princeton: Princeton University Press.

———. 1994. "Introduction" to *Women as Subjects: South Asian Histories*, edited by Nita Kumar, 1–25. Charlottesville: University Press of Virginia.

———. 1995 (1988). *The Artisans of Banaras: Popular Culture and Identity, 1880–1986*. New Delhi: Orient Longman.

———. 2007. *The Politics of Gender, Community, and Modernity: Essays on Education in India*. Oxford: Oxford University Press.

Kumar, Subas. 1998. "The Tourism Industry in India: Economic Significance and Emerging Issues." In *Tourism in India and India's Economic Development*, edited by Kartik Roy and Clement Tisdell, 21–46. New York: Nova Science.

Kusserow, Adrie. 2004. *American Individualisms: Child Rearing and Social Class in Three Neighborhoods*. New York: Palgrave.

Lacy, Julie, and William Douglass. 2002. "Beyond Authenticity: The Meanings and Uses of Cultural Tourism." *Tourist Studies* 2(1): 5–21.

La Fontaine, J. S. 1998. "Ritual and Satanic Abuse in England." In *Small Wars: The Cultural Politics of Childhood*, edited by Nancy Scheper-Hughes and Carolyn Sargent, 277–294. Berkeley: University of California Press.

Laidlaw, James. 1996. "The Uses and Abuses of Theology: Comments on Jonathan Parry's Death in Banaras." *South Asia Research* 16(1): 31–44.

———. 2000. "A Free Gift Makes No Friends." *Journal of the Royal Anthropological Institute* 6(4): 617–634.

Lakoff, George, and Mark Johnson. 1980. *Metaphors We Live By*. Chicago: University of Chicago Press.

Lamb, Sarah. 2000. *White Saris and Sweet Mangoes: Gender, Aging, and Body in North India*. Berkeley: University of California Press.

———. 2002. "Love and Aging in Bengali Families." In *Everyday Life in South Asia*, edited by Diane Mines and Sarah Lamb, 56–68. Bloomington: Indiana University Press.

Lareau, Annette. 2003. *Unequal Childhoods: Class, Race, and Family Life*. Berkeley: University of California Press.

Lasch, Christopher. 1978. *The Culture of Narcissism: American Life in An Age of Diminishing Expectations*. New York: W.W. Norton.

Lett, J. 1983. "Ludic and Liminoid Aspects of Charter Yacht Tourism in the Caribbean." *Annals of Tourism Research* 10: 35–56.

Lever, Janet. 1976. "Sex Differences in the Games Children Play." *Social Problems* 23: 478–487.

LeVine, Robert. 2007. "Ethnographic Studies of Childhood: A Historical Overview." *American Anthropologist* 109(2): 247–260.

Liechty, Mark. 2003. *Suitably Modern: Making Middle-Class Culture in a New Consumer Society*. Princeton: Princeton University Press.

Liddle, Joanna, and Rama Joshi. 1989. *Daughters of Independence: Gender, Caste, and Class in India*. New Brunswick: Rutgers University Press.

Lindholm, Charles. 2001. *Culture and Identity: The History, Theory, and Practice of Psychological Anthropology*. New York: McGraw-Hill.

Loker-Murphy, L. 1996. "Backpackers in Australia: A Motivation-based Segmentation Study." *Journal of Travel and Tourism Marketing* 5(4): 23–45.
Loker-Murphy, L., and P. Pearce. 1995. "Young Budget Travelers: Backpackers in Australia." *Annals of Tourism Research* 22: 819–843.
Lutz, Catherine. 1988. *Unnatural Emotions: Everyday Sentiments on a Micronesian Atoll and Their Challenge to Western Theory.* Chicago: University of Chicago Press.
Lynch, Caitrin. 2007. *Juki Girls, Good Girls: Gender and Cultural Politics in Sri Lanka's Global Garment Industry.* Ithaca: Cornell University Press.
Lynch, Owen. 1990. "The Mastraam: Emotion and Personhood among Mathura's Chaubes." In *Divine Passions: The Social Construction of Emotion in India*, edited by Owen Lynch, 91–115. Berkeley: University of California Press.
MacCannell, Dean. 1976. *The Tourist: A New Theory of the Leisure Class.* London: Macmillan.
———. 1992. *Empty Meeting Grounds: The Tourist Papers.* London: Routledge.
Madan, T. N. 1991. "Auspiciousness and Purity: Some Reconsiderations." *Contributions to Indian Sociology* 25(2): 287–294.
Majumdar, Rochna. 2002. "Self-Sacrifice versus Self-Interest: A Non-Historicist Reading of the History of Women's Rights in India." *Comparative Studies of South Asia, Africa and the Middle East* 22(1–2): 20–36.
Maoz, Darya. 2004. "The Conquerors and the Settlers: Two Groups of Young Israeli Backpackers in India." In *Global Nomad: Backpacker Travel in Theory and Practice*, edited by G. Richards and J. Wilson, 109–122. Clevedon, UK: Channel View Publications.
———. 2005. "Young Adult Israeli Backpackers in India." In *Israeli Backpackers: From Tourism to Rite of Passage*, edited by C. Noy and E. Cohen, 159–188. New York: State University of New York Press.
———. 2007. "Backpackers' Motivations: The Role of Culture and Nationality." *Annals of Tourism Research* 34(1): 122–140.
Marglin, Frédérique. 1977. "Power, Purity, and Pollutions: Aspects of the Caste System Reconsidered." *Contributions to Indian Sociology* 11(2): 245–270.
Markus, Hazel, and Shinobu Kitayama. 1991. "Culture and the Self: Implications for Cognition, Emotion, and Motivation." *Psychological Review* 9(2): 224–253.
Marriott, McKim. 1968. "Caste Ranking and Food Transactions: A Matrix Analysis." In *Structure and Change in Indian Society, 133–171,* Chicago: Aldine.
———. 1976. "Hindu Transactions; Diversity without Dualism." In *Transaction and Meaning: Directions in the Anthropology of Exchange and Symbolic Behavior*, edited by Bruce Kapferer, 109–142. Philadelphia: Institute for the Study of Human Issues.
———. 1990. "Constructing an Indian Ethnosociology." In *India through Hindu Categories*, edited by McKim Marriott, 1–39. New Delhi: Sage Publications.
———. 1998. "The Female Core Explored Ethnosociologically." *Contributions to Indian Sociology* 32(2): 279–304.
Marriott, McKim, and Rondald B. Inden. 1977. "Toward an Ethnosociology of South Asian Caste Systems." In *The New Wind: Changing Identities in South Asia*, edited by Kenneth David, 227–238. The Hague: Mouton.
Maseide, P. 1990. "The Social Construction of Research Information." *Acta Sociologica* 33(1): 3–13.
Mauss, Marcel. 1990 (1954). *The Gift: The Form and Reason for Exchange in Archaic Societies.* Translated by W. D. Halls. New York: W. W. Norton.
Mayall, B. 1994. *Children's Childhoods: Observed and Experienced.* London: Falmer.
McClintock, Anne. 1995. *Imperial Leather: Race, Gender, and Sexuality in the Colonial Conquest.* New York: Routledge.
McGregor, R.S., ed.1993. *The Oxford Hindi-English Dictionary.* Oxford: Oxford University Press.

Mead, George Herbert. 1934. *Mind, Self and Society*. Chicago: University of Chicago Press.
Mead, Margaret. 1928. *Coming of Age in Samoa: A Psychological Study of Primitive Youth for Western Civilization*. New York: William Morrow.
Medick, Hans, and David Warren Sabean, eds. 1984. *Interest and Emotion: Essays on the Study of Family and Kinship*. Cambridge: Cambridge University Press.
Mellinger, Wayne. 1994. "Toward a Critical Analysis of Tourism Representations." *Annals of Tourism Research* 21(2): 792–729.
Mills, C. Wright. 1959. *The Sociological Imagination*. Oxford: Oxford University Press.
Mines, Mattison. 1988. "Conceptualizing the Person: Hierarchical Society and Individual Autonomy in India." *American Anthropologist* 90(3): 568–579.
———. 1994. *Public Faces, Private Voices: Community and Individuality in South India*. Berkeley: University of California Press.
Misri, Urvashi. 1985. "Child and Childhood: A Conceptual Construction." *Contributions to Indian Sociology* 19(1): 115–132.
Mitchell, Juliet, ed. 1987. *The Selected Melanie Klein*. New York: Free Press.
Morton, Helen. 1996. *Becoming Tongan: An Ethnography of Childhood*. Honolulu: University of Hawai'i Press.
Munday, E. 1979. "'When Is a Child a Child'? Alternative Systems and Classification." *Journal of the Anthropology Society of Oxford* 10(3): 162–172.
Munn, Nancy. 1992 (1986). *The Fame of Gawa: A Symbolic Study of Value Transformation in a Massim (Papua New Guinea) Society*. Durham: Duke University Press.
Muzaini, Hamzah. 2006. "Backpacking Southeast Asia: Strategies of 'Looking Local.'" *Annals of Tourism Research* 33: 144–161.
Nash, Dennison. 1996. *Anthropology of Tourism*. Oxford: Pergamon Press.
Natrajan, Balmuri. 2005. "Caste, Class, and Community in India: An Ethnographic Approach." *Ethnology* 44(3): 227–241.
Ndjio, Basile. 2008. "Mokoagne Moni: Sorcery and New Forms of Wealth in Cameroon." *Past and Present* 199(3): 271–289.
Noy, Chaim. 2004. "This Trip Has Really Changed Me: Backpackers' Narratives of Self-Change." *Annals of Tourism Research* 3(1): 78–102.
Obeyesekere, Gananath. 1981. *Medusa's Hair: An Essay on Personal Symbols and Religious Experience*. Chicago: University of Chicago Press.
O'Flaherty, Wendy Doniger. 1976. *The Origins of Evil in Hindu Mythology*. Berkeley: University of California Press.
Olsen, Kjell. 2002. "Authenticity as a Concept in Tourism Research." *Tourist Studies* 2(2): 159–182.
Opie, I., and P. Opie. 1969. *Children's Games in Street and Playground*. Oxford: Oxford University Press.
———. 1977 (1959). *The Lore and Language of Schoolchildren*. Oxford: Oxford University Press.
Ortner, Sherry. 1999. *Life and Death on Mt. Everest: Sherpas and Himalayan Mountaineering*. Princeton: Princeton University Press.
Östör, Ákos, Lina Fruzzetti, and Steve Barnett, eds. 1992. *Concepts of Person: Kinship, Caste, and Marriage in India*. Delhi: Oxford University Press.
Padilla, Mark, Jennifer S. Hirsch, Miguel Munoz-Laboy, Robert Sember, and Richard G. Parker, eds. 2007. *Love and Globalization: Transformations of Intimacy in the Contemporary World*. Nashville: Vanderbilt University Press.
Parish, Steven. 1994. *Moral Knowing in a Hindu Sacred City*. New York: Columbia University Press.

Parry, Jonathan. 1980. "Ghosts, Greed, and Sin: The Occupational Identity of the Benares Funeral Priests." *Man* 15(1): 88–111.

———. 1985. "Death and Digestion: The Symbolism of Food and Eating in North Indian Mortuary Rites." *Man* 20(4): 612–630.

———. 1986. "The Gift, the Indian Gift, and the 'Indian Gift.'" *Man* 21(3): 453–473.

———. 1989. "On the Moral Perils of Exchange." In *Money and the Morality of Exchange*, edited by Jonathan Parry and Maurice Bloch, 64–93. Cambridge: Cambridge University Press.

———. 1994. *Death in Banaras*. Cambridge: Cambridge University Press.

———. 1999. "Lords of Labour: Working and Shirking in Bhilai." *Contributions to Indian Sociology* 33(1–2): 107–140.

———. 2000. "The 'Crisis of Corruption' and 'The Idea of India': A Worm's-Eye View." In *Morals of Legitimacy: Between Agency and System*, edited by Italo Pardo, 27–56. New York: Berghahn Books.

———. 2008. "The Sacrifices of Modernity in a Soviet-built Steel Town in Central India." In *Religion on the Margins*, edited by J. Pina-Cabral and F. Pine, 233–262. Oxford: Berghahn Books.

Parry, Jonathan, and Maurice Bloch. 1989. "Introduction: Money and the Morality of Exchange." In *Money and the Morality of Exchange*, edited by Jonathan Parry and Maurice Bloch, 1–32. Cambridge: Cambridge University Press.

Pearce, Phillip. 1982. *The Social Psychology of Tourist Behavior*. New York: Pergamon Press.

Pearce, Phillip, and Gianna Moscardo. 1986. "The Concept of Authenticity in Tourist Experiences." *Australian and New Zealand Journal of Sociology* 22(1): 121–133.

Pinney, Christopher. 1999. "On Living in the Kal(i)yug: Notes from Nagda, Madhya Pradhesh." *Contributions to Indian Sociology* 33(1–2): 77–106.

Pizam, A., and S. Sussmann. 1995. "Does Nationality Affect Tourist Behavior?" *Annals of Tourism Research* 22: 901–917.

Polanyi, Karl. 1957. *The Great Transformation: The Political and Economic Origins of Our Time*. Boston: Beacon.

Postman. Neil. 1994 (1982). *The Disappearance of Childhood*. New York: Vintage Books.

Povinelli, Elizabeth. 2006. *The Empire of Love: Toward a Theory of Intimacy, Genealogy, and Carnality*. Durham: Duke University Press.

Pratt, Mary Louise. 1992. *Imperial Eyes: Travel Writing and Transculturation*. London: Routledge.

Qvortrup, Jens. 1994. "Childhood Matters: An Introduction." In *Childhood Matters: Social Theory, Practice and Politics*, edited by Jens Qvortrup, Marjatta Bardy, Giovanni Sgritta, and Helmut Wintersberger, 1–24. Aldershot: Avebury.

Raheja, Gloria. 1988. *The Poison in the Gift*. Chicago: University of Chicago Press.

———. 1994. "Women's Speech Genres, Kinship and Contradiction." In *Women as Subjects: South Asian Histories*, edited by Nita Kumar, 49–80. Charlottesville: University of Virginia Press.

Raheja, Gloria, and Ann Grodzins Gold. 1994. *Listen to the Heron's Words: Reimagining Gender and Kinship in North India*. Berkeley: University of California Press.

Ramanujan, A. K. 1991. "Is There an Indian Way of Thinking? An Informal Essay." In *India through Hindu Categories*, edited by McKim Marriott, 41–58. New Delhi: Sage Publications.

———. 1994. "Toward a Counter-System: Women's Tales." In *Gender, Genre, and Power in South Asian Expressive Traditions*, edited by Arjun Appadurai, Frank Korom, and Margaret Mills, 33–55. Delhi: Motilal Banarsidass.

Rawlins, Roblyn. 2002. "'Long Rows of Short Graves': Sentimentality, Science, and Child-Saving in the Construction of the Intellectually Precocious Child, 1870–1925." In *Symbolic Childhood*, edited by Daniel Cook, 89–108. New York: Peter Lang.

Reynolds, Patricia. 1989. *Childhood in Cross-Roads: Cognition and Society in South Africa*. Grand Rapids: Eerdmans.

Reynolds, Vernon. 1974. "Can There Be an Anthropology of Children? A Reply." *Journal of the Anthropological Society of Oxford* 5(1): 32–38.

Richardson, S., and J. Crompton. 1988. "Vacation Patterns of French and English Canadians." *Annals of Tourism Research* 15: 430–448.

Riley, P. 1988. "Roadculture of International Long-Term Budget Travelers." *Annals of Tourism Research* 15: 430–448.

Ritter, W. 1987. "Styles of Tourism in the Modern World." *Tourism Recreation Research* 12(1): 3–8.

Rojek, Chris. 1993. *Ways of Escape: Modern Transformations in Leisure and Travel*. London: Macmillan.

Rojek, Chris, and John Urry. 1997. "Transformations of Travel and Theory." In *Touring Cultures: Transformations of Travel and Theory*, edited by Chris Rojek and John Urry, 1–19. New York: Routledge.

Rosen, David. 2005. *Armies of the Young: Child Soldiers in War and Terrorism*. New Brunswick: Rutgers University Press.

Sahlins, Marshall. 1972. *Stone Age Economics*. Chicago: Aldine.

———. 1976. *Culture and Practical Reason*. Chicago: University of Chicago Press.

———. 1981. *Historical Metaphors and Mythical Realities*. Ann Arbor: University of Michigan Press.

———. 2004. *Apologies to Thucydides: Understanding History as Culture and Vice Versa*. Chicago: University of Chicago Press.

Said, Edward. 1979. *Orientalism*. New York: Vintage Books.

Scheper-Hughes, Nancy. 1992. *Death without Weeping: The Violence of Everyday Life in Brazil*. Berkeley: University of California Press.

Scheper-Hughes, Nancy, and Daniel Hoffman. 1998. 'Brazilian Apartheid: Street Kids and the Struggle for Urban Space." In *Small Wars: The Cultural Politics of Childhood*, edited by Nancy Scheper-Hughes and Carolyn Sargent, 352–388. Berkeley: University of California Press.

Scheper-Hughes, Nancy, and Carolyn Sargent. 1998. "Introduction: The Cultural Politics of Childhood." In *Small Wars: The Cultural Politics of Childhood*, edited by Nancy Scheper-Hughes and Carolyn Sargent, 1–34. Berkeley: University of California Press.

Schoss, Johanna. 1995. "Beach Tours and Safari Visions: Relations of Production and the Production of 'Culture' in Malindi, Kenya." Ph.D. dissertation, University of Chicago.

Scott, James. 1976. *The Moral Economy of the Peasant: Rebellion and Subsistence in Southeast Asia*. New Haven: Yale University Press.

Seizer, Susan. 2000. "Roadwork: Offstage with Special Drama Actresses in Tamilnadu, South India." *Cultural Anthropology* 15(2): 217–259.

Selwyn, T. 1993. "Peter Pan in South East Asia. Views from the Brochures." In *Tourism in Southeast Asia*, edited by M. Hitchcock, V.T. King, and M.J.G. Parnwell, 117–37. London: Routledge.

Sennett, Richard. 1976. *The Fall of Public Man*. New York: W. W. Norton.

———. 1998. *The Corrosion of Character: The Personal Consequences of Work in the New Capitalism*. New York: W. W. Norton.

Seshadri, P. 1930. *Benares*. Cawnpore: City Press.
Seymour, Susan. 2002. "Family and Gender Systems in Transition: A Thirty-five Year Perspective." In *Everyday Life in South Asia*, edited by Diane Mines and Sarah Lamb, 100–115. Bloomington: Indiana University Press.
Sherring, M. A. 2001. *Benares: The Sacred City of the Hindus in Ancient and Modern Times*. New Delhi: Rupa.
Shweder, Richard, and Edmund Bourne. 1984. "Does the Concept of the Person Vary?" In *Culture Theory: Essays on Mind, Self, and Emotion*, edited by Richard Shweder and Robert LeVine, 158–199. Cambridge: Cambridge University Press.
Shweder, Richard, and Joan Miller. 1991. "The Social Construction of the Person: How Is It Possible?" In *Thinking through Cultures: Expeditions in Cultural Psychology*, edited by Richard Shweder. Cambridge: Harvard University Press.
Silver, Ira. 1993. "Marketing Authenticity in Third World Countries." *Annals of Tourism* 20(2): 302–318.
Singh, Rana P. B., Vrinda Dar, and S. Pravin. 2001. "Rationales for Including Varanasi as Heritage City in the UNESCO World Heritage List." *National Geographical Journal of India* (Varanasi). 47: 177–200.
Snodgrass, Jeffery. 2001. "Beware of Charitable Souls: Contagion, Roughish Ghosts and the Poison(s) of Hindu Alms." *Journal of the Royal Anthropological Institute* 7(4): 687–703.
Sörensen, A. 2003. "Backpacker Ethnography." *Annals of Tourism Research* 30: 847–867.
Staples, James. 2003. "Disguise, Revelation, and Copyright: Disassembling the South Indian Leper." *Journal of the Royal Anthropological Institute* 9: 295–315.
Steedman, Carolyn. 1995. *Strange Dislocations: Childhood and the Idea of Human Interiority 1780–1930*. Cambridge: Harvard University Press.
Stephens, Sharon. 1995. "Children and the Politics of Culture in 'Late Capitalism.'" In *Children and the Politics of Culture*, edited by Sharon Stephens, 3–50. Princeton: Princeton University Press.
Stirrat, R. L. 1989. "Money, Men, and Women." In *Money and the Morality of Exchange*, edited by Jonathan Parry and Maurice Bloch, 94–116. Cambridge: Cambridge University Press.
Sukul, Kubernath. 1974. *Varanasi down the Ages*. Varanasi: Bhargava Bhushan.
Swain, Margaret. 1989. "Gender Roles in Indigenous Tourism: Kuna Mola, Kuna Yala, and Cultural Survival." In *Hosts and Guests: The Anthropology of Tourism*, edited by Valene Smith, 247–264. Philadelphia: University of Pennsylvania Press.
———. 1995. "Gender in Tourism." *Annals of Tourism Research*. 22(2): 247–266.
Taussig, Michael. 1980. *The Devil and Commodity Fetishism in South America*. Chapel Hill: University of North Carolina Press.
Taylor, Charles. 1989. *Sources of the Self: The Making of Modern Identity*. Cambridge: Harvard University Press.
Thompson, E. P. 1967. "Time, Work-Discipline, and Industrial Capitalism." *Past and Present* 39: 56–97.
———. 1971. "The Moral Economy of the English Crowd in the Eighteenth Century." *Past and Present* 50(1): 76–136.
Thurot, Jean, and Gaetane Thurot. 1983. "The Ideology of Class and Tourism: Confronting the Discourse of Advertising." *Annals of Tourism Research* 10(1): 173–189.
Toomey, Paul. 1990. "Krishna's Consuming Passions: Food as Metaphor and Metonym for Emotion at Mount Govardhan." In *Divine Passion: The Social Construction of Emotion in India*, edited by Owen Lynch, 157–181. Berkeley: University of California Press.

Toren, C. 1989. "Drinking Cash: The Purification of Money through Ceremonial Exchange in Fiji." In *Money and the Morality of Exchange*, edited by Jonathan Parry and Maurice Bloch, 142–164. Cambridge: Cambridge University Press.
Tourist Statistical Book. 1997. Lucknow: Directorate of Tourism.
Towner, J. 1985. "The Grand Tour. A Key Phase in the History of Tourism." *Annals of Tourism Research* 15:47–62.
Trawick, Margaret. 1990. *Notes on Love in a Tamil Family*. Berkeley: University of California Press.
———. 2007. *Enemy Lines: Warfare, Childhood, and Play in Batticaloa*. Berkeley: University of California Press.
Trilling, Lionel. 1971. *Sincerity and Authenticity*. Cambridge: Harvard University Press.
Tucker, Hazel. 1997. "The Ideal Village: Interaction through Tourism in Central Anatolia." In *Tourists and Tourism: Identifying with People and Places*, edited by Simone Abram, Jacqueline Waldren, and Donald V. L. Macleod, 107–128. Oxford: Berg.
Turner, L. and J. Ash. 1975. *The Golden Hordes: International Tourism and the Pleasure Periphery*. London: Constable.
Uriely, N., Y. Yonai, and D. Simchai. 2002. "Backpacking Experiences: A Type and Form Analysis." *Annals of Tourism Research* 29: 520–538.
Urry, John. 1990. *The Tourist Gaze: Leisure and Travel in Contemporary Societies*. London: Sage Publications.
———. 1995. *Consuming Places*. London: Routledge.
Van der Veer, Peter. 1985. "Brahmans: Their Purity and Their Poverty. On the Changing Values of Brahman Priests in Ayodhya." *Contributions to Indian Sociology* 19(2): 303–321.
Vatuk, Sylvia. 1990. "'To Be a Burden on Others': Dependence Anxiety among the Elderly in India." In *Divine Passions: The Social Construction of Emotion in India*, edited by Owen Lynch, 64–88. Berkeley: University of California Press.
———. 1992. "Forms of Address in the North Indian Family." In *Concepts of the Person: Kinship, Caste, and Marriage in India*, edited by Ákos Öṣtör, Lina Fruzz Etti, and Steve Barnett, 56–98. Delhi: Oxford University Press.
Vatuk, Ved Prakash, and Sylvia Vatuk. 1971. "The Social Context of Gift Exchange in North India." In *Family and Social Change in Modern India*, edited by Giri Gupta, 207–232. Durham, N.C.: Carolina Academic Press.
Wadley, Susan. 2002. "One Straw from a Broom Cannot Sweep: The Ideology and Practice of the Joint Family in Rural North India." In *Everyday Life in South Asia*, edited by Diane Mines and Sarah Lamb, 11–22. Bloomington: Indiana University Press.
Wadley, Susan, and Bruce Der. 1990. "Eating Sins in Karimpur." In *India through Hindu Categories*, edited by McKim Marriott, 131–48. New Delhi: Sage.
Weightman, Barbara. 1987. "Third World Tour Landscapes." *Annals of Tourism Research* 14: 227–239.
Weiner, Myron. 1991. *The Child and the State in India*. New Delhi: Oxford University Press.
Weisgrau, Maxine. 2007. "Sickly Men and Voracious Women: Erotic Constructions of Tourist Identity." In *Raj Rhapsodies: Tourism, Heritage and the Seduction of History*, edited by Carol Henderson and Maxine Weisgrau, 123–140. Aldershot: Ashgate.
Westerhausen, K. 2002. *Beyond the Beach: An Ethnography of Modern Travellers in Asia*. Bangkok: White Lotus.
Whiting, Beatrice, ed. 1963. *Six Cultures: Studies of Childrearing*. New York: John Wiley and Sons.
Wickens, Eugenia. 2002. "The Sacred and the Profane: A Tourist Typology." *Annals of Tourism Research* 29(3): 834–851.

Willis, Paul. 1977. *Learning to Labor*. Farnborough: Saxon House.
Winnicott, Donald. 1989 (1971). *Playing and Reality*. New York: Routledge.
Zelizer, Viviana. 1985. *Pricing the Priceless Child: The Changing Social Value of Children*. New York: Basic Books.
———. 1994. *The Social Meaning of Money*. New York: Basic Books.
———. 2005. *The Purchase of Intimacy*. Princeton: Princeton University Press.

INDEX

An n after a page number indicates a note on that page.

Aashaa, 176
affective economy, 140
Alex (Australian tourist), 69
Alexandra (Swiss tourist), 78–79
Alicia (English tourist), 79
Altekar, A. S., 190n2
ambivalence: of human interaction, 187–188; of sex worker customers, 143; of tourists, 143–144, 150; of value of children, 71; of views on children by locals, 8–9, 99–100, 184–185
antipathies of customers, 131, 132, 140
anxiety: of boys on ghat, 58, 127; of locals toward changes, 23, 25, 92, 102, 106, 115; persecutory, of tourists, 87, 115; of tourists, 4, 50, 78, 87, 90, 183–184
Appadurai, Arjun, 136
appropriation, 148, 161, 180, 185–186, 202n20
Apu Bhai, 124
Ariès, Philippe, 67
Artisans of Banaras, The (Kumar), 174
asexuality, 37, 191n4
Assi Ghat, 10
authenticity: bounded, 157; dialectic of, 201n15; of noble savage, 72–73; through relationships, 144–49; tourist desire for, 5–6, 137
authentic Other, 6, 70, 152, 194n5, 201n20
autonomy and rebellion, 196n14

Babaji (*sadhu*), 88
backpackers, 10, 13, 26, 147, 149, 155, 169
backstage, 137, 159
Back to Life Program, 42
bahri alang, 174, 175, 203n10
Bakhtin, Mikhail, 131, 134
balanced reciprocity, 135, 198n13
Banaras: description of, 9–11; growth of tourism in, 29–30; history as tourist destination, 22–30; in 1980s, 28–29; riverfront, map of, 11; sacred geography of, 193n22

Banarsipan, 174
barren money, 167–168, 179
Baudrillard, Jean, 7, 147, 200n2
bazaar, as world above, 59, 61, 129
Bean, Susan, 202–203n7
beggars, 41, 55, 63, 84, 86, 156
Benares (Seshadri), 22
Benares, the Sacred City (Havell), 22
Bernstein, Elizabeth, 157, 160
Bhabha, Homi, 194n5
blank slate, 77, 95, 107, 195n5
Bloch, Maurice, 165, 179–180
Bluebond-Langner, Myra, 187, 192n15
boatmen: creation of trustworthiness by, 198n12; Mallah caste, 12, 99, 108, 120; power relations among, 120; rights and rules among, 120–121
boli system, 120
Bollywood, 38, 58, 177
bounded authenticity, 157
Bourdieu, Pierre, 55
boys clothing, girls use of, 37, 42
boys on ghats, 51–64; age restrictions, lack of, 65; boldness (*tez*) of, 102–103, 196n13; consciousness of peripheral status of, 58–59; and conditional love, 54, 192n19; as demanding, 99–100; and domestic devotional economy, 54–55; fear or shame, lack of, 101–102; freedom of, 56, 59, 65, 139; as little professionals, 82–83; locals' view of, 99–100, 101–105, 109–112; and moral code, 64; outsiders, 53, 66, 120–121, 129, 198n4; and play, 59; pleasures of working with tourists, 55–57; police harassment of, 60–61, 193n23; praise of, 82–83, 104–105; precocity, causes of, 109–112; and respect, 47, 60–64, 126–127; social fear, lack of as virtue, 103–104; spending and saving practices of, 138–140; surveillance by kin, 59–60;

boys on ghats (continued)
　troubles at home as reason for working, 52, 53–54. See also guiding/commission work
Brian (U.S. tourist), 72

Caine, W. S., 21–22
Cantonment Area, 23, 24, 25, 26
capitalism, and consumption, 162, 200n2
Carla (Canadian tourist), 161, 162
Casey (U.S. tourist), 77
caste: caste-based insults, 65–66; Chamar caste, 93; Dome caste, 108; in Hindu culture, 107–108, 196n15; Mallah caste, 12, 99, 108, 120; ritual specialist caste, 196n16
Chacha, Lalu, 99–100
Chakarabarty, Dipesh, 168, 176
Chamar caste (untouchable), 93
Charles (U.S. tourist), 74, 76, 81
Charlotte (Irish tourist), 74
cheating and lying, 128, 170, 171
Chevrillon, André, 20–21
child: classification of, 4–5; as deficient but desirable, 77–79; as evocative symbol for locals, 9, 184–185; expressive value of, 68; on ghats compared with Western, 70, 71–72, 83–84; as innocent being, 68–79, 92; instrumental value of, 54–55, 68; as "little adult," 4, 79–84; as "little professional," 82–84; Lockeian model of, 77, 95, 107; as noble savage, 4, 69–73, 95; as pathologically precocious, 79–82, 92; Romantic conceptions of, 4, 76, 92; Rousseauian model of, 69, 77, 95; sentimental value of, 55, 68, 80; significance of playfulness of, 73–77; as sincere/trustworthy, 68–69; as transitional object, 194n7; "upper-class" Indian, 72, 73; value in global sphere, 182–183; value in industrial society, 71, 193n1; view of, as diatribe against government of India, 84–87. See also boys on ghats; girls on ghats; locals, view of children on ghats
Child and the State in India, The (Weiner), 113–114
child prostitution, 50
children's culture, 5, 187, 189n3
Chris (Canadian tourist), 86
class. See social class
Cohen, Lawrence, 80, 93–94, 195n4, 196n9
Cohn, Bernard, 20
colonial mimicry, 194n5
colonial travel writings of Banaras, 19–22
commission agent (dalal), 12; child as competition for, 111–112; notoriety of, 29. See also guiding/commission work
commodification: of places and people, 6, 161; of relationships, 148, 152; of sexualized transactions, 143
competition, informal rules to mitigate, 121–123
comportment, 192n10
conditional giving, 158–160
conspicuous consumption, 139
conspicuous parsimony, 139
consumption: by boys, 139, 174–175, 177–179, 180–181; in capitalist society, 200n2; conspicuous, 139; by girls, 40, 140, 180; as mimicry, 177; in precapitalist society, 199n18; shift in nature of tourist practices of, 161–164; sign value of, 147–148; and symbolic value of money, 165; through intimate interactions, 7, 142–143; through personal relationships, 144–149, 185–186
Cook, Daniel, 7
cooking of money, 204n18
Copeman, Jacob, 193n21
Corrosion of Character, The (Sennett), 162
Culler, Jonathan, 89
cultural capital, 6, 55, 162

dalal (commission agent), 12, 29, 111–112
dalali (commission work), 36. See also guiding/commission work
dan, 170, 171, 202n4
Daniel, Valentine, 196n15
Dasashwamedh: transformation to low-budget tourist hub, 24–29; travel writings on, 22–23
Dasashwamedh Ghat: children and adults of, 12; physical description of, 10. See also boys on ghats; girls on ghats; guiding/commission work
data collection, present study, 16
David (French tourist), 137
Death in Banaras (Parry), 10
defense mechanisms, of tourists, 4, 87–91, 115, 183
denial, 4, 82, 87–91, 90, 183, 184
depressive position, 90–91, 194n12
Derné, Steve, 99, 103
dialectic of authenticity, 201n15
Diane (English tourist), 86–87
digestive idiom, 128
diplomacy, use by boys, 125
dirtiness of foreigners, physical, 169
Dispesh, 128, 135

division of labor, 8, 121
diya, description of, 12
dogla (mongrel/deceitful person), 61, 62
Dome caste, 108
domestic helpers, 192n16
Doron, Assa, 10, 119, 120–21, 122, 123, 198n12
drugs, 110, 168, 172, 179
Dube, Leela, 36

Edensor, Tim, 147
education: lack of, 44, 107, 112–113; and social class, 113–114
elders, respect for, 59–60, 99–100, 102
emotional investment, by tourists, 146–147
emotional labor, 7, 199n17
enclavic tourist spaces, 199n1
ephemeral precocity, 80, 113
Erin (U.S. tourist), 81–82, 89
Etty Mama (Israeli tourist), 73, 80–81
exchange, symbolic, 144, 152–153
expressive value, of child, 68

Fall of Public Man, The (Sennett), 162
fame, emphasis of boys on, 56–57, 65
Fame of Gawa, The (Munn), 57
female adult entertainers/sex workers, 7, 143, 146, 157
feminine capacity to suffer and empathize, 95–98
fighting metaphor, 127
food: eating away from home, 175–177; Hindu view of, 203n14
four *yugas* (ages), 197n21
Frank, Katherine, 142–43, 149
freedom: and boys, 56, 59, 65, 139; and girls, 36–37, 51, 66
friendship making, as sales strategy, 133–134, 148
Frommer's Adventure Guides: India, Pakistan, and the Himalaya, 30
fun, emphasis of boys on, 55, 56, 65

Gawa, 57
gender differences: in child as evocative symbol for locals, 184–185; in consumption, 40, 139, 140, 174–175, 177–179, 180–181; in contributions to household economy, 166–167, 180–181; role in emotional capacities, 95–99; role in shaping experiences, 64–65; in social expectations, 7–8, 115; in spatial freedom/constraints, 7–8, 35–37, 66; in spending practices, 138–140; in work trajectories, 35–36, 121. *See also* boys on ghats; girls on ghats
generalized reciprocity, 135, 198n13

George (Australian tourist), 134–135
ghats: description of, 10; as world below, 61–62, 127–128
gift giving, by tourists: money, 146, 148, 152, 153–154, 156–159; motivation for, 146; payment vs. gift, 148
girls on ghats, 35–51; age restrictions, 35, 44, 50–51, 65; criticism of tourists by, 49–50; domestication of ghats as strategy to avoid stigma, 41–44; as evocative symbol, 9; freedom of/constraints on, 35–37, 51, 66; lack of social fear as vice in, 105–106; moral superiority, showing through class stereotypes, 40, 43–44, 66; norms and expectations for, 40–42, 192n8; play, role in lives of, 40, 48–49; praise of, 9, 96–97, 98–99, 100, 139, 165, 180, 186; reconsideration of reasons to work, 44–48; sexual purity of, 36–37, 191nn2–3; spending and saving practices of, 138–139, 140; taunting by boys, reaction to, 40–42; troubles at home as strategy to avoid stigma, 38, 39, 41, 45–47, 97; virtue of necessity as strategy to avoid stigma, 37, 39–40, 65, 139
Godolia bazaar, 29
Goswami, Rani, 106–107, 108, 177
Grima, Benedicte, 97
G-Strings and Sympathy (Frank), 142–143
guiding/commission work: guide–shop owner relationships, 129–130; inappropriate spending of monies from, 173; as increasing addiction to money and drugs, 179; as increasing love of luxury and comfort, 175–176; informal rules for, 122–123; money from as ill-gotten, 170–172; as morally problematic, 168–169; as not real work, 169–170; preference for child guide, 156, 163; professional guides, inferiority of, 22, 78; remuneration as more than necessary, 173–174; role of seniority in, 196n9; and traditional concept of pleasure, 174–175; unlicensed, 58, 60–61, 168–169; view of locals on, 167–179. *See also* boys on ghats
guilt, of tourists, 4, 27, 82, 92, 137–138; defense mechanisms to deal with, 87–91, 115, 183

Harvey, David, 143
Havell, E. B., 22
Heber, Reginald, 20
heterogeneous tourist spaces, 199n1
Hewamanne, Sandya, 184

Higonnet, Anne, 76
hippie invasion, 24–26, 27–28
Hochschild, Arlie, 199n17
hot house development, 80
humor and jokes, as sales strategy, 132–133
Hutnyk, John, 148, 149, 200n4

idealization, 4, 87–91, 183, 184
idioms of addiction, 179
illegal drugs, 168
imagination, 48, 55–56, 65, 71, 177, 188
independent travelers, 13. *See also* backpackers
Indian men, Western tourists on, 78–79
institutionalized neglect, of children, 113–114
instrumental value, of child, 54–55, 68
intergenerational reciprocity, 138–139, 140, 193n20
interiority, 163–164
interoperability concept, 193n21
intersubjective spacetime, 57
intimacy, 134–136, 142–143, 162

Jacqueline (French tourist), 144–146, 148, 149, 162
James, Allison, 68
Japanese tourists, 190n12
Jay (U.S. tourist), 84–86, 86–87
Jenks, Chris, 68
Johnson, Mark, 81
Jorgen (Dutch tourist), 77–78, 82–83, 141, 154–161, 163
Joshi (Mr.), 25–26, 169
Joyce (U.S. tourist), 79

Kali Yuga, degenerative age of, 111–112
karma, 29, 95, 169, 195n5
Kashi. *See* Banaras
Kathmandu, 58
Kaushal, on reputation of boys on ghat, 104
Kevin (U.S. tourist), 69
Kimberley (Canadian tourist), 79
Kirsten (German tourist), 74–75, 132
Klein, Melanie, 87, 194n12
Kumar, Nita, 41, 64, 65, 174, 175

labor of leisure, 192n9
Lakoff, George, 81
Lamb, Sarah, 111
Laurien (U.S. tourist), 75–76, 79, 132
Liechty, Mark, 58
life-cycle stages, 112–113
locals, view of children on ghats: ambivalence of, 8–9, 99–100, 184–185; anxiety of, 23, 25, 92, 102, 106, 115; bad family effects, 106–108; boys, 99–100, 101–5, 109–112; caste effects, 107–108; child as problematic/pathological, 79–82, 92; daughters vs. sons, 95–97; gender effects on household economy, 166–167, 180–181; girls and social fear, 105–106; goodness/godliness of children, 94–95; guiding and commission work, 167–179; modernity effects, 8–9, 110–111; poverty effects, 99, 100, 106, 115; social fear, 103–106; Western corruption/cash effects, 108–109, 110
Lockeian model of the child, 77, 95, 107
Lonely Planet guidebook, 28–29, 151
low-budget guest houses, 25–26, 185, 190n2
lying and cheating, 128, 170, 171
Lynch, Caitrin, 184

MacCannell, Dean, 6, 137, 159, 185, 201n15
Mahabrahman funeral priests, 171, 173
Main Ghat. *See* Dasashwamedh Ghat
making friendship, as sales strategy, 133–134, 148
Mallah (boatman) caste, 12, 99, 108, 120. *See also* boatmen
man, Nepali concept of, 195n1
Manmandir, 12, 66
Maoz, Darya, 13
marginality, 58–59
Marion (U.S. tourist), 150–154
Mark (U.S. tourist), 69
masti, 175, 178
Max (Australian tourist), 81
McClintock, Anne, 192n9
Mead, George Herbert, 44
metaphors, consequences of, 81
methodological challenges, present study, 14–16
Mike (U.S. tourist), 83–84, 86
Mills, C. Wright, 188
mimicry, 73, 113, 177, 194n5
Modernist ideas of youth, 92
modernity, ills of, 8–9, 80, 94, 110–111, 166, 177, 185, 187
money: barren, 167–168, 179; as gift of tourists, 146, 148, 152, 153–154, 156–159; as *the* issue in transactions, 154; symbolic value of, 165–166, 179–181
Moore, Henrietta, 36
moral economy, 8, 140, 197n1
moral lessons, teaching: through gifts, 149; through monetary rewards, 152, 156
mortuary industry, 10, 171, 172

Mukherjee, Bharati, 178
Mukherjee, Devika, 59, 108, 158–159, 178, 179, 184
Mukherjee, Jaggu, 55, 59, 60, 77, 135, 178
Mukherjee, Mohan: and competition, 128; desire for fame and recognition, 57; earning strategies of, 55; father's view on work of, 178; on guiding as hard work, 63; on illegal drugs, 168; and Jorgen, 77, 78, 82–83, 141, 155–161; as little professional, 82–83; and respect, 60, 101–102; surveillance of, 59
Mukherjee, Rana, 178
Munn, Nancy, 57

Nagwa, 93, 94
narcissism, 6, 163, 185
negative reciprocity, 170
Newar culture, 95, 195n1
Nicholas (U.S. tourist), 82
noble savage, 4, 69–73, 95
nuga (heart), 195n1
Nusan (Israeli-American tourist), 74

Obeyesekere, Gananath, 115
observational/travel modalities, 19–20
"old voice," 93–94, 195n4
one-item rule, 121, 122, 124
ontological insecurity, 69, 204n3
outsiders, 53, 66, 120–121, 129, 198n4. *See also* Pandey, Keshwar; Yadav, Jay

Pandey, Arjun, 112–113
Pandey, Dipesh, 132–133, 134–315
Pandey, Diraj, 72, 77
Pandey, Keshwar, 54, 122, 124–126, 140
Pandey, Vinod, 108–109, 170–171
paranoid-schizoid position, 194n12
Parish, Steven, 95, 195n1
Parry, Jonathan, 10, 128, 165, 168, 170, 172, 179–180, 193n22, 196n16, 203n17
paternalistic relationships, 160–161
performative deference, 100, 139
persistence, as sales strategy, 131–132
person-centric, Hindu culture as, 196n15
pestering, as sales strategy, 90, 131–132, 161
Peter (Canadian tourist), 83–84
Peter (English tourist), 26–28, 70–73
Picturesque India (Caine), 21–22
pilgrimage, 9–10, 15; industry, 12, 168, 198n4
pollution, 202n7
positioning, researcher, present study, 16–17
post-Fordism, and consumption, 162

poverty: card, 55; as fascination for tourists, 149, 200n10; as reason to work on ghats, 99, 100, 106, 115; and volunteer tourism, 200n4
power relations: among boatmen, 120; between children and tourists, 5, 146–147, 148; in commodified sexual transactions, 143, 146; between older and younger boys, 122, 123–124; between parent and child, 5
Pradeep, 121, 126
praise, 136; of boys, 104–105; of girls, 9, 96–97, 98–99, 100, 139, 165, 180, 186; in Hindu culture, 136; as little professionals, 82–83, 133; by parents, 5, 54, 96–97, 99–100, 139
presociological model of child, 68, 79, 94
professional guides, inferiority of, 22, 78
Prout, Alan, 68
psychodynamics of classification, 4–5, 87–91; idealization and denial, 87–91
psychological warfare, 82, 132
psychosocial factors, 186
puja (evening ritual ceremony), 10, 48, 132
purity: of play, 73–77; and pollution, 101–102, 202n7; sexual, 36–37, 191nn2–3

Raheja, Gloria, 170
Raju, 60, 61, 126–127
Rakhel (Israeli tourist), 86–87
Ramesh, 60
Ravi, 55
Rawlins, Robin, 80
rebirth, liberation from cycle of, 10
reciprocity/emotional intimacy as sales strategy, 134–136
respect: and boys on ghats, 47, 60–64, 126–127; for elders, 59–60, 99–100, 102
right to earn, 8, 119; and cheating and lying, 171; vs. fight to earn, 127–130; through allowable items, 121–123; through informal division of labor, 121
Ritthi, 150, 166
ritual specialist caste, 196n16
Robert (Canadian tourist), 141
Rohan, 109–110
Rohit, 170–171
Romantic child, 4, 76, 92
Ross (U.S. tourist), 76–77
Rousseauian model of the child, 69, 77, 95

sacrization effect, 157
Sahani, Anand, 165, 167, 169–170, 181
Sahani, Anita, 48, 70, 71, 133

226 INDEX

Sahani, Arun, 128
Sahani, Ashish, 174–175
Sahani, Avi, 109, 111, 179
Sahani, Bali, 73, 98, 129, 168, 173, 176
Sahani, Basanti, 41
Sahani, Diraj, 35, 94, 95, 111–112, 167, 173
Sahani, Ganesh, 101–102
Sahani, Gappa, 62–63, 169
Sahani, Gopal, 171
Sahani, Harsha, 122, 151–154
Sahani, Jaila, 45–46, 49, 81, 106, 150, 166
Sahani, Kailash, 135, 136, 175–176
Sahani, Malika: compared to Goddess Laxmi, 165, 166; compassion and understanding of, 95–97, 106; criticism of tourists by, 49–50; gifts from tourists, 137, 138; reason for working on waterfront, 37–40, 41; retirement from riverfront, 51; saving practices of, 139
Sahani, Mukesh, 128
Sahani, Pramod: earning strategies of, 133–134, 135, 136; encounter with tourist as business transaction, 151–154; Jorgen teaches moral lesson to, 156; on lying and cheating, 128, 171; playfulness of, 77; and power dynamics, 144–147; praise by tourist, 83; on reasons to work on ghat, 54, 56–57; and respect, 47, 60, 64, 103–104
Sahani, Rahul, 109, 170, 179
Sahani, Rakhi, 132
Sahani, Rita, 51
Sahani, Sangeeta, 49, 119, 126
Sahani, Sharmila, 51, 95–97, 98, 137, 165, 166
Sahani, Suriya, 105
Sahlins, Marshall, 136, 183, 198n13
sales strategies, 130–136; humor and jokes, 132–133; making friendship, 133–134, 148; persistence and pestering, 131–132, 161; reciprocity and intimacy, 134–136; sales pitches and speech genres, 131; strategic hospitality, 137–138
Sara (Canadian tourist), 74, 101–102, 132, 137, 149–150
Sargent, Carolyn, 67–68, 71
Scheper-Hughes, Nancy, 67–68, 71
schooling fees, 158–159, 200n12
Scott (U.S. tourist), 68
Seenu, 150
self-discovery, by tourists, 190n7, 201n20
self-interest, of boys, 173–174, 203n17
self-loathing, by tourists, 89
self-reflection, by children, 46, 66
self-restraint, by girls, 167, 191n3

Sennett, Richard, 162–163
sentimental value, 55, 68, 80
Seshardi, P., 22–23
sexual interest in child by tourist, 50
sexual purity, 36–37, 191nn2–3
sex workers, 7, 143, 146, 157
short- and long-term transactional order, 180
sign objects, 6–7, 147–148
sign value of consumption, 147
sin, pollution, contagion, 168–169
sincerity, 68–69, 193n2
social class: and education, 113–114; indifference to poor, 113–114; insults based on, 65–66; and moral superiority, 40, 43–44, 66; role in shaping emotional capacities of child, 98; social fear as value among upper, 103
social fear: and boys, 103–104; and girls, 105–106
social weakness (*kamzori*), 94, 196n9
socioeconomic change, views of locals on, 184–185
sociological imagination, 188
Sophia (French tourist), 137
speech genres, 131, 135
spending practices, gender differences in, 138–140
splitting, 4, 90, 183, 184
Srivastav, Anjali, 42–44, 51, 97–98, 105–106, 138–139, 166–167
Srivastav, Gulab, 42, 166–167
Srivastav, Madhuri, 97–98, 138–139, 166–167
Srivastav, Maneesh, 42, 98, 166–167
Srivastav, Mona, 42, 49, 81, 139, 166–167
Srivastav, Priya, 46–48, 49, 75, 80, 81, 131–132
Srivastav, Sanju, 123–126
Steedman, Carolyn, 163–164
Stephens, Sharon, 72–73
Steven (Australian tourist), 132
strategic hospitality as sales strategy, 137–138
strip clubs, 142–143, 154
Sudesh, 109
Suitably Modern (Liechty), 58
Sukul, Kubernath, 24–25
symbolic exchange, 144, 152–153
symbolic interactionism, 91, 204n4
sympathies of customers, 131, 140

tabula rasa (blank slate), 77, 95, 107, 195n5
Tanya (U.S. tourist), 79

Temporarily Yours (Bernstein), 157
territorial boundaries, 120, 121, 198n4
tez (boldness), 102–103, 196n13
Titu, 102
Tourism Police Task Force, 60
tourist: ambivalence of, 143–144, 150; anxiety of, 4, 50, 78, 87, 90, 115, 183–184; and authenticity, 72–73; becoming/remaining customer, 144–149; as benevolent benefactor, 149–161; as child, 163, 186, 189n4, 194n13–195n14; criticism by girls on ghats, 49–50; defense mechanisms to deal with guilt of, 87–91, 115, 183; emotional investment by, 146–147; gift giving by, 146, 148, 152, 153–154, 156–159; guilt of, 4, 27, 82, 92, 137–138; overview of, 13–14; power relations with children, 5, 146–147, 148; self-discovery by, 190n7, 201n20; sexual interest in child by tourist, 50; shared repertoire of responses to children, 14, 67, 74–75; shift in nature of consumption, 161–164; shift in object of consumption, 185–186; volunteer, 200n4
tourist gaze, 30, 162, 185–186
touristic turn inward, 6, 143, 161–164, 185–186, 186–187
tourist police task force, 110
travel writings, on Banaras, 19–23
Trilling, Lionel, 193n2
trustworthiness, 68–69
Tulu, 177
tyranny, territorial disputes as reason for, 123–125

unlicensed guiding, 58, 60–61, 168–169, 193n23

Urry, John, 143, 162, 185, 201–202n20
Usha (German tourist), 87–91, 92

value(s): of child in global sphere, 182–183; creation of, in island society, 57; economic, 7, 9, 55; instrumental/expressive of child, 54–55, 68; as interoperable, 55; production of, 119, 140; role in shaping price, 155, 157–158; sentimental, 55, 68, 80; sign value, 147; and social class, 44; traditional, 7, 9, 44, 55, 80, 120, 167, 168, 176
van der Veer, Peter, 168
Varanasi. *See* Banaras
Varanasi down the Ages (Sukul), 24–25
Vatuk, Sylvia, 36, 112
Vinod, 170–171
Vishnu, on tourism industry, 110
volunteer tourism, 200n4

wandering work, 61, 63
weakness, social, 94, 196n9
Weiner, Myron, 113–114
Winnicott, Donald, 48, 194n7
world above, 59, 61, 66, 91, 129

Yadav, Arun, 176
Yadav, Jay, 52–54; criticism of girls working on ghat, 45–46, 105–106; on informal rules of ghat, 122–123; outsider status of, 53, 126; on reality of money in encounters, 154; on reasons to work on ghat, 53–54; and respect, 61–62, 63–64, 126–127
Yadav, Manoj, 129–130
Yadav, Raj, 52–53, 114
Yadav, Soni, 172–173

Zelizer, Viviana, 157

ABOUT THE AUTHOR

JENNY HUBERMAN is an assistant professor of anthropology at the University of Missouri–Kansas City.